ties. It also offers an absorbing narrative about what we mean by the social, and how we can think about it, weaving in discussions of the personal, the political and social change, along with concepts, questions and vivid contemporary examples.

This welcome new edition is fully updated with the latest references and data. It offers enhanced discussions of theory and engages with current pressing social challenges, such as war and terrorism; migration; sustainability and the environment; and deepening social inequalities. With its strong thematic structure and engaging end-of-chapter activities, it consolidates its position as the perfect entry-point to the field – at once supportive of the reader new to sociology and engaging for those who are taking their studies to university level for the first time.

Ken Plummer is Emeritus Professor of Sociology at the University of Essex, UK, and is internationally known for his research on sexualities and narrative. He is author of many books, including the bestselling *Sociology: A Global Introduction* (with John Macionis, fifth edition, 2012). His most recent book is *Cosmopolitan Sexualities* (2015).

The Basics

SOCIOLOGY
THE BASICS

Ken Plummer

Routledge
Taylor & Francis Group

LONDON AND NEW YORK

First published in 2010
by Routledge

This second edition published in 2016
by Routledge
2 Park Square, Milton Park, Abingdon, Oxon OX14 4RN

and by Routledge
711 Third Avenue, New York, NY 10017

Routledge is an imprint of the Taylor & Francis Group, an informa business

© 2010, 2016 Ken Plummer

British Library Cataloguing in Publication Data
A catalogue record for this book is available from the British Library

Library of Congress Cataloging-in-Publication Data
Names: Plummer, Kenneth, author.
Title: Sociology : the basics / Ken Plummer.
Description: 2 Edition. | New York : Routledge, 2016. | Series: The basics |
    Revised edition of the author's Sociology, 2010. | Includes bibliographical
    references and index.
Identifiers: LCCN 2015046127 | ISBN 9781138927445 (hardback) |
    ISBN 9781138927452 (pbk.) | ISBN 9781315682594 (e-book)
Subjects: LCSH: Sociology.
Classification: LCC HM585 .P58 2016 | DDC 301—dc23
LC record available at http://lccn.loc.gov/2015046127

ISBN: 978-1-138-92744-5 (hbk)
ISBN: 978-1-138-92745-2 (pbk)
ISBN: 978-1-315-68259-4 (ebk)

Typeset in Aldine401 BT-RomanA
by Apex CoVantage, LLC

MIX
Paper from
responsible sources
FSC® C013056

Printed and bound in Great Britain by
TJ International Ltd, Padstow, Cornwall

For all my students who taught me much

CONTENTS

ILLUSTRATIONS

Figures

Tables

SOCIAL HAUNTINGS

So these are the hauntings of social things.
Attuning to people and drenched with their presence,
We do things together. We move with the other –
The living, the dead, the soon to arrive.
Sociality becoming the air that we breathe.

Our life's social worlds, so stuffed with the possible.
Proliferating multiples and things on the move.
Yet, here we all dwell in the rituals we make;
The pounding of patterns to engulf and entrap us.
These worlds not of our making that haunt till we die.

The tiniest things and the grandest of horrors.
Inhumanities of people and generations at war;
Gendered classed races, sexy nations disabled;
Excluding, exploiting, dehumanizing the world.
The stratified hauntings of pain we endure.

Standing amazed at this chaos and complexity
We celebrate, critique and cry in our shame.
Our utopian dreamings of empowering lives.
Each generation more justice, a flourishing for all?
Sociology: the endless challenge for a better world.

PREFACE TO THE FIRST EDITION
WELCOME TO THE SOCIAL MAZE

Two roads diverged in a wood, and I took the one less travelled by.
Robert Frost, 'The Road Not Taken', 1916

Welcome to the social maze. At the heart of this maze is a new way of thinking and imagining social life. We will start on eight journeys to a possible grasping of these new ways for thinking about human social worlds. Never mind if you do not arrive at the centre of the maze, I hope you will enjoy some of the journeys. On the first exploration, in Chapter 1, I want you to get a glimpse of sociology's imagination – the domain of the social – and I give lots of examples. I will encourage you to develop a critical consciousness, to become an 'outsider' and suggest that sociology can look at anything – anything that engages you (from sport to science to sex). The second journey will examine just what we mean by the social and how we can think about it. It will look at some of the images we create to think about social things. It is an invitation to social theory. Chapter 3 will move us into the hurly-burly of teeming human life as it emerges across the world in the twenty-first century and looks at some of the significant changes taking place in it. Many of these changes suggest the world is hurtling to a disaster! How can we possibly find ways of grasping this complexity? Our next puzzle (Chapter 4) will be to consider how sociology, the discipline designed to look at the social, developed in the Western world to deal with just this problem. It is a short history. Chapters 5 and 6 will then start laying out some road maps for doing sociology – for thinking about theory and research. I cannot give precise satnavs for this but will aim, from a vast literature on all this, to distil a few wisdoms that will help you orientate yourself to what sociologists try to do. The seventh pathway looks at a topic which haunts most of the other pathways – the human sufferings and inequalities we find along our way. It is just one key area of sociological investigation but one which most sociologists would agree is central. On my final journey (Chapter 8), I ask why we should bother with all this anyway. I ask: why? What's the point of it all? What role does sociology have to play in the modern world? Each chapter is a pathway that can stand on its own, and any one alone just might take you to the holy grail of sociology.

Like all books in this series, I am only looking at the basics of sociology. A short introductory book can hardly do justice to a complex and inexhaustible subject. I have had to be very selective for a reader who I assume is a beginner and knows little about the subject. My hope is that what I can say in a short space will tempt you to expand your ways of thinking about the social and explore further the workings of the social in the world we live. Each chapter will end with some advice on going further (and each chapter will also provide boxes to help your thinking).

Ken Plummer
Wivenhoe, January 2010

PREFACE TO THE SECOND EDITION

The first edition was written in 2008 and published in 2010. This second edition was revised in 2015 and published in 2016. The book remains the same as the first edition in its structure, but it has been reworked a little page by page. The core changes are threefold: (1) It updates all facts, references and arguments, where needed, from 2008 to 2015. (2) It adds new sections in several places. This includes new sections on violence, terrorism, digital change, Big Data, migration and the environment. (3) It 'improves style' wherever I thought it was needed. In addition, I have developed more on the website, organized by pages of the book, which will give you sources and leads to follow things up further. I do recommend you look at it.

I wrote the first edition in the aftermath of a major transplant surgery. Ten years on, I remain deeply grateful to the many who saved my life.

Ken Plummer
Wivenhoe, February 2016

IMAGINATIONS: ACTING IN A WORLD I NEVER MADE

Men make their own history, but they do not make it as they please; they do not make it under self-selected circumstances, but under circumstances existing already, given and transmitted from the past. The tradition of all dead generations weighs like a nightmare on the brains of the living.

Karl Marx, *The Eighteenth Brumaire of Louis Bonaparte,* 2000 [1851]

At birth, we are – each one of us – hurled into a social world we never ever made. We will have absolutely no say about which country we are born into, who our parents and siblings may be, what language we will initially speak, or what religion or education we will be given. We will have no say about whether we are born in Afghanistan, Algeria, Australia, Argentina, or one of several hundred other countries in the world. We will have no say whether we are born into villages, nations or families considered super-rich or in abject poverty. We will have no say whether our initial family is Muslim, Christian, Buddhist, Jewish, Hindu, or any one of several thousand other smaller religions found across the world. What is significant here is that we are born into a world that pre-exists us and will continue after us. These days this world is increasingly a global, digital world. Yet we are 'thrown into' this everyday social world that was quite simply not one we had any say in making. And it is this very world which sociologists study. Every day we confront social facts and social currents which 'come to each one of us from outside and . . . sweep us along in spite of ourselves'. We look at worlds we cannot wish away – worlds that await us and shape us. They are **'social facts'** over and above us.[1]

But then, very soon, most of us learn to find our own feet in this 'thrown into world'. Most significantly, we start to become aware of other people in this world (usually initially our dear – or not so dear – mothers, fathers and siblings): we start to become attuned to them. We learn how to please them and others, and indeed how to annoy them. We slowly start to imagine the worlds that they live in and how they may respond to us. Like it or not, we become increasingly socialized to act towards them, to develop a primitive empathy or sympathy towards others. If we do not – if we fail to learn this empathy – then we will not be able to communicate, we will not be able to routinely go about our daily social life in any kind of satisfactory way. Sociology is also charged with studying this everyday life of adjustment – how the billions of people who dwell on Planet Earth get through the day living with each other. How do we adapt and conform, rebel and innovate, ritualize and withdraw? We look at the complicated relations between our bodies, our inner worlds (or 'subjectivities') and our ways of behaving with others in this living of everyday life so that social worlds can proceed in a fairly intelligible and orderly fashion most of the time. It will of course also be subject to serious conflict and breakdown, and sociology looks at this too.

What is fascinating about this everyday world is that we – that little child thrown into a strange but given world – actually also make parts of it ourselves. It turns out that from the moment of birth, when we first confront this constraining world, till the moment we die and life comes to a dramatic end, we are given an active energy to keep going – to move through the world with a tremendous potential

---

1 This is a reference to the sociologist Émile Durkheim. (Durkheim, 1982, pp. 52–3). There are very few further footnotes or references in this book as they are hereafter provided page by page, often with links, on the website that accompanies this book. See http://kenplummer.com/sociology

and creative ability to act in it and on it. We little human animals are the creators of social life all the time: we are active agents who make social worlds. Socialized into it, we then make it work for us. And sociology studies this too. Sociologists ask how people come to assemble their social lives and social worlds in radically different ways in different times and places. Yet whilst some of us can develop ways of being the active agents of their lives, many others may be restricted in doing so. While no one is determined, we are not all capable or knowledgeable actors in the world to the same degree. And here is a key problem for sociologists: **inequalities** (we will return to this often and especially in Chapter 7).

SOCIOLOGY AS CONSCIOUSNESS: OUTSIDERS ON THE MARGINS?

Sociology brings a fresh imagination for seeing social life. As sociologists we enter the human social worlds of others, and are likely – at least momentarily – to feel challenged by the differences of others. *For people – in other groups, countries and times – live different lives to yours.* To see this clearly, I will need to temporarily abandon my own taken-for-granted view of the world and develop an empathy with the worldview of others. As sociologists, we have to suspend our own world and for a while hold back on all judgements about others. At this most basic level, there are some sociologists (like Harold Garfinkel in *Studies in Ethnomethodology*) who have conducted 'breaching experiments' to make our everyday life experiences very strange. Garfinkel invited his students to question everything going on around them, to ask and probe every convention of the daily round. A friend says 'how are you'? They ask back: 'what do you mean by that'? They go to a shop and barter over the price of goods (in many cultures, this is the norm; but it is not so in the UK or North America). They move their face right up to the face of the person they are speaking to, almost rubbing noses. They sit with friends and question everything that is said. These little experiments in breaking the routine soon show how much our society depends on trust, kindness and understanding each other. Others are soon threatened by strange questionings.

This leads us to one of sociology's key problems: the need to challenge **ethnocentrism** and the closely linked issue of ego-centrism. Here are stances that put our own 'taken-for-granted' ways of thinking at the centre of the social world, as if we are always right and know *the* truth. Ethnocentrism assumes that our culture (our *ethno* – way of life) is at the centre of the world; whereas egocentrism assumes that the world revolves around us. We need to purge ourselves from their influence. Sociology demands as a pre-requisite that we get rid of this self-centred view of the world and that, as the contemporary and influential sociologist Zygmunt Bauman puts it, we learn to *defamiliarize ourselves with the familiar*. It stresses the need to always see the differences (and value) of other lives and cultures and, indeed, the value of the differences of other standpoints. At its strongest, it absolutely forbids us to pronounce on other's worlds and instead to take them seriously on their own terms. It makes us humble in the face of the world's differences.

To take the simplest example of this in everyday life: you are going on a holiday to a country you do not know. You are the outsider, the stranger. Now you can of course just go to another culture and 'trample' on it: assume your own culture is best and not bother with what you find there. You would become one of those ignorant, crass holidaymakers that are an embarrassment to everyone! You would speak only in your own language; not bother to learn any of the new customs expected of everyone; and take little interest in what is going on that makes that culture historically different – its politics, its religion, its family life. Worst of all, you will probably extol the virtues of your own country when you face different foods, different ways of queuing, different modes of talking to each other. You will be, in short, a narrow-minded, uncouth holidaymaker abroad!

But if you are a more sensitive soul, then travelling can be very difficult. You often come to feel a complete fool as you stumble against a language you cannot speak and customs, mores and folkways you do not understand. I know that I sometimes feel I am like a very young child when I cannot even say 'excuse me' or 'where is this or that?' in the host language. Or simply when I want to ask for a cup of coffee and cannot express myself. What a bumbling, incompetent fool I am! How can they – why should they – bother with me? People are usually kind and they try to help. But without a basic knowledge of a culture's language, it is hard to move around easily in it. And it goes much further than that. The meanings of cultures lie deep: the meaning of the garden in Japan, the bullfight in Spain, the veil in Iran. (Kate Fox's *Watching the English* (2005) is a field study of the English which gets at the taken-for-granted oddities of English culture.)

Here is the social as outsider, not insider: outsiders are people who do not belong, who dwell on the margins, who are deviants and strangers. The social is defined not just by who belongs, but by who does not. Often it is best studied and analyzed *not* through the eyes of the people who belong and are in it – but rather through the eyes of those outside. It is only the outsider who can see (and question) what is truly taken for granted. Hence sociology takes seriously the voices and eyes of immigrants, the strangers in town, the 'invisible man', the alienated young, the disenfranchised and deviant, the gothic and the queer. Their differences throw a sharp light on what is taken for granted and normal.

THE SOCIOLOGICAL IMAGINATION AS CRITIQUE AND WONDER

The physicist looks at the skies and stands in amazement at the universe. The musician listens to Mozart, Beethoven or Stravinsky – or ABBA or Adele – and stands in amazement at the magnificent works that little human beings can produce on earth. The sportsperson finds their adrenalin gushing at the thought of running or going to a football stadium. And the sociologist gets up every day and stands in wonder at the little social worlds – and indeed human societies – that we have created for ourselves: their meaning, order, conflict, chaos and change. For the sociologist, social life is sometimes sensed as something quite inspiring, and sometimes as something quite horrendous which brings about disenchantment, anger and despair. Sociologists stand in awe and dreading, rage and delight at the humanly produced social world with all its joys and its sufferings. We critique it and we critically celebrate it. Standing in amazement at the complex patterns of human social life, we examine both the good things worth fostering and bad things to strive to remove. Sociology becomes the systematic, sceptical study of all things social.

THE DARK SIDE OF SOCIETY: THE MISERIES AND SUFFERINGS OF HUMAN SOCIAL LIFE

So here is the bad news. On a bad day I can hardly get out of my bed. The weight of the world and its suffering bears down upon me: the human misery, as it has confronted the billions before me. Luckily, I am not a depressive so I have my ways of getting up and springing into action. But lying there some mornings, I see the long historical march of humanity's inhumanities, the horrors of the world and the sufferings of humankind, and I squirm. How can it be that for so long and with such seeming stupidity and blindness, human beings have continued ceaselessly to make human social worlds in which so very many suffer – that are so manifestly dehumanized and inhuman? Here is a world full of wars and violence, poverty and inequality, despotisms and corruption. Here is the horrendous treatment of other peoples who are different from us and the vast neglect and denial of these sufferings. Billions of people throughout history have gone to their deaths with *wasted lives*. Studying this is one of the routine topics for sociology.

For sociology might be seen as borne out of an awareness of human fragility, vulnerability and suffering. Everywhere it seems societies cast 'others' into the roles of enemies and monsters – creating hierarchies of 'the good' to value and 'the bad' to dehumanize. It was, after all, human beings that designed slavery for much of history – a system that still exists (the Global Slavery Index in 2015 claims there are some 35.8 million in forced labour, child labour and trafficking in 167 countries today). It was also human activity – apparently supported by gods – which created the 'caste' system of social stratification, as Aryan-speaking people moved into India around 1500 BCE, creating a group of people called the untouchables who were to be designated outside of regular human life and left with all the dirty jobs (see Chapter 7). It is all a history of kings, rulers and popery dominating in splendour over the vast immiserated masses. There has been no period free from wars – over land, status, wealth and religion – and by all accounts the twentieth century was the bloodiest century of all, with its genocides, world wars, purges, revolutionary mass slaughters, its 'fascisms' and its 'communisms'. There is controversy over how to count the number of actual 'mega-deaths', but somewhere between 180 million and 200 million is a number often cited. That is to say that probably one in ten of the population of the world born around 1900 were slaughtered through war or genocide in the twentieth century. And the widespread problems of wars, poverty, hunger, Holocaust and disease throughout time have only been marginally diminished in the current time. To all this must now be added the growing awareness of global warming and a widely predicted potential ecological catastrophe before too long. We humans do not seem to have made a very good job of living together peacefully, happily and productively. All this is the stuff of great literature, poetry and filmmaking – and sociology.

Sociology, then, generates concern at the billions of wasted and damaged lives engulfed by 'man's inhumanity to man'. Sociologists are interested in the social conditions which can produce human social suffering. We are concerned with the ways in which private and individual sufferings have origins from within our societies: how what might seem to be *personal problems* are also *public issues*. We may grasp the problems of refugees through understanding the problems of an individual life, but we can also show how this connects to much wider structural problems of state conflicts, nationalism, racism, religions and economic inequalities. Sociology is charged with linking the personal to the social, the private to the public. And the analysis of human suffering is a central interest.

ALWAYS LOOK ON THE BRIGHT SIDE OF LIFE: THE JOYS AND POTENTIALS OF HUMAN SOCIAL LIFE

Given this, it's not surprising to find many saying that sociology is the dismal science – a dark, bleak, pessimistic discipline. Don't hang around with sociologists, they say, because the trade of sociologists makes them pretty gloomy people. Indeed, all this may have been enough to make you put this book down. But hold on. Is it really all such bad news? Critical we sociologists are. But at the same time, we cannot stop seeing – most of the time – how people also go about their daily rounds in society working with each other, caring for each other, loving each other and much of the time in ease and co-operation. Societies are often remarkable human achievements.

A few years ago, as I lay in my modern hospital bed shortly after ten hours of major life-saving surgery, I pondered just how all this had come to be. My life-threatening illness – chronic liver cirrhosis – had killed millions of people throughout history; but over the past sixty years or so, the invention of transplant surgery through modern science had come to save thousands of lives. A life-threatening illness had been tamed. But it was so much more than this. Here I was in a modern hospital – a hugely expensive bureaucracy employing thousands of workers in multitudes of different ways in a massive division of labour in order to save my life and the lives of thousands of others. All around me I could see social acts of great, learned skill and scientific knowledge, myriad social acts of humane and loving care, multiple social acts of practical activity: workers cleaning the floors, pushing trolleys with patients, providing food, keeping the plumbing going, welcoming the outpatients, organizing beds, orchestrating a million little daily routines. This was no small human *and social* endeavour. How had this come to be? As I lay there, I celebrated the wonder of human social organization and the way it had fashioned this whole experience. I pondered – in a flash – the history of hospitals, the training of doctors and nurses from all over the world, the social meanings of caring for others, the generosity and altruism of many people, the skills of surgeons passed on from generation to generation, the daily organization of timetables and roles – for nurses, doctors, porters, ambulance drivers, social workers, pharmacists, phlebotomists, physiotherapists, transplant co-ordinators, volunteers, administrators, ward managers and the rest. I pondered indeed my own social timetable on the ward and my daily encounters with a myriad of health professions, a string of rituals from x-ray to medication. And I thought: this is what sociologists want to understand. Just how did this all come together? Just how does this work? And all of this so I – and all the others – could live?

Yet this is just one of hundreds of stories I could tell of my sociological amazement over many years. There are many marvels of human creativity, care and imagination. Of science, medicine, art, sport, music: the clothes we fashion, the food we create, the music we delight in, the knowledge we have accumulated over the millennia – the museums and libraries, the technologies that get people on to the moon and allow them to speak to people all over the world. It goes on and on. Sociologists also look in sheer wonder at human social world making, at the ways in which we solve problems, do daily life and often treat each other with care, respect, kindness and love. And all in a sort of orderly way. We look at the social organization of everyday living and the fortunate and fulfilled, even privileged, lives that some lead. And we ask about the social conditions under which the good, humane and happy social life can be lived.

THE GOOD NEWS AND THE BAD NEWS

Sociologists, then, are Janus-faced. In one direction, we look for the problems and suffering and are highly critical. In the other direction, we look for the joys and humanity of the social world and are (cautious and critically) celebratory. This has been a longtime problem in the thinking about society. It is found, for instance, quite strikingly in the Enlightenment philosopher Voltaire's famous satire *Candide* (1759). Here the hero follows his teacher Dr Pangloss's philosophy that 'everything is for the best in the best of all possible worlds' (the Panglossian philosophy), only to encounter everywhere he travels the horrors of rape, bestiality, exploitation, murder, war and catastrophe. Concluding, he is led to say that this is not the best of all possible worlds, but we do make our own lives. We had better, he says, cultivate our own gardens. And here we may find some happiness in the world.

THINK ON: TRAVELLING IN THE AIR

And so here is the good news and the bad news.

I am waiting for a plane at a major international airport, and I stand in awe. How did it come to be that millions of *Homo sapiens* can now travel daily across the globe in the air? This was not really possible even a hundred years ago. A new 'aeromobility' has helped organize the modern global world. And I ponder the sheer complexity of this social action, the sheer inventiveness and creativity of human beings to make all this happen – to 'invent' planes, flying, airports, travel.

Think of a journey. From millions of little individual lives, decisions are made to get from A to B (say Buenos Aires to Cairo, but anywhere). Phone calls are made, websites are searched and tour operators are brought in. A massive worldwide system of booking involving thousands of business operations is brought into play. This is human endeavour at a manifestly global level. Bookings are made. Arrivals and departures are fixed. And airport terminals are reached: here are huge complex enterprises where it would seem possible for so much to go wrong – queuing, ticketing, baggaging, passporting, security, boardings, take off, landings. In 2014, there were some *3.3 billion passengers* across the world. At London's Heathrow alone, some 74 million people moved through it. (Atlanta is the world's busiest with 96 million passengers per year, followed closely by Beijing.) Here are amazingly complex timetables in place – in major international airports, planes take off and land every few seconds! And these places – spaces – are now built as huge cathedrals of consumption, as places where you do not just want to fly, but somehow need to buy a wide bunch of expensive commodities. I have often pondered why nearly all major airports have a fascinating bar where caviar, smoked salmon, seafood and champagne is served (it is the last thing I fancy before going up into the air: is it status food for the wealthy?). But there must be a demand for this. Airports are fascinating objects of study: they are transient communities, vast shopping malls, landscapes of surveillance and places of work. They show massive divisions of labour, multiple complex social encounters, the social organization of spaces. There are sign systems that need to be understood, practical activities to be done, architecture to be tacitly understood. It is a world of markets, communication, conflicts, change and above all social order. And with it, there is a whole 'underworld' of airports that we know little about but which we sometimes read about. And we haven't even got up into the air yet.

Once we take off, a series of other wonders come into play. Who could have imagined 200 years ago that we would invent large metal cans to house some 600 people which can then fly in the air across space at nearly 1,000 kilometres an hour? And even more than that: in these cans we would be served hot meals (vegetarian low-cholesterol fusion Thai would be my meal of choice) and have a seemingly endless choice of films, games and music? (Heaven forbid that we should be bored in our eight-hour trip across thousands of miles.) A whole world of autopilots, airport mechanics, ground staff and of course flight attendants comes into play. And finally, I ponder what this means to the millions of individual lives and pathways criss-crossing round the world to meet business appointments and loved ones? To watch the faces at the arrival gates tells a lot. The ending of the Richard Curtis film *Love Actually* (2003) shows the arrival gate of Heathrow and the screen slowly opens up to show hundreds of expectant faces meeting and greeting each other from their travels. Here indeed is a social structure at work – thousands of people doing things together in patterned ways – making social order at airports, making society work.

But hold on, you rightly say: there is also very bad news here too. Most of the world's population have never been near a plane or an airport – suggesting a massive inequality of the world.

It has been estimated that a mere 1 per cent of the world's population do 80 per cent of the world's flights – and only 5 per cent alive today have ever been on a plane! More than this, airports and planes wreak huge havoc on the environment – destroying habitats and emitting large quantities of carbon (even as they are planned to double in size in the next few decades). But more than this, since the attack on the Twin Towers of the World Trade Center and the Pentagon on September 11, 2001 (with some 3,000 victims (and nineteen jihadi hijackers) killed as four planes were crashed), they have become sites of fear, suspicion, surveillance and danger. Many of my friends now hate flying because security has made the journey awful. Airports have now become astounding centres of simultaneous crass commercialism (you have to walk through an endless shopping mall to get to the planes), surveillance (you are watched all the time) and incivility (people get nasty). Sociologists have documented how airports have become centres of distinctly unpleasant and dehumanized life.

For more on all this, see John Urry's *Mobilities* (2007: Chapter 7), Harvey Molotch's *Against Security* (2012: Chapter 2) and Rachel Hall's *The Transparent Traveler* (2015).

One more example must suffice and it is a much more general one. Although sociologists see and write about terrible things in the world, I have long been impressed – in literature and life – at the myriad little ways in which people construct their own little social worlds and go about their everyday lives, wherever they can, not being too nasty or disruptive to other people, and very often being kind to their neighbours and friends. Yes, we know there is conflict, there are bad neighbours and, according to some sociologists, the decline of community. But there are also the ubiquitous little worlds of human care, kindness and sensitivity to others. If you look at much great literature, you will certainly find tragedy and drama, hatred and jealousy. But you will also frequently find a celebration of ordinary people going about their ordinary lives. George Eliot's nineteenth-century novel *Middlemarch* is a marvellous example. Generally considered to be one of the world's greatest novels, it tells the story of industrialization and change coming to a small nineteenth-century community, with all the class and gender divisions you would expect to find. But it also tells the story of everyday heroism, of people getting on with their lives, sometimes looking after others, sometimes doing altruistic acts – and all the little personal foibles this generates. This is the social organization of everyday life, it is everywhere and it is truly astounding. Sociologists thus also study the little acts of everyday life, how people care for each other – and indeed love each other. There is then a sociology of everyday life, a sociology of care and a sociology of altruism, as well as a sociology of play, a sociology of love and a sociology of happiness.

A SOCIOLOGY OF EVERY DAMNED THING

So in the end, it seems, sociology can study anything and everything – both the big things and the little things. Traditionally, it is studied through a series of key institutions such as religion, education and the economy. Look at any school or college textbook on sociology (a good way to get the sense of the taken for granted in a field of study) and you will find chapters on social things like the family, the government and the workplace. But sociology actually studies a lot more: its range is the whole of social life. Since everything that human beings do involves social things, everything and anything can be analyzed sociologically.

This certainly means it clearly studies all the *big* issues of social life – terrorism, environmental catastrophe, the new digital technologies, the drug trade and migration. But it also means that sociologists can be interested in absolutely anything at all, including all the little things of everyday life. So here is a quick alphabet of a few topics. You can find a sociology of age, a sociology of bottled water, a sociology of consumption, a sociology of drugs and deviance. There are sociologies of education, of food and football, of global things, of horror films. Sociologists study Ireland and Italy, Jamaica and Johannesburg. They investigate the sociology of knowledge, love, music and norms. They study Oriental despotism, patriarchy, queer politics, rape, suicide, transgender, the upper classes and urban life, voting behaviour, welfare, X-treme sports, youth and zero-tolerance policies. There can indeed be a sociological approach to any damned thing you can think of – even the most unlikely sounding subjects. If it involves people coming together socially, then it can be studied sociologically. Wherever there are social things, sociologists can study them. This means that sometimes sociology is mocked as a rather wild and silly discipline because it can study the most seemingly ridiculous things and seem to be trivial in the extremes. I hope to show you that this itself is a very silly view. Sociologists can bring their imaginations to study all that is social in human life, and that means everything.

SO IS SOCIOLOGY SILLY? THE THREE 'T'S

Let me give three of these seemingly 'silly' examples quickly. I will call them the three 'T's: the sociology of tomatoes, the sociology of toilets and the sociology of telephones – the 'tomatoes, toilets and telephones' problem! Now you may laugh, and at first sight some might say this is typical and just what gives sociology a bad name. A sociology of tomatoes, or a sociology of toilets indeed? Think on. Here are their concerns.

What does *a sociology of tomatoes* look like? I have one colleague who has – for many years now – specialized in the sociology of tomatoes. He is a professor and he runs a research centre at a major university. He is a very serious man, and if you get him talking about tomatoes, he will not stop. Why? He can trace the history of tomatoes, from the earliest Aztec salsa through to the famous Heinz Ketchup bottle and on to the latest fashionable pizza and Bloody Mary cocktail. He can show how the tomato has been continually transformed in the ways it has been produced, exchanged and consumed. He looks at its role in recent capitalist societies and shows how 'it' was an early pioneer in mass production and a contemporary contributor to the creation of global cuisines. These days, it has become even more interesting as the variety of tomatoes found in our supermarkets becomes simultaneously more and more standardized and yet of a much wider range than people could have ever bought before. How can we get such standardization and yet such diversity at the same time – and often just round the corner? *How has capitalism organized the tomato?* How the world has changed. Just go to the tomatoes and have a look next time you are in a supermarket. What is the chain of people that got the tomatoes there? Why are they in this form? Who is buying them and who is making money out of them? Before you know it, you are discussing the historical nature of the global economic system under capitalism. And we haven't even started to discuss genetic modification and the environmental issues.

OK, but toilets? What can *a sociology of toilets* possibly be about? Well, I have another colleague, Harvey Molotch, a dear friend as it happens, and a world leader in 'urban sociology', who in recent years has taken to studying what he calls 'stuff'. He looks at all the social things we use daily – from toasters to chairs – and asks questions about their social history (where did they come from), their social appearance (why do they come to look like they do) and how they are used in everyday life. Our worlds are cluttered with objects – you could make a quick list of the things surrounding you right now, from computers to pens to books to mobile phones and so on. These are all social objects and they all have a sociology. Well a few years back, he got interested in toilets (and jokingly, he and his colleagues call it 'shit studies'). Now surely I can't be serious. A sociology of toilets? Shit studies? Again, think on.

Toilets raise a major spectrum of issues. Over the past century, they have become basic to our modern world. (Which reader does not use one?) Yet the flush toilet (WC) is recognized globally as an icon of modernity – an emblem of wealth – for an estimated 2.5 billion of the world's population lives without even a latrine! One billion have to resort to 'open defecation' in fields, mud, forests and bushes. Think alone of the smell and sights but also the consequences for health. The lack of sanitation breeds diseases. When we socially reorganize sanitation, we change the smells, sights and health of a society. So a sociology of toilets raises the big issues of *health and modernity* – how did changes in sanitation in the nineteenth century prove to be a decisive factor in changing health and morbidity levels? – and of *social inequalities* today – who in the world get the 'decent' toilets, even luxury bathrooms, and how do the poor so often dwell in such appalling sanitary conditions?

But now move to the more mundane level of everyday life. Spend a week observing your behaviour and those of others in toilets; look for the tacit and overt social rules that organize your behaviour and also the little social rituals you have developed. These things have been studied by sociologists to suggest ways in which our everyday lives are regulated by fine systems of rules and rituals, many of which we hardly notice. Think about the long queues often found for women's toilets; think generally about the gender differences – men rarely talk in toilets, women often do. Think about the adjustment of dress and the comportment of body. Maybe watch Paromita Vohra's documentary film *Q2P* (2006), which can be found on YouTube. Set in Mumbai, it looks at who has to queue to pee and shows how gender and class inequalities are revealed through toilets. Sometimes, too, sociologists look into the so-called deviant patterns – where rules are broken. In one remarkable classic and controversial sociological study, *Tearoom Trade* (1975), the sociologist Laud Humphreys (1930–1988) showed how toilets could be used by heterosexual men for homosexual pickups with routine users remaining unaware of the homosexual activities that were taking place. There is much then to be said about toilets sociologically.

Finally, consider *a sociology of telephones*. What might this look like? Probably no means of communication has revolutionized the daily lives of ordinary people more than the telephone. Invented around 1876, it diffused gradually from a few thousand elite users to a widespread way of communicating across the social classes and the world. (Herbert Casson's *History of the Telephone* is a classic published in 1910 and covers the first thirty-five years. There have been many such histories since.) Portable and mobile phones arrived in the 1980s and were popular by the 1990s. Smart phones arrived in the 2000s, and the iPhone was announced in 2007. They have now become ubiquitous and universal. By 2014, some 4.55 billion people worldwide were using mobiles. In the UK alone, 93 per cent owned a mobile phone by 2014, and 61 per cent of adults owned a smart phone (see http://media.ofcom.org.uk/facts). In just a few decades, the mobile phone has become a worldwide global necessity of modern living.

What has this meant? For most of human history, commun. tion has been direct and face-to-face. But with the phone, hum. interactions started to be more and more mediated by technologies – shifting *who* we could speak to, *when* we could speak to them and indeed *where* we could speak with them. But with the smart and mobile phone, everyday life is revolutionized. It raises new issues here for the twenty-first century to confront. Space, for example, gets reorganized: friendships now can easily glide across the globe. Time gets transformed: there is instant accessibility and the possibility for many of 'perpetual contact' through a mobile phone. Information becomes vast, readily available and ubiquitous. The self comes to be presented in new and different ways – through 'selfies', for example. The visual changes as we use Skype and can look at the people we speak with. Language gets altered as new forms of texting and writing appear. The public/private reconfigures: issues once private become more and more publicly visible. Inequalities sharpen as a new hierarchy of access to phones appears: those who have access to all this across the world, and those who do not. New global issues are raised of regulation (how states control these new communications) and surveillance (how states monitor what is going on). There is, as you can see, a lot to be analyzed about 'telephones', and sociologists have indeed written much on it. The changes will go on. We are now arriving in the land of 'the internet of things', 'Big Data' and the world of artificial intelligence. I will return to all this throughout the book.

SUMMARY

Sociology cultivates an imagination to study the systematic, sceptical and critical study of the social. It investigates the human construction of social worlds and its sufferings and joys, creating a bridge between the personal life and the public one. It can study anything from the big issues (like war, migration and poverty) to the smaller things (like tomatoes, toilets and telephones) and can be both critical and celebratory. It grapples with the idea that even as we are born into a world we never made, we are capable of acting on it and changing it. Sociologists adopt an outsider stance; once encountered, the world will never be seen in quite the same way again.

l your sociological imagination by linking to the
: on Sociology as Consciousness (pp. 3–5) and
....peccing your own assumptions. Think about whether you
can suspend belief in them, at least for a while.

2 In starting to get clear some of the 'basics' of sociology, why
not build up your own sociology blog, diary or Facebook page
and even share with others? Following on from the examples given in the chapter of tomatoes, toilets and telephones,
think of a few areas of social life that interest you (the six 'D's,
for example – dance, dress, dogs, democracy, drugs or drink!)
and start to build up your own sociological analyses of them.
By the end of reading this book, you should be starting to
think sociologically and will have produced your own first
small-scale sociological studies.

3 As you read each chapter of this book, build up a few more
observations, a little collection of relevant links and maybe
some key words. Note that words in **bold** throughout the text
are gathered together in a glossary at the end of the book and
are key words to understand. You may like to build your own
glossary of key words for your blog.

FURTHER READING

An inspiration now for several generations has been Charles Wright
Mills, *The Sociological Imagination* (1959). Other classic 'short' introductions to sociology are Peter Berger, *Invitation to Sociology* (1966);
Norbert Elias, *What Is Sociology?* (1978); and Zygmunt Bauman,
Thinking Sociologically (2001, second edition with Tim May). Berger's book turned me on to sociology in the 1960s, and he tells his
personal story of sociology in a very readable way in Peter Berger's *Adventures of an Accidental Sociologist* (2011). Important addi-
tional introductions include Ben Agger (1952–2015), *The Virtual
Self* (2004); Richard Jenkins, *Foundations of Sociology* (2002); and
Charles Lemert, *Social Things* (2011, fifth edition). Textbooks are
also often a good way to sense the range of topics covered and get a
feel for a discipline. Amongst many texts, see Anthony Giddens and

Phillips Sutton, *Sociology* (2013, seventh edition); Robin Cohen and Paul Kennedy, *Global Sociology* (2013, third edition); John Fulcher and John Scott, *Sociology* (2011, fourth edition); or my own, John Macionis and Ken Plummer, *Sociology: A Global Introduction* (2012, fifth edition). A valuable collection of readings with clear commentary can be found in Daniel Nehring, *Sociology: An Introductory Textbook and Reader* (2013). On tomatoes, see Mark Harvey *et al.*, *Exploring the Tomato* (2002). A recent study on the sociology of the toilet is Dara Blumenthal's *Little Vast Rooms of Undoing* (2014). On telephones, see Rich Ling, *New Tech, New Ties: How Mobile Communication Is Reshaping Social Cohesion* (2008); Nancy Baym, *Personal Connections in the Digital Age* (2015); Ben Agger, *Oversharing: Presentations of Self in the Internet Age* (2015).

2

THEORY: THINKING THE SOCIAL

> Society is not a mere sum of individuals. Rather, the system formed
> by their association represents a specific reality which has its own
> characteristic . . . The group thinks, feels, and acts quite differently
> from the way in which its members would were they isolated.
>
> Émile Durkheim, *The Rules of
> Sociological Method*, 1895

So just what is this thing called 'the social' which sociologists study
and how can it be analyzed? This is a key place to start. Many people prefer to start with viewing human life as biological, individual,
economic or religious, but for sociologists, the starting point has
to be with the social. It is why it is an 'ology'. It is a difficult idea
with multiple meanings – indeed, when I first came to study it some
fifty-odd years ago as an exuberant young gay man, I naively knew
three others words that connected strongly to it: *social* partying, *social*
work and *social*ism. At that time, I liked all three and thought it had
to be a good subject to study! But I soon learnt it was oh so much
more than that. In this chapter, we will start to explore the idea of
the social and ponder a little of the ways sociologists think about
society.

WHAT IS THE SOCIAL?

What I hope to get clear is that, at its best, sociology studies a distinctive reality of life. The ideas of both 'social' and '**society**' derive from the Latin *socius*, which originally meant friend or companion. This suggests both an active companionship and friendship. Ideas of the 'social' were developed in the nineteenth century to mean, more and more, a cluster of human associations and communities that mediate human experience: family, village, parish, town, voluntary association and class. They often indicated associations of people coming together for friendly purposes (as in the friendly societies, self-help and trade unions). Since then, the idea of 'society' has grown to become a central idea for sociologists – highlighted, even constructed, by them as they made it their object of study. The social comes to capture the idea of people functioning together in associations outside of the workings of the state (what is now often called 'civic society'). And in recent times, the idea of society itself has been challenged and re-debated. This chapter seeks to raise some of these ideas.

CONNECTING SOCIOLOGY TO OTHER STUDIES: MULTIDISCIPLINARITY

Sociology is part of a wide spectrum of human and social sciences. Its own emphasis is on the social, and the task of this book is to show what this means. But sociology should not stand apart from other ways of thinking. It is part of a wider, *multidisciplinary project* that wants to make sense of our world, drawing frequently from these other disciplines whilst also contributing to them. Connections always need to be made to disciplines like *anthropology, criminology, economics, humanities, history, philosophy, psychology* and more.

Thus, we need an *anthropologist's* eye to see the ways in which societies can be so different yet so similar as they evolve their webs of meaning into contrasting cultures and symbols across the world. We need a critical *economist's* analysis to get to the heart of the working of modern finance and global capitalism and its contrasting economic systems. We need an *historian's* sensibility to sense where we are coming from – recognizing that everything we examine evolves and emerges from a past. How did this 'social thing' come about? We need a link with *psychology* to grasp how the dynamics of 'inner lives' connect to the wider world. We need a *philosopher's* mind to deal with some pretty profound issues around the meaning of knowledge (**epistemology**), the nature of human social life (ontology) and even the ultimate values of our existence (ethics). We need a bit of the *artist* to glimpse at the complexity and imaginations of unique human beings as they go about their myriad multiplicities of day-to-day creativities and doings. We need to read books and *literature* to expand our horizons of other lives. All this is a tall order, indeed, and a sheer impossibility for any one discipline (or person alone) to do. But bit by bit, and person by person, it can be put together. Sociology is really at its very best when it takes seriously all these other disciplines and works them into a deeper understanding.

Take an example. You want to study education. The sociologist will ask 'macro' questions about how schools link to the wider society and inequalities, as well as 'micro' questions about the culture of the school. The anthropologist will show us how education exists and works in different kinds of society across the world; criminologists will ask questions about 'troubled cultures' in schools and universities. The economist will look at supply and demand and the working of budgets for education; the humanities will direct us to films, art and novels about schools, universities, teachers and students to give us imaginations and insights. Historians will ask how educational systems have grown and changed over time. Philosophers will turn our attention to the purpose and meaning of education, whilst psychologists will direct us to the development of children and youth. A deeper understanding will come from bridging the disciplines of which sociology is one vital part.

SOCIAL FACTS/DOING THINGS TOGETHER

Simply put, for sociologists 'the social' has two meanings: it can depict a reality that comes to exist independently on its own (*sui generis*), or it can depict a reality of interactions and communications between people.

The view that the social has a life of its own was famously claimed by the much-celebrated founding French sociologist Émile Durkheim (1858–1917). For him, society stood uniquely as a collective reality over and above any individual. In a way, it works like a crowd: society comes to have a life of its own and we get coerced to behave in certain ways through it. Sociologists, hence, study this social as a fact external to individuals which constrain us. (Durkheim famously called these '**social facts**'.)[1] These days, social facts are both global and digital.

By contrast, another influential early sociologist, Georg Simmel (1858–1918), had a different view, seeing the social as embedded in relations and interactions. He claimed that 'society is merely . . . a constellation of individuals who are the actual realities'. For him, communicating with others in the same species became a distinctive **social form** of life (the human species could have been unsocial). The social is human interaction, and it is the study of this interaction which is at the heart of sociology. An early leading sociologist, Max Weber (1864–1920), asked: how do we come to 'take into account the behaviour of others'? A more recent leading contemporary sociologist, Howard S. Becker (1928–) suggested that sociology means studying people 'doing things together'. The social becomes a relationship, and we ask about the ways in which we connect to each other. How do we live with each other, and how might we survive without others? There are echoes here of *Robinson Crusoe*, the famous novel by Daniel Defoe (and the modern version of this has become the digital network, with Robinson Crusoe being perhaps the earliest star of *I'm a Celebrity . . . Get Me Out of Here!*). Sociologists ask: *how is a society possible and how can human beings come to live together?* Social beings cannot survive and meet their needs other than

---

1 Words in bold can be found in the glossary at the end of the book and are developed more on the website.

through social co-operation and association. In this sense, the social lives in our imaginations as we come to live through the minds of the others – a process which sociologists sometimes call **role-taking** and the **inter-subjective**. How then might this happen?

ACQUIRING THE SOCIAL: SOCIALIZATION AND THE SELF

A newly born baby, full of bodily desires, is a very human animal – but it is not a very social one. As every good parent across the world knows, it takes a while to care for a baby and to help to make it properly social and empathetic. These processes (often called early or primary **socialization**) are performed very differently across different cultures and across histories: children are raised by wet nurses, nannies, in communes and large families, by single parents, residential homes, gay parents and so on. There is much diversity in child-rearing habits and much research which charts how children come to construct their language, their sense of self and their social habits – for good or bad. What seems clear is that if they are left on their own, without the formative impacts of other people, then they will simply not develop. Many studies of feral children left living in isolation and then discovered later show that they simply cannot then function as social beings.

One of the commonest controversies raised in social science is that of the so-called 'nature–nurture' debate: do we become who we are because of our biology (genes and the like), or do we become who we are because of our upbringing and wider environmental factors? After a century and a half of endless dispute, this now seems to be a false debate (even though many prolong it). *Both* environment *and* genes play significant roles in the shaping of human lives. It is true that different researchers and disciplines will inevitably emphasize different aspects, but most will now agree that the interaction between the two is a crucial matter. *There are always evolutionary pushes, specific biological and genetic influences alongside the workings of the brain at the same time as there are always also specific historical and cultural shapers.* In this book about sociology, it is these social shapers that take pride of place, as they are often overlooked.

AWARENESS OF OTHERS: THE SELF AND INTERACTION

One core idea here is that of the developing human **self** – an idea profoundly shaped by the ideas of the psychologist William James (1842–1910), the sociologist Charles Horton Cooley (1864–1929), the philosopher George Herbert Mead (1863–1931) and the sociologists now commonly known as **symbolic interactionists**. There is a very long intellectual tradition of examining sympathy, empathy and the self – their character, sources, transformations and the role they play in creating social orders and making our 'human natures' coherent. Sympathy and empathy speak to fellow feeling, while the self asks who we are in social action; it serves to create a necessary bridge between the truly unique person and the more general social being. Having some sense of self and self-awareness helps us to evolve more as coherent, even flourishing, social people.

This self suggests that the ways we communicate socially (through empathy and sympathy with other people across life) lie at the core of our social beings. But we have to learn it from our earliest childhood experience. It starts when the baby begins to realize there is something beyond its own world of instinctual gratification, as it comes to recognize and identify with the faces and hands around it (on which it depends). Bit by bit, it moves from a pulsating little bundle of egocentric desires towards the recognition of others and ultimately a much wider social world. The early stages of this self may simply happen when the child responds mechanically to others, but gradually the child comes to identify with parents and ultimately to broaden and create a wider sense of others – friends, communities, societies. Mead talks about this as moving through various phases – imitation, playing the roles of others, acquiring a sense of others to play games, and ultimately a much wider sense of community: the generalized others. In Mead's work, we have a key early account of the core dynamics of how we become social. We can use the analogy of learning a sport or a game of chess: think how they require taking the role of others to play adequately. All our interactions in social life are like this. Failure to take the roles of others competently is a major source of social breakdown.

The idea of self suggests an inner being (often called an 'I') who is engaged in a constant dialogue with an outer world of expectations (sometimes called the 'me'). This is a process in which we are ceaselessly having a conversation with ourselves and others and through which we are struggling to understand who we are and to make sense of our lives and worlds. This conversation depends on the prior existence of the social and communication bonds. To do this, we are always connecting, even balancing, our inner resources given to us in our bodies and emotions (partly genetic) with those we find all around us in other people – near and far – whose significance helps give meaning to our lives. *We are never alone with a self.* Who we are is always being reflected back to us, like a mirror image, by other people, and we come to dwell in the mind of others. We weave mirror-like webs of communications, flows of symbols and signs (**semiotics**), where 'others' are always shaping our next moves. In this sense, then, socialization continues from birth to death and is a life-long process. (Sociologists often refer to this as adult socialization and secondary socialization.) What matters here is that we come to live in the thoughts of imagined others even when we are unaware of this, and our social lives are constantly being shaped by this. The **self** is reflective and reflexive and tries to make sense of social life in a perpetual conversation with itself.

These others can be initially seen as a kind of continuum which spans the following:

Individuals/ action	Self	Groups	Society	World
subjects	interactions	organizations	states	global
Micro		*Meso*		*Macro*

Figure 2.1 A continuum of the social

Sociology studies all this. We can approach these social others from the smallest units (micro) of individuals and selves to the largest (macro) of society and world, through a range of middling units of groups and organizations (often called the meso). This gives us three different kinds of sociology. **Micro-sociology** looks at social actions, face-to-face interactions and contexts – examining how people make sense of the worlds they live in. **Macro-sociology** looks at whole societies, often comparing features of social structures (or stable patterns) and key social institutions (or organized habits) like the economy or education. **Meso-sociology** looks at the patterns that connect them – the interactions in organizations like workplaces, schools or hospitals.

Any aspect of life can be analyzed through these levels. Take, for instance, the issue of crime. Looking at the *micro level*, a key concern is the way in which much crime is learned conduct – we pick up 'deviant' patterns of behaviour from the groups we hang around with or through being within situations which offer opportunities for crimes. Situations, stresses and social group learning become key tools for understanding law breaking and other 'deviances'. Sociologists are not especially interested in crimes as purely individual – as biological (bad seeds, criminal types, criminal genes) or as personality types (psychopaths, sick people, dangerous people). Rather, their interest lies in group learning and the ways in which deviant selves are acquired. They also focus on the *interactional*, how does a crime actually take place in a situation. How does a gang member pull a knife in a particular situation? How do delinquents see society and each other? What kind of situation allows some people to think it is OK to fraud on their taxes? What surrounds acts of theft, rape, homicide, drunken driving, drug taking and terrorism that facilitates their happenings? How do people come to see themselves in this situation, and what stories and language might they bring to it that help it move the way it does?

Moving on to the *meso level*, sociologists take an interest in the ways in which police, courts and prisons function as huge bureaucracies – and the ways in which people get processed through them. At the wider, *macro* or *structural level*, the focus turns to the way in which crime is bound up with the normal conditions of social life. There is a definite pattern to it, and it is found in all societies. Patterns can soon be detected: look at criminal statistics and you will soon sense that crimes are not random. Overwhelmingly, they are usually committed by young men – and often from lower class and ethnic backgrounds. How is this so – or is it even true? Maybe the statistics measure something else – the making of statistics are social acts themselves? We can also ask questions about the institutions of law, policing, prisons and the like which are organized and structured in varying ways across time and history, and we can ask how they play a role in shaping crime – maybe preventing it, maybe structuring crime itself. At an even wider level, we have the global. Here we look at the different rates of crime across societies: why is crime very low in traditional Muslim countries, Japan and Switzerland, and why does it soar in others? Why is it taking on increasingly global forms like trafficking, smuggling, money laundering and the drug trade?

Sociology then examines all things social – the wide range of connections that people make with each other. It encourages a way of thinking that sees that the air we breathe is social: 'the social' is everywhere. We are always linked to others, so the wider whole is always greater than the part. Typically, *we search for underlying patterns in these relations, examine the meanings that people give to their lives in cultures, and see all of this as flowing in a constant and perpetual stream of social actions.* There is no such thing as an isolated individual. In John Donne's famous poem, 'No man is an island'; in Stephen Sondheim's musical *Into the Woods*, 'No one is alone'. Even the most seemingly natural things – like our individualities, our bodies, our feelings, our senses – change enormously under different social situations. Yet this is probably *not* how most people routinely see their daily world.

The largest unit of the social is often seen to be '**society**'. All societies – old or new, big or small – have to organize resources to live: food, shelter, clothing, things, 'capital'. They have to keep some level of order with each other. If everybody just did their 'own thing', chaos and breakdown would probably ensue. Certainly, conflicts need to be managed. Further, because human animals, above all other animals, have developed elaborate languages and ways of talking, they need to organize both their beliefs and their ways of communicating with each other. And finally, they have to pass this on and reproduce their society from one generation to the next or they might die off. In short, all societies need (a) economies, (b) political and legal systems – governance, (c) cultures, beliefs and communication, as well as (d) mechanisms of socialization. These are the building blocks of all social organization. Such concerns will keep reappearing throughout this book.

THE BODY AS SOCIAL

Let's consider a very telling example: *the human body*. It is telling because as we look at fleshy individuals – those seemingly most individual of things – sociologists find them drenched in social relations. Our 'social bodies' display how people 'do things together' – always, everywhere, bodies are profoundly 'social'. Our bodies, our feelings and our senses change enormously under different social situations. We see the world differently, experience the body differently, even walk differently in different societies. *Bodies change under the rule of the social*.

The body is a good example because common sense leads us to think of it as being overwhelmingly biological and natural. And it is, of course: biologists (and many psychologists) rightly focus primarily on the biological workings of our brains, our inherited genes, our hormones. They need to look at the evolution, structures and functions of our biological body. The taken-for-granted assumption is that of the 'natural body'. There surely is no case in sociology to reject biology in any way, and indeed a lot of sociologists work closely with biologists, sometimes doing 'sociobiology', sometimes looking at the social life of animals, sometimes critically examining the role of 'nature' and the natural in social life, and often these days linking to important environmental issues. Despite all this, sociologists look at the body and biology as something that must also always be seen as something profoundly social for human beings. So in what ways are bodies social?

The simple response is that we do things to our bodies because other people matter. We relate our bodies to others. As we connect to others, so social expectations are built up for how we should move our bodies and adorn them. Ultimately, our bodily conducts can come to take on a life of their own – coercing the way we act. At the simplest level, consider how we adorn and display our bodies through our clothes, hair styles, tattoos and body piercings. What a fuss many of us make! We *have* to dress in certain ways and not others. It is not biology that drives us to wear fashion but culture. Indeed, we identify people through their modes of dress and the fashions and styles that tie them to their cultures and generations. Youth in 2016 do not dress like youth did in 1950; the Mahi tribe do not dress like Victorian patriarchs. We obviously do things with our bodies that have social implications. But the ways we do this – 'embodiment', 'body projects' – extend way beyond this simple example. There is now a well-developed *sociology of the body*, and the box provides some examples for you to think about.

THINK ON: THE SOCIAL BODY

Consider the many ways in which the body is social. For example:

1 We purify and clean our bodies through a range of activities – bathing and hairdressing, cosmetics and hygiene. Different societies expect different regimes of cleanliness. There are often very strong differences of class and gender in these practices – we are back to the sociology of toilets here! (see pp. 15–16).

2 We repair and maintain our bodies through medical work (nursing, surgery, environmental health) and body modification (tattoos, plastic surgery, transgender surgery). Again, there are major differences here in class and gender, and many millions of people in the industrial world are employed to work on our bodies through major health (body) organizations.

3 We discipline and regulate our bodies – dieting, exercising, training and taking them to the gym. Here, sociologists study fitness regimes, medical regimes and educational regimes of all kinds. They are busy studying the gym, the health spa and Weight Watchers.

4 We represent our bodies in different ways – think of the ways the body is portrayed in art, film, writing, fashion and advertising.

5 We develop the world of our senses – think how they are shaped by social circumstances. What we can *eat and taste* varies greatly across cultures (snakes, snails and semen) along with contrasting ways we eat (with hands, sticks, plates). Likewise, how people *hear* (the new iPod sounds block out the sounds of the birds in the woods), *see* (the new world of rapid YouTube images is different from watching the slow sunset), and *touch* differ across groups and societies ('touchy' cultures and 'hands-off' cultures). There is indeed a developing *sociology of the senses* which focuses on each of our senses.

6 We commodify our bodies: our bodies are turned into commodities for sale, from the sale of whole people into

slavery through to the sale of body parts and on to 'sex work'. Everything from skin, bone and blood to organs and genetic materials of 'the other' are now up for sale, and there is a massive international market of global trafficking (which is almost invariably in one direction: from the poorest to the richest).

7 We transform and extend our bodies. In some ways, humans are cyborg creatures – the part-animal and part-machine creatures. We do not leave our 'natural bodies' alone. Instead, we extend them *outwards* through tools, machines, clocks, computers. The computer keyboard is joined in cybernetic system with the screen to our bodies, the neurosurgeon hands are guided by fibre-optic microscopy during an operation and the body of the game player in the local video arcade connects their body with a machine for play. Likewise, we extend our body *inwards* with a vast array of prosthetic devices – from contact lenses and artificial limbs to full-blown transgender surgery or transplant surgery. We enter the world of posthuman, transhuman and technological bodies.

8 We also present and perform our bodies – in drama and in interviews, and in all kinds of body rituals.

9 We do sex. We turn our bodies into objects of pleasures and desires, and give them multiple different meanings for doing this. From reproduction to violence, we use our bodies sexually for social purposes.

For a lively and wide-ranging collection of discussions and examples on all this, see Bryan S. Turner (ed.), *Routledge Handbook of Body Studies* (2012).

In short, across history and across cultures we put our bodies to social uses of all kinds. It is never just or simply a biological force which determines our behaviour. Groups and different cultures make sense of their bodies in different ways. The body has different histories – we quite literally live our bodies in different ways at different times. A slave body is not the body of a modern super-rich;

a black woman's body drenched in abject poverty is not the same as the multi-billionairess pop stars Madonna and Lady Gaga sexing their wealthy way through the world.

In a telling and influential study, the much celebrated German-English sociologist Norbert Elias (1897–1990) made important contributions to the study of both sociology and social change. A refugee from Hitler's Germany, his studies of *The Civilizing Process* (originally published in Germany in 1939, a critical year in the denial of humanity in European history) suggested how from the Middle Ages onwards in most of Europe people came to exert greater self-control over their behaviour and their bodies. Through a series of studies of ways of eating, sleeping, dressing, spitting, having sex, defecating and dying, he charts the changing ways of life.

Thus, medieval life was unpredictable, highly emotional, often chaotic and indulgent, and there were few codes around bodily functions. Bodies were volatile, endangered, short-lived, surrounded by disease, death, violence and a putrid stench; they encountered torture and killings. But Elias claims that court society slowly started to change all this by bringing about etiquette for body management, locations for defecation and for sleeping. Restraint appeared in codes such as those managing table manners. The state developed side by side with a 'civilized' system of self-control. This 'civilized society' has self-discipline, self-control, higher levels of shame and embarrassment. People are taught to hide natural functions like defecating and urinating. We become less emotional; we come to see ourselves and our bodies as distinctively separate. (The sociological followers of Elias – of which there are many – have suggested that more recently there has been further changes on the body. It has now become informalized, i.e. we have made many things very casual in our approach to the body.) Changes in our bodies then walk in parallel with changes in society.

MAKING SENSE OF THE SOCIAL: METAPHORS OF THE SOCIAL WE LIVE BY

The work of Elias moves from detailed description of social life to a wider understanding of **social structure** and process. All sociology will sooner or later bring you to the issue of sociological **theory**, whose core task is to deliberate upon how best to understand and even explain these wider workings of the social – of how we are 'coerced by social facts' and 'do things together'. There are many introductions to sociological theory, and this short book does not aim to duplicate them in any way. (A few are suggested at the end of this chapter.) It is an invitation for you to start to develop a feel for just a few of the imageries that might help us make these wider connections to the social. (Table 2.1 summarizes and suggests some more.)

Generally, behind every major social theory, there is an imagery (a trope, a metaphor) or way of seeing the social world. These suggest ways of explaining just how 'the social' works and provide ways to open your eyes for seeing the social world in new ways. Each imagery provides one way of seeing – and *every way of seeing is also always a way of not seeing*. The limits of our language are often the limits of our visions. They are not mutually exclusive and they are often mixed up, but here I just flag a few to help you become sensitive to them. If you spend a few hours looking around the world through some of the different languages here, you may find yourself starting to 'think sociologically'.

Table 2.1   Metaphors of the social that we live by: some opening images to start thinking sociologically

	Think of the social and society as if they were:	Theories and words/concepts to look out for:
1.	Ways of connecting: as a social bond, belonging and creating community, solidarity and togetherness.	**Functionalism**; community studies; (some) network theory; social bonding; institution; attachment; breakdowns in **anomie**, social disorganization. *(Introduced in this chapter.)*
2.	Structure: as patterns and organization; like an organism, a machine or a system.	**Structuralism**; functionalism; evolutionary theory; some Marxist theories; systems theory; cybernetics. *(Introduced in this chapter.)*
3.	Conflict: as wars, struggles, tension, schisms, coercion, power.	Conflict theory; Marxism; inequalities; **feminism; ethnicity; queer; post-colonialism; critical theory**. *(Introduced in this chapter.)*

Table 2.1 continued

	Think of the social and society as if they were:	*Theories and words/concepts to look out for:*
4.	Drama: as theatrical, performance, script.	**Role theory**; **dramaturgy**; performance theory; identity theory. *(Introduced in this chapter.)*
5.	Language: as discourse, signs, speech and conversations.	**Semiotics**; **ethnomethodology**; conversational analysis; discourse theory; **narrative** sociology; **dialogic** theory. *(Introduced in this chapter.)*
6.	Meaning: as culture, self and action.	**Hermeneutic** sociology; **symbolic interaction**; phenomenological sociology; **social constructionism**; interpretative sociology; **habitus**; cultural theory. *(Introduced in this chapter and Chapter 5.)*
7.	Rationality: as rational choice and utilitarian action.	**Rational choice theory**; exchange theory; games theory; strategic theory. Linked to utilitarianism and **neo-liberal** economic theory. *(Introduced in this chapter.)*
8.	Interaction: as emergence, relations, self and others.	Interactionism; formal sociology; relationalism; networks; ritual chains. *(See earlier in this chapter.)*
9.	Unconscious: as masked, hidden and repressed meanings.	Psychoanalysis; depth psychology; Freud; trauma theory; gender; repression. *(Introduced in this chapter.)*
10.	Multiplicities: as pluralities, complexities, flows, networks, cosmopolitanism and chaos.	Relationalities; networks; rhizomes; mobilities; assemblages; matrix; circuits; complexities; holograms; liquid; elastic; complex society; **postmodernism**. *(Introduced in this chapter.)*
11.	World interconnectedness: as international, transnational.	**Globalization**; world systems theory; post-colonialism; transnational theory. *(See Chapter 3.)*

THE SOCIAL AS A BOND: METAPHORS OF COMMUNITY
AND CONNECTING TO EACH OTHER

The social immediately suggests our solidarities and interconnectedness, the ties we make to others. We ask who bonds with whom, how, where and when? And what indeed are the implications of not bonding? There is a strong historical connection here to what has been philosophically called 'social contract theory': the pact between the members of a society to help make it work. This social bond is found most at work in families, communities, gangs, friendships and civic groups of all kinds (choirs, teams, religious groups, sporting associations, workplace unions), and sociologists try to explain the ties, the connections, the belongings and companionships which humans create with each other. Often it has an economic base – common workplace, common consumption. Always it suggests some kind of normative bond, i.e. people share economic situations and **norms**. A great deal of sociology looks at these bonds in different kinds of groups and organizations and how we do things together.

One concern of sociologists working with this imagery has been with the so-called decline of community, with **anomie** and the breakdown of the social bonds in the modern world. Robert D. Putnam's influential work *Bowling Alone* (2000) follows this pattern. He suggests that since the 1960s, people in the US have withdrawn from civic life: there has been a breakdown of the social bond and with this a breakdown of trust. The title of the book suggests it all; when once people went out bowling together and belonged together, now they have become lonely bowlers. Here we see the decline of community, the breakdown of the family, a broken society. At the same time, there are others who say this is not true: what is actually happening is a reworking of the bonds. Families now are not like families of the past; they still bond but now in different ways – families are smaller, more intense and the bonds may be tighter. Think of the mobile phone. Far from breaking relationships, it now often makes families link up twenty-four hours a day. Internet and mobile phone communications have fostered new 'networks', wider global connections and a widening of our bonds. Likewise, while the old locally based (and often craft-based) communities may have collapsed and declined, new communities have appeared everywhere – shaped by social movements, interests and, of course, internet networking. We still need the bonds even as they change their shape.

The idea of **social capital** highlights how life is organized through social connections; having social capital means you are well connected. It suggests not just that bonds are created through others but that these bonds serve as valuable assets in life. They do not just provide cohesion and togetherness but also enable people to gain mutual advantages from each other. The term 'capital' has traditionally been an economic term, but the emphasis on the 'social' highlights the fact that resources also accrue to people through their networks and mutual acquaintances. People look after their own from womb to tomb; good connections advance some people more than others. Privileged people maintain and advance their privileges through connections with other privileged people; different kinds of bonds give very different kinds of returns. So, for example, going to Oxbridge or the Ivy League universities can set up connections and links for life. Social bonds may simply secure advantages of some groups over others, generating and amplifying social inequalities (see also Chapter 7). A good introduction to all this, and the work of its key proponents Pierre Bourdieu, James Coleman and Robert Putnam, is John Field's short account in *Social Capital* (2008).

THE SOCIAL AS STRUCTURE, FUNCTION AND INSTITUTION: THE METAPHORS OF THE ORGANISM

Another set of images of the social (with a long history) is derived from seeing the social holistically as a functioning structure. Here we ask questions about a society's parts and how they **function**: the social is studied through its major institutions and the roles these play in solving problems and helping make a society work. Table 2.2 suggests the most basic way in which this works.

Most famed for this argument in the nineteenth century was the eccentric, founding British sociologist Herbert Spencer (1820–1903). Heavily influenced by the work of Charles Darwin, he saw societies evolving like animal bodies. Just as bodies have identifiable structures (hearts, brains, skin, legs, livers) so societies have identifiable structures (economies, political systems, legal systems, families, religions). Just as bodies have structures with clear functions (hearts

Table 2.2 Problems in living and their institutions

Problems in social life: key concerns	Structures, institutions, practices
Getting basic resources – food, shelter, fuel	Economy, energy, work, consumption, cities, housing
Getting organized – achieving goals	Polity, governance, organizations
Keeping things orderly	Law, socialization, culture
Reproducing the society	Families, education, communities
Caring for each other and the world	Civic life, citizenship, welfare
Developing communications	Language, media, digitalism
Acquiring and developing knowledge	Science, arts, social sciences, education
Cultivating a spiritual side to life	Religion, therapy, transcendence
Others, e.g. looking after the body	Medicine *(Note: there are other concerns and this list is not comprehensive)*

pump the blood, brains co-ordinate activities and provide intelligence, livers cleanse the body), so societies have identifiable functional structures. Economies help us organize resources and adapt to the environment, politics helps societies achieve goals, communities help socialize and integrate the diverse components, and law regulates and controls a society. More, just as a body evolves over time from the simplest organism to the most complex through a process of differentiation and adaptation, so societies have developed over a long period of time and become increasingly differentiated and adaptable. The work of the mid-twentieth-century giant of sociological theory, Talcott Parsons (1902–1979), helped further develop such ideas, which we will look at a little in Chapter 4.

THE SOCIAL AS CONFLICT OF INTEREST: POWER, WAR AND STRUGGLE

Unlike the images of the social bond or functioning organism or machine, many see the social less benignly: as a war of endless political conflicts between different group interests. Here we ask about human struggles and conflicts in social relations. Indeed, the history of societies can easily be seen as the history of one damn war after another. From the wars of the Romans and the Greeks to the wars around the world today (there are currently over forty trouble spots in the world from Afghanistan to Zimbabwe), it is not hard to see conflicts and turmoil as the stuff – the very dynamic – of so much of the social. In contrast to the image of bonding, our focus now moves to our differences. Society now is seen as a war between conflicting interests.

Some have focused on the general interests of society and the nature of **power** and conflict. Niccolò Machiavelli (1469–1527) wrote *The Prince* in 1513 as a guide book of rules and war strategies for the Medici prince whose favour he courted, whilst Thomas Hobbes (1588–1679) was immersed in debates over civil wars and revolutions when he wrote *Leviathan* in 1651. Both were early influential political thinkers who saw human beings in need of strong governments. Machiavelli claimed that left on their own people would be 'ungrateful, fickle, lying, hypocritical, fearful and grasping'. Hobbes claimed that without strong governments, left in a natural state, lives would be 'solitary, poor, nasty, brutish and short'. Both saw the need for strong government. Even if people's own interests were squashed, for the social to function well there had to be a strong ruler. Such debates came to an extreme head in the subsequent conflicts in the French and Russian Revolutions and set the contexts for much of the debate today about democracy.

The sociologist most identified with this image of society is Karl Marx (1818–1883). Of all the social thinkers you will fleetingly encounter in this short book, he has had the greatest world influence. For much of the twentieth century, his ideas shaped life in at least a third of the world (and especially Russia and China). Marx focused on the material needs of people and their labour, and suggested that the history of all societies was the history of class struggle. People fell into conflict as they came to recognize the denial of their human interests and their exploitation in classes. But it is broader than this. As well as class conflicts, many have highlighted the long battle between the sexes and the abuse of women, the cruel conflicts between the races, and, of course, the bloody wars and violence between the nations. We need to understand who dominates

Table 2.3 Conflict is everywhere in society (Ideas explored more in Chapters 5 and 7.)

Conflicts in interest and their power struggles	*Emerging hierarchies and stratification*
Economic	Class, caste, slavery, globally excluded
Ethnicity	Race, racialization, **racism**
Gender	Patriarchy, gender order, sexism
Age	Generations and ageing
States and nations	Colonization, nationalism, genocides
Sexuality	Heterosexism and homophobia
Health	Disablement and illness

and how power and autonomy is taken from many people (see Table 2.3). Some, like Simmel, have even suggested that conflict is endemic in all human interaction and can be found everywhere in everyday life. Others even suggest that conflict may well be a necessity for societies to work. Conflict, then, has long been of great interest to sociologists and provided much of its imagery.

THE SOCIAL EXPLAINED AS EVERYDAY DRAMA: ACTING TOGETHER

When sociologists want to focus on the doings of the social – how social life is lived daily – the most common images evoked are those of drama. Social life is a theatre. We are seen to play social roles as we glide across our lives – we become actors, playing parts, using props, rehearsing the parts we have to play, sometimes embracing our roles and sometimes 'distancing' ourselves from them. **Identities** become masks as ultimately we ask questions about the disparities between the real and its presented appearance. Its key sociological thinker has been Erving Goffman (1922–1982), the most influential 'micro-sociologist' of the twentieth century. As we have seen, micro-sociology is less concerned with large-scale **social structures** such as the state and the economy and examines instead the close-up, small-scale, face-to-face social life in which people encounter each other. In a stream of books published mainly in the

1960s, Goffman showed us how societies may be seen as partially constituted through these face-to-face encounters in which people manage the impressions they give to each other. In his first book, intriguingly called *The Presentation of Self in Everyday Life* (1956), he observed the lives of people on a Hebrides island and documents the myriad ways in which people play roles and present themselves in different ways (front stage and back stage) as they move across different social situations, working hard to manage the impressions they give off of themselves. The book becomes a kind of manual of the skills we all employ in our daily lives. In his later book *Asylums* (1961) – a sociological bestseller – he went on to examine the underlife of people living in hospitals, concentration camps, prisons and what he calls 'total institutions' where people are cut off from the routines of normal everyday life. Again, his focus is on the drama of life – in this case with how the self gets mortified in these extreme situations, and how people rework a sense of who they are. (Goffman has much to say; a useful guide to his work is Greg Smith's *Erving Goffman* (2007).)

There is, however, nothing new about this drama image. That people hide behind masks and veils is present in Greek drama. It is present through all the rites and ceremonies of many tribal societies. It is there in masquerades and carnivals that form part of religious ceremonies enacted to contact with spirits and ancestors. Shakespeare frequently uses the stage as a metaphor for life: 'All the world's a stage, and all the men and women merely players; they have their exits and their entrances; and one man in his time plays many parts.' (Jacques in *As You Like It*, II, vii). Or even more dramatically: 'Life's but a walking shadow, a poor player, that struts and frets his hour upon the stage and then is heard no more; it is a tale told by an idiot, full of sound and fury, signifying nothing.' (*Macbeth*, V, v). Much of this is also captured in the twentieth-century play *Six Characters in Search of an Author* (1921) by the Italian playwright Luigi Pirandello.

THE SOCIAL AS LANGUAGE: THE DISCOURSES OF THE SOCIAL

Closely linked to the drama image is another which also borrows heavily from the humanities and from theories of communications.

This is the idea that society is structured like a language and can be analyzed as a **discourse**. Here the social is regulated through a series of finely balanced rules in much the same way as our speech and talk is. At the most general level, the social is seen as a discourse and a key thinker here has been the French philosopher of ideas Michel Foucault (1926–1984). His ideas are complicated but very influential. In a much quoted passage from a key early book, *The Order of Things* (1969), he describes a discourse about classifying and defining things from a Chinese encyclopedia. Here is a classification of animals. They are:

> (a) Belonging to the Emperor, (b) embalmed, (c) tame, (d) suckling pigs, (e) sirens, (f) fabulous, (g) stray dogs, (h) included in the present classification, (i) frenzied, (j) innumerable, (k) drawn with a fine camel hair brush, (l) et cetera, (m) having just broken the water pitcher, (n) that from a long way off look like flies.

Now I am pretty sure that this classification will make no sense to you, but this is the point. Societies depend upon classifications like these – languages, discourses – that help them make sense of

Table 2.4 A basic guide to Foucault's key writings

Examine the discourses of	To show power relations inside institutions like	Key book
Criminology	Prisons, courts, law, policing, surveillance	*Discipline and Punish* (1975)
Health	Hospitals	*The Birth of the Clinic* (1963)
Mental illness and psychiatry	Asylums, classification systems, welfare	*Madness and Civilization* (1961)
Sexology, psychology, social science	Therapy, prison, governmental interventions, law	*The History of Sexuality* (1976)
The humanities, literature and history	Academic life, universities	*The Archaeology of Knowledge* (1969)
Religion, politics, education	Government, schools	Found in many of his interviews and essays

themselves to themselves. *But they are usually unintelligible to those outside.* They are not – as we often like to think – supremely rational, God-given or natural. They are, rather, unmistakably tied up with the specific historical context. Foucault wants us to look at these vast systems of ideas, thoughts, knowledge and the institutions that they work through. He claims that when you do look at them, you will always find that it is power which organizes them. Power is everywhere in language. Table 2.4 indicates the range of his work.

THE SOCIAL AS A SEARCH FOR MEANING: HUMAN CULTURES

Human sociality is marked by its complex symbols: we are the meaning-making, symbol-manipulating animal that creates **culture**, history, memory, **identity** and conversation. We pass our meanings on from generation to generation. Of course all animals communicate, but they do not – as far as we can tell – develop such intricate signs and linguistic systems. What other animals have so many gods, explore the scientific universe, write the histories of their lives and times, develop art and music, or write Shakespearean tragedies? Human social life is cultural life.

Let's be clear. It is not that other animals are disengaged from meaning – all animals have versions of communication and even languages. But as far as we can tell, most living creatures are guided by instincts, a biological programming over which they have little control. A few animals – notably chimpanzees and related primates – have the capacity for limited culture: researchers have observed them using tools and teaching simple skills to their offspring. But only humans build complex systems of meaning making: spinning complex cultures, fostering religious, philosophical, scientific (even sociological) ideas about themselves and their societies. Only humans weave complex **narratives** about the nature of their own identities and personhood. Only humans cultivate linguistic skills for telling and memorializing history, their 'dead' and other times – and indeed transmit histories and ideas to each other over long periods of time. We are the symbolic, narrating animal, and sociology has long taken this to heart. If sociology wants to understand the humanly social, then it is charged with inspecting closely the nature, content and consequences of the ways in which human activities create little social worlds of human meanings.

I return to this often in this book, but for the moment consider a short quote from Raymond Williams (1921–1988), a UK cultural sociologist:

> Culture is ordinary: that is the first fact. Every human society has its own shape, its own purposes, its own meanings. Every human society expresses these, in institutions, and in arts and learning. The making of a society is the finding of common meanings and directions, and its growth is an active debate and amendment under the pressures of experience, contact, and discovery, writing themselves into the land. . . . Culture is ordinary, in every society and in every mind. (1989)

This world of meanings manifests itself in many ways, but one striking way is in its search for spirituality. Religious or spiritual experience can provide both extreme and commonplace examples of these meaningful worlds or cultures. In Haitian Voodoo, Gede spirits come to possess the bodies of the living. In India, Hindu worshippers find Bhadra Kali. Pentecostal churches round the world come to 'speak in tongues'. In Appalachia, the handling of poisonous snakes produces religious experiences. In Hong Kong, people worship their ancestors. Religions build special languages, wonderful symbols, elaborate rituals and fascinating stories about their people and their gods which are often wondrous to behold. Many millions of Jews believe in the story of Moses who parted the seas and – standing on the top of a mountain – was sent 'the Ten Commandments' through thunder, lightning and the sound of a trumpet. Likewise, many millions of Muslims believe that a human, Mohammad, was visited by an angel, Gabriel, who flew him on a horse to Jerusalem where he met Moses, Jesus and Abraham – and there climbed a ladder into the seven levels of heaven. Many millions of Christians have daily rituals to celebrate a saviour who was conceived by an unmarried and unpregnated woman and who was killed (crucified) but then arose from the dead – and lives on. Virgin births, the rising dead, heavens and hell. In addition, multiple new religions come and go, only lasting a few generations or so. There is an ever expanding list of new religions – of Scientologists, Swedenborgians, Pentecostals, Moonies – and across the world, people search for meaning in a multiplicity of religions. This search for meaning in human life – and the growing strength of many new religions as one route into this – is a key topic for sociologists.

THINK ON: HOW BRANDING AND LOGOS PROVIDE NEW METAPHORS FOR SOCIAL LIFE

An early image of the modern world grasped society as a gigantic machine, vividly portrayed in Fritz Lang's classic science fiction silent film *Metropolis* (1927) and in Charlie Chaplin's *Modern Times* (1936). (Both may be viewed on YouTube.) It was also found in major literary writings such as Kafka, Dickens and others. We have gone on looking for images to capture society, and recent metaphors have often taken a lead from logos and brand names. As consumption and shopping has grown under global capitalism, so world brands such as Coca-Cola, McDonald's, American Express, Nike, Disney, Wal-Mart, Apple and Google have come to symbolize a much wider social organization. Social scientists now write about Wal-Mart, Coca-Cola, Google, the Nike shoe or iPhone as if they provide a key to understanding how a society works. Understand Google and you have a key to the way information works. Understand Wal-Mart and you understand the workings of modern capitalism. Social scientists now write about *The Disneyization of Society* (Bryman), *Coca-Globalization* (Foster) and *The Googlization of Everything* (Vaidhyanathan).

George Ritzer's bestselling sociological work *The McDonaldization of Society* is a prime example. First published in 1993 (with an eighth edition in 2014), it has spawned many debates. Ritzer developed Max Weber's ideas of rationality and bureaucracy and takes the fast-food company McDonald's as a point of entry for thinking not just about fast food in itself but as a metaphor for the ways in which much consumer behaviour is organized. For Ritzer, society is becoming McDonaldized and there are four key features of this. Everywhere across the world – not just in McDonald's, but in university courses, religious groups, in sports – you will find the same themes: efficiency, calculability, predictability and uniformity, and control through automation. The world is starting to act like a giant McDonald's. We have McUniversities, McMedia, McReligions and even McChildren.

THE SOCIAL AS RATIONAL CHOICE: EXCHANGE, GAMES AND GIFTS

A widespread way of thinking about the social has been through the idea that people are rational beings who make calculations about the costs and benefits of alternative actions: the social here is rational and based on self-interest. This is an image derived from classical **Enlightenment** utilitarian theory ('the greatest happiness for the greatest number'), and it is closely allied to classical economic theory, behaviourist psychology and philosophies of rational man. People make decisions according to the 'logic of the situation' (a term used by the philosopher Karl Popper). In sociology, this idea has become best known as 'rational choice theory'. It is identified in the United States with the work of George Homans (1910–1989), Peter Blau (1918–2002) and James Coleman (1926–1995); in the United Kingdom with John Goldthorpe (1935–); and in Norway with Jon Elster (1940–).

Images that flow from this approach often see the social life as a game, exchange or strategic contest; it highlights reciprocity, gifts, 'maximizing profits' and 'winning'. Social life is seen as an (often calculated) exchange in which people act in order to gain rewards – such as money, love, status or political support – maximizing their rewards though employing the strategies and tactics that are often found in games. A key early example of exchange can be found in the idea of *The Gift*, originally studied by the French anthropologist Marcel Mauss (1872–1950) in the early 1920s to show how gifts become a key feature of building and sustaining reciprocal social relations.

These various ideas have been applied in a wide range of research areas like human groups, relational inequalities, social mobility, education, families, economies, criminal behaviour, organizations and power. Yet while the theory has been very influential, critics suggest the theory is often limited because it often fails to deal with emotions and affect, bodies, irrationality and the unconscious.

THE SOCIAL AS REPRESSED UNCONSCIOUS: ON FREUD AND SOCIAL THINKING

Sigmund Freud (1856–1939) was one of the key thinkers of the twentieth century, giving us the imagery and metaphor of the repressed unconscious and its dynamics in human life. Yet he had a curious relationship with sociology. Some sociologists have shown no interest in his ideas, and many have been very critical. But there are a few who take him very seriously, recognizing the importance of the unconscious in shaping the social.

In his earlier work, Freud highlighted the importance of personal development and psychodynamics, showing how human life is shaped by repressed desires, early childhood traumas and conflicts over gender. He claims this creates psychic struggles, anxieties and a repressed unconscious that shapes the inner worlds of childhood and adult life. Much of this leads to an understanding of how gender, sexuality, mothering and violence – key topics for sociology – happen in everyday life. A later strand of his work focused more and more on how societies themselves could become traumatized through instinctual conflicts and their repression, especially around violence, sex and the fear of death. Societies can become 'wounded' through wars, economic crises, slavery and other 'traumas', leaving hidden collective wounds that may well shape social life for generations to come. The social unconscious may play a key, if concealed, part in the conflicts of a society. (See Elliott, 2013; Alexander, 2012.)

THE SOCIAL AS MULTIPLICITIES: SOCIETIES AS COMPLEXITIES AND MOBILITIES

Another way of seeing the social is to grasp the image that a society or group is never a unified, static or linear thing. It is, rather, a multiplicity of fragments in constant movement, a perpetually changing and emerging flow. In this imagery, nothing is fixed and everything is interacting with everything else. As a version of society, it has a long history (at least from the sixth-century BCE philosopher Heraclitus and often identified with the Greek sea god Proteus). It now has many modern proponents, including William James (1842–1910), Gilles Deleuze (1925–1995) and those who follow actor network theory. The metaphors used here have to evoke a sense of social complexity and movement: common images have included those of labyrinth, helix, matrix, mosaic, assemblage, liquidity, circuits, networks, contingencies and rhizomes.

Three recent usages can be highlighted: assemblage, liquidity and complexity. To see society as an assemblage is to highlight its fragile nature in being put together from many parts. (It is used by the philosopher Deleuze but is developed sociologically in the writings of many sociologists such as Sassen and Walby.) To see society as liquid is to highlight how it is not solid but open to constant change and movement. All societies may be liquid, but recently, it can be said to have accelerated and become a key feature of society. Zygmunt Bauman (1925–) claims that the modern liquid society becomes more fragile, ambivalent, precarious and open to constant change. We face *Liquid Modernity* (2000), *Liquid Love* (2003), *Liquid Life* (2005), *Liquid Times* (2007) and *Liquid Surveillance* (2012). To see society as *Global Complexity* (Urry, 2003) is to draw from physics and complexity theory and suggest an underlying moving chaos in the world where small events can have big changes (and vice versa): a world of contingency and unpredictabilities.

SUMMARY

This chapter provides an introduction to the notion of the 'social' (both as an external fact – like a crowd – that coerces us to behave in certain ways and as a relationship with others) and to 'sociological theory'. I have chosen to prepare the way for thinking more deeply about theory by introducing some of its ideas through some key images – socialization, the social as a bond, as conflict, as drama, as discourse, as culture, as rational, as multiple, as interaction, as machine, as logo. All of these (and there are many more) will give you starting points for entering the study of the 'theory of the social'.

EXPLORING FURTHER

MORE THINKING

1 Think of your own uses of the term 'social' in daily language and, making connections to the opening sections of this chapter, define and clarify the different meanings of the word 'social'. Think now of a topic that interests you sociologically (see Chapter 1, p. 13) and ask what is social about it.

2 Consider what metaphors are and indeed what is meant by the idea *'metaphors of the social we live by'*. Now take some of the images raised in this chapter and think about the language they use – try and apply it to the world around you, and to the things that interest you. Do these images help you see the world differently? How might different ways of seeing also be ways of not seeing? Think of major brands and logos: how might their study help you see how society works?

3 What is sociological theory, and what does it try to achieve? Look at some of the books below. Start a blog page that maps out the different schools of social theory: a vertical axis on history and a horizontal axis on cultures and continents.

FURTHER READING

Social theory is at the heart of all sociology courses and research, and this chapter provides a 'light' introduction to it. Also written with beginners in mind are Paul Ransome's *Social Theory for Beginners* (2010), Shaun Best's *A Beginner's Guide to Social Theory* (2002) and William Outwaite's *Social Theory: Ideas in Profile* (2015). Gregor McLennan provides a 'first companion to social theory' in his *Story of Sociology* (2011), and Ralph Fevre and Angus Bancroft's *Dead White Men and Other Important People* (2010) is written as a novel from the point of view of a student starting sociology, introducing 'sociology's big ideas'. More fully, the classic set of readings is Charles Lemert's *Social Theory* (2013, fifth edition). Anthony Elliott's *Contemporary Social Theory* (2014, second edition) is a 400-page blockbuster that is very up to date and lively. Other guides include David Inglis and Christopher Thorpe's *An Invitation to Social Theory* (2012), Rob Stones's *Key Sociological Thinkers* (2016, third edition) and Steven Seidman's *Contested Knowledge* (2012, fifth edition).

An erudite discussion of just what is meant by the idea of society can be found in Anthony Elliott and Bryan S. Turner's *On Society* (2012). They focus on just three images: structure, solidarity and creation. On the body, Bryan S. Turner's *The Body and Society* (1984; 2008, third edition) is the classic that initiated this as a major field of sociological enquiry. Daniel Rigney's *The Metaphorical Society* (2001) continues the idea of metaphor developed in this chapter and suggests eight key metaphors. You might like to follow up on some of the metaphors. On changing social bonds, see Robert Bellah *et al.*, *Habits of the Heart* (2007). On drama in everyday life, the classic is still Erving Goffman's *The Presentation of Self in Everyday Life* (1956). Readings on conflicts are found at the end of Chapter 7. The classic example (and easiest to read) of Foucault and discourse is his study of the changing nature of prisons and control in *Discipline and Punish* (1991). On the logo and branding of society, the very readable classic is George Ritzer's *The McDonaldization of Society*, which in 2014 was in its eighth edition!

SOCIETIES: LIVING IN THE TWENTY-FIRST CENTURY

> In the history of mankind, the amount of time civilization has existed is minute . . . it is very much an immature and ongoing experiment, the success of which is by no means proven.
>
> Colin Turnbull, *The Human Cycle*, 1984

At the heart of sociology lies the central challenge of understanding global human social life as it teems across Planet Earth. Here, I outline some of the earliest attempts to do this, suggest some key areas that sociologists have to understand today, and discuss the directions that global twenty-first-century societies are taking. The chapter signposts many 'problems' of the modern world and ultimately asks you to consider just where we might be heading.

COSMOS AND EVOLUTION: ON CREATING HUMAN WORLDS

Let's start at the very beginning. Understanding our contemporary twenty-first-century world requires that we know a little of our past, and this is a very humbling history. As every school child is taught, Planet Earth is some 4.5 billion years old in a universe some 14 billion years old, and it is but one member of billions of galaxies in the universe. (The Hubble Space Telescope data estimates between 125 billion in 1991 and 170 billion in 2015: a lot, then, and growing!) No life of any kind at all appeared for a long time on Planet Earth, and it was billions of years before dinosaurs ruled the earth – and then disappeared. Sixty-five million years ago, primates emerged, followed by the great apes around twelve million years ago. Studying fossil records, it seems that cultural fundamentals like fire, tools, weapons, simple shelters and basic clothing started to appear around two million years ago. Modern humans started to appear around 100,000 years ago in Africa and bordering southwest Asia. There are signs that after the last great ice age, the earth's human population may have been around five million, but by 500 BCE it had probably leapt to 100 million. Major civilizations of the past (including Egypt, Chinese (Sinic), Arab and the Mesoamerican) only began 5,000 years ago, and most come and go, not lasting for long in the grand scheme of things. The major societies that developed from then were nomadic, agricultural and feudal. But the industrial world as we know it began a mere 300 years ago. *It is with this tiny part of societal history that most of contemporary sociology is concerned.* So here we have world history in scarcely twenty lines! Of course, millions will disagree with this story – 'creationists', for example, still want people to believe the history of the earth is much simpler: made by God in a few days, or no more than a few thousand.

THE EMERGENCE OF SOCIOLOGY ON A PLANET OF THE APES

Sociology developed around the time that Charles Darwin's (1809–1882) ideas of evolution and emergence were developing as a major, if partial, explanation of human life. Ultimately, what sets primates apart from other teeming earth life is intelligence, based on the largest brains (relative to body size) of all living creatures. And just as Darwin was busy studying and comparing different kinds of plant and animal life across the world, so many of the earliest sociologists, historians and anthropologists were busy drawing out comparisons between different kinds of societies in the past and present, seeking a greater appreciation of their own past through looking at ancient Greek, Roman and Eastern antiquities. Others looked out to non-European peoples, whose ways of life differed strikingly from those of Europeans. Indeed, often these were countries that Europe had invaded, colonized and Christianized. With full-blown **ethnocentrism**, they often saw these cultures as inferior to their own.

The history of societies in part can be seen as the evolution of food – no food, no society. In early societies, one key task involved roaming around the earth to find food sources (hunter-gatherers). Once food stocks were depleted, there was a need to move on. But once the idea of cultivating food was struck upon, societies could become more settled. Geographic differences in both local vegetation systems and animals were more or less available for 'domestication'. Water systems needed to be developed; plants needed to be grown in settled areas; animals needed to be reared. The rise of food production varied around the world, but where food production was developed and advanced, many other skills could be developed: writing, germ control, technology, political systems.

It is very humbling and important to remember the scale of all this past: when we make grand claims for today, we should always remember the much grander claims of our past. Sociology, then, may now be seen as the product of major changes in the very recent Western past, including the Industrial Revolution, the French Revolution and the American Revolution. All were linked to major shifts in living conditions (as people moved from the land to the city, to factory life and capitalism, and migrated in large numbers around the world) and political expectations (as people challenged old authorities and sought freedoms, equalities and rights). Here, in this newly emerging 'modern world', with its entrenchment of a new kind of mass urban poverty and class system, sociology was born. Much early sociological work was concerned with charting these major changes – and indeed much work today continues to look at continuing change. At the outset, it may help to provide a brief summary of some of these suggested changes. (See Table 3.1.) The sociologist Krishan Kumar once claimed that 'for all practical purposes it is not misleading, therefore, to regard the enterprise of nineteenth-century sociology as the anatomy of a distinctive type of modern industrial society' (1978). We might say that since its inception, sociology has been interested in drawing up **'ideal type'** versions of different kinds of societies and sometimes suggesting an evolution from one to the other. Sociologists use versions of

Table 3.1 Emergent human social worlds – a classic basic typology ('ideal types') of Western societies
We all dwell simultaneously in traditional, modern and postmodern worlds – though to very different degrees.

	Traditional (agrarian)	Modernizing (industrial capitalism)	Twenty-first century (global capitalism)
Economy and work	Agricultural; herding; fishing maritime	Mercantile capitalism; factory	Global capitalism; service and information technology; unemployment; offshoring; robotics
Technology	Human and animal energy	Industrial energy sources	Post-industrial; information; digital; energy crisis; low carbon
Population	High birth and death rates; low population	Falling death rates; high birth rates, rapid growth	Low death rates; low birth rates; slowing and ageing populations
Governance	Slavery; feudal war lords; kings	Nation-states and new social movements (NSMs)	World organizations; cosmopolitanism; digital activism
Environment	'Natural disasters'	Industrial pollution	Eco-catastrophe, environmental movements, low-carbon society
Religions	Superstition; polytheism to monotheism	From monotheism to secularism	Post-secular; fundamentalist; multifaith; 'a God of one's own'
Communications	Signs; speech and early writing	Print to electronics	Mass-media and digital culture; mediatization and digitalism
Community	Tribal; village; face-to-face; local	Cities; associations; secondary	Global networks

continued

Table 3.1 continued

	Traditional (agrarian)	Modernizing (industrial capitalism)	Twenty-first century (global capitalism)
Knowledge and ideas	Religion; folk superstition	Rise of science	Relativism; reflexivity; relationalism; chaos and complexity
Control and law	Punitive; repressive; 'natural'	Increase of laws and formal institutions; restitutive	Litigation society; heavily organized and financed
Health	High death rate	Environmental health and 'sick model'	Managed care; pharmaceutical society; high-tech medicine
Values	Traditional	'Make it new'	Postmodern pluralism
Groups	Primary	Secondary	Networked
Roles and self	Ascribed	Achieved	Individualism, open, choice
Culture	Folk	Mass culture	Multicultural, hybrid, postmodern, cosmopolitan
Society	Simple	Industrial	Complexity (chaos)
Time and change	Very slow	Speeding up; invented traditions	Rapid, fast, 'speed'
Military	Centrality of warfare but limited and focused	Mass national armies; all the people: 'Liberté, égalité, fraternité, and internal revolution	'New wars': end of monopoly of state, degenerate, fragmented, de-institutionalized

these ideas in many of their arguments, but there are many dangers of oversimplification and overgeneralization. Sociologists have to beware of the dangers of historicism – of seeing necessary, predictable change. Societies develop contingently and unpredictably and are never homogenous. These models can also be criticized for usually being derived from *the standpoint of Western cultures* and will not be so applicable elsewhere. The schema can, however, be useful as starting points for understanding deep contrasts and changes in society.

Nowadays, sociology has developed a global agenda – an analysis that moves way beyond the West. (I trace this history of this sociology in Chapter 4, but here I will look at some of these wider global changes.)

SIGHTINGS OF OUR TWENTY-FIRST-CENTURY WORLD, *CIRCA* 2016

The modern, and largely Western, world is often divided into the 'long' nineteenth century (1789–1914), running from the French Revolution to the start of the First World War, and the 'short' twentieth century (1914–1989), running through two World Wars, a cold war, the collapse of the Soviet Union, the fall of the Berlin Wall and the Tiananmen Square massacre in 1989. This latter period is often seen as a struggle between the liberal, democratic West and totalitarian regimes, or as the struggle between capitalism and communism. Sociologists, historians and politicians debate these changes in enormous detail, but whichever account is preferred, most will agree that the twentieth century was an unmistakably bloody century. Our big-brained animal is also pretty dumb. In his later years, the leading German philosopher and world leading sociologist Jürgen Habermas (1929–) would remark tellingly in his book *The Postnational Constellation*:

> [This was] a century that 'invented' the gas chamber, total-war, state-sponsored genocide and extermination camps, brainwashing, state security apparatuses, and the panoptic surveillance of entire populations. The twentieth century 'generated' more victims, more dead soldiers, more murdered civilians, more displaced minorities, more torture, more dead from cold, from hunger, from maltreatments,

> more political prisoners and refugees, than could ever have been
> imagined. The phenomena of violence and barbarism mark the dis-
> tinctive signature of the age. (Habermas, 2001)

The twenty-first century, so far, is not faring much better. We still
have wars, genocide, religious intolerance, pandemics, mass poverty. World conflicts are ubiquitous, especially in the divide between
Arab cultures and Western ones and in the rise of 'terrorism'
since 9/11. Global environmental warming has become a major
world issue, and many predict humanity will not survive the coming century. The economic world tilts to China, even as capitalism
itself falls into deep crisis, creating a world of massive inequalities
and injustice. So what is this twenty-first world we live in now
actually like?

As I write, in 2015, there were roughly 200 major societies in the
world and some 7.3 billion people. Some societies cover expansive
land mass and have teeming populations. The largest are China,
Russia, the United States and India. At the other extreme, some of
the smallest countries are mere islands. Some forty countries have
less than one million people, and the Vatican itself – located right in
the middle of Rome – has a population of a scant 1,000. (Ironically,
it may be the smallest in size and numbers, but it exerts enormous
influence on the world as the centre of the Catholic Church.) Other
small countries like Tuvalu, Nauru and Palau (only a few thousand)
are not very well known, but places like Cyprus, Barbados and Iceland (slightly larger) are. There are a multitude of islands with populations of less than 100!

The twenty-first-century world can be mapped in many ways,
and these days you can have a lot of fun playing with world maps
on the internet, starting with Google maps. In the recent past, societies have often been divided into the rich North and the poorer
South, the more democratic West and the less democratic East. For a
good part of the twentieth century, people spoke of the three worlds:
the first (industrial), the second (transitional) and the third world
(relatively undeveloped and poor). A fourth was later added (new
industrial countries – NICs), linked to the Pacific Rim and so-called
'Asian values'. With continuing rapid social change, such distinctions can no longer be so easily or clearly made. Sociology, oddly,

has usually focused its attention on only a very, very small number of these countries (the so-called 'West'), often giving a very skewed view of the global situation. Much of what I say in this book shows the restricted nature of sociology in the past. Still, in the twenty-first century, there are signs that sociology is becoming more global, as you will also see.

Anthony Giddens – one of the world's leading sociologists – can set us on our path. In 1999, he delivered a series of lectures on *Runaway World* for the prestigious annual BBC Reith Lectures. He gave these lectures across the world – in Washington (on the family), in London (on democracy), in Hong Kong (on risk) and in Delhi (on tradition). You can find them all on the BBC's website under Reith Lectures and in the short book *Runaway World* (1999). His central thesis suggested the modern world was fast running out of control and that we needed a sustained analysis in order to possibly get it back under control. He used the image of a huge juggernaut rolling rapidly out of control down a hill and remarked:

> We are the first generation to live in this society, whose contours we can as yet only dimly see. It is shaking up our existing ways of life, no matter where we happen to be. This is not – at least at the moment – a global order driven by collective human will. Instead, it is emerging in an anarchic, haphazard, fashion, carried along by a mixture of economic, technological and cultural imperatives. It is not settled or secure, but fraught with anxieties, as well as scarred by deep divisions. Many of us feel in the grip of forces over which we have no control. Can we re-impose our will upon them? I believe we can. (Giddens, 1999: Lecture 1)

Sociologists want to understand this new emerging order and have written many studies that try to capture this change. In the 1960s, it was most commonly called the *post-industrial society* (developed by the prominent US sociologist Daniel Bell to suggest a productive system based on service work, knowledge, information and high technology). In the 1980s and 1990s, a range of new conceptualizations suggested we lived in a *post-modern society* (Jean Baudrillard, Krishan Kumar) or a *late modernity* (Anthony Giddens, Ulrich Beck), suggesting a break with the **Enlightenment** and **modernity** and the arrival of fragmentation, difference and **pluralism.** Others spoke of *a late capitalism, a disorganized capitalism* and *a casino capitalism*, suggesting a continuation of the themes first analyzed by Marx. At the turn of the millennium, a sense of fragmentation and vulnerability heightened as globalization and digitalism became prominent and sociology developed analyses of the *Risk Society, Individualization* and *World at Risk* (all book titles of the prominent German sociologist Ulrich Beck (1944–2015)) and of *Liquid Modernity* (Zygmunt Bauman's term). We were entering *The Information Age* and *The Network Society* (Manuel Castells), *The Global Age* (Martin Albrow), the *Surveillance Society* (David Lyon), the *Post-modern Society* (Jean Baudrillard) and the *Postnational Constellation* and the *Post-Secular Age* (Jürgen Habermas). Sociologists wrote about *Informalization* (Cas Wouters), *The McDonaldization of Society* (George Ritzer) and *The Disneyization of Society* (Alan Bryman). Often, academics wrote apocalyptically: *The Dark Side of Modernity* (Jeffrey Alexander), *The End of History and the Last Man* (Francis Fukuyama) and *The End of the World as We Know It* (Immanuel Wallerstein). Still further, as the twenty-first century rolled on into 9/11 and the 2008 crash – and all the talk was of 'terrorism', 'new wars', 'rampant inequalities', 'environmental catastrophe', 'economic breakdown' and the failures of 'neo-liberal policies' – a new breed of studies started to write about *Expulsions* (Sasskia Sassen), *Financialization* (Thomas Palley), *Offshoring* (John Urry), *The Rise of Disaster Capitalism* (Naomi Klein), the *Seventeen Contradictions and the End of Capitalism* (David Harvey) and *Crisis* (Sylvia Walby). Others started highlighting how digitalism and 'the internet of things' were bringing *Postcapitalism* (Paul Mason), a new *Empathic Civilization* (Jeremy Rifkin) and the *Networks of Outrage and Hope* (Manuel Castells).

As you can see, there is an enormous amount of analysis of our changing times! But whatever terms we use, it is generally agreed that somewhere back in the mid-twentieth century, a new 'second great transformation' started to emerge – for good or bad – one that continued with capitalism but found itself confronting **globalization** and a variety of emerging **multiple modernities** (following the sociologist Shmuel Eisenstadt (1923–2010)). Modern societies have become increasingly globally and digitally interconnected and the pathways of capitalisms are paved with crisis, but the search for any one pattern of modernity is now strongly refuted. It is more complex than that. Rather, taken together, we see a new world emerging from plural pasts that lead to multiple futures often full of ever-increasing rapid change, uncertainty, risk, openness and individualism alongside continuing violence, wars, exploitation, religious intolerances and inequalities. There are many different emphases. Some see dark, pessimistic dystopias; others provide more optimistic, positive utopian images (see Table 3.3). Given there is so much analysis of this change with so many different themes highlighted and developed, I can only highlight a few briefly here.

One critical theme to be noted at the outset is *the growth of inequalities* – the fact that a billion or so people live below the poverty line while a tiny number of very rich people own most of the wealth and have the power that seems to have come with it. Inequality was decreasing in the mid-twentieth century, but in recent years it has been sharply on the increase. I discuss this more in Chapter 7, but here I want to introduce a wide range of other critical issues.

MAKING THE WORLD ONE PLACE: ON GLOBALIZATION AND GLOCALIZATION

In the twenty-first century, no country can stand in isolation from others. Modern communications – global media, digital networking and speedy transport – put people from different parts of the world in touch with each other instantly. The world has become both faster and smaller. Time speeds up and space is compressed. Hitherto in history, movements across countries have been very slow and cumbersome. All that has now changed. **Globalization** refers to this process, and its twin, **glocalization**, refers to the way big global trends are nevertheless modified by local communities, making new and distinctive forms.

Globalization is most commonly seen as economic, as *global capitalism*. It refers to the *global trading, global finance, global consumerism* and offshoring. It is linked to the extension of capitalist markets round the world and, indeed, often to inequalities. But sociologists see globalization at work everywhere: not just the World Bank but also the United Nations, Greenpeace and Disney World. From international marathons and *global concerts* to mass tourism and the internet, we can see more and more people moving in networks not bound to a fixed spatial community. People network across the globe, making the global, their local and their local, the global. Some see themselves as '*global citizens*'. All social institutions have been touched by it. There is *global education* (think 'overseas' university students), *global health* (think HIV, Ebola and Zika), *global politics* (think digital social movements and the United Nations), *global religion* (think multifaith and religious conflicts), *global crime* (think organized crime, drug trafficking and cybercrime), *global conflict* (think terrorism), *global human rights* and *global work* (think migration and even sex trafficking). Think too of the world problem of '*global crisis migration*' with millions of people becoming 'displaced'. Or *global families*, 'distant partners' where families and partners live apart from each other in different countries – a growing phenomenon. And then there are major issues of the *global environmental crisis*. As this world becomes more uncontrollable, we face *global risk*.

All these global changes happen across every sphere of human social life, bringing controversies in each. All of sociology has become *global sociology*.

POPULATION: AGEING SOCIETIES ON AN OVERCROWDED PLANET

A first striking feature of our global world is that it is truly teeming with human life – 7.3 billion people in 2014, projected to grow by a further billion in the next twelve years, and reaching nearly 10 billion by 2050. We live in the pressures of being 'overcrowded' – and getting more so. Of course, there are real differences across continents: China, India and Africa account for around 50 per cent of the world. In 2016, China and India were by far the largest, with populations of around 1.4 billion and 1.3 billion, respectively. They are followed by the US with 322 million, Indonesia with 222 million and Brazil with 205 million. The population of Africa is expected to more than double by 2050 to 2.3 billion. By contrast, Europe, North America, Japan and Australia have declining birth rates. Although the world growth rate has declined a little since the 1970s, it is still around 1.2 per cent per year, which actually means adding 70 million more people to the world's population each year – many more people than you would find in countries like the UK (with around 64.6 million at mid-2014).

Though there are major problems of measurement with such a count, one thing is sure: it is very large, and it has been growing dramatically over the past couple of centuries, as the striking Table 3.2 shows.

Table 3.2   World populations in summary

1750	791 millions
1800	978 millions
1900	1,650 millions (1.6 billion)
1950	2,500 millions (2.5 billion)
1999	6,000 millions (6 billion)
2015	7,300 millions (7.3 billion)
2050	9,700 millions (prediction of 9.7 billion)

Source: United Nations, *World Population Prospects*, 2015 Revision
See: http://esa.un.org/unpd/wpp/Publications/Files/Key_Findings_
WPP_2015.pdf

For most of the world's history, our planet has looked very empty with just a few million people roaming around it. There were a million perhaps in the Paleolithic Age? Ten million in the Neolithic? Maybe a hundred million by the Bronze Age? Recurrent wars and plagues would wipe populations out. By 1350, after the Black Death, it was estimated to be around 350 million. But once industrialization set in, we started hitting a billion. Now – just two hundred years on – it is well over seven billion, over three billion of which has happened in the last thirty years! This suggests an astounding change in the nature of social life. Some say to greater prosperity, others to a dangerously overcrowded planet. Since the pioneering work of Thomas Malthus (1766–1834) on the exponential growth on population and the problems it would bring, there has been an ongoing debate about the social significance of demographic change. *Whatever problems the world now faces are amplified by the huge numbers of people involved.*

For sociologists, many important issues are raised: falling fertility, 'ageing societies' (the title of a key book by Sarah Harper), changing population pyramids and a world environmental crisis in an overcrowded planet. For some, there are still problems of too many people and the need for population control; for others, the issue is how to handle the growing problems of elderly care, health, pensions and retirement for an ageing population. (According to the United Nations (2013), the world population of older people (60 or over) grew from 9.2 per cent in 1990 to 11.7 per cent in 2013 and will more than double between 2013 (with 841 million) to some two billion in 2050.) Whilst demographers analyze these population changes, sociologists are charged with making sense of their social implications.

FROM RURAL LIFE TO THE GLOBAL CITY: A PLANET OF SLUMS

This population growth has implications for where we live. While much of the world still lives in small communities, villages and isolated islands, more than half of the world's peoples are now urbanized. The growth in just fifty years has been astonishing – from 746 *million* in cities in 1950 (30 per cent) to 3.9 *billion* in 2014. And some are startlingly large. When cities first appeared – in the Middle East and elsewhere – they held only a small cluster of the world's population. By 1700, London – the largest city in Europe – had what seemed a staggering half a million. But now, in 2015, it stands at over 8.5 million (and some 14 million as a metropolitan area). Yet while it is a major global city for finance, it now only ranks at twenty-fifth on the scale of world cities by size. In 2014, Tokyo was the world's largest city with an agglomeration of 38 million inhabitants, followed by Delhi with 25 million, Shanghai with 23 million, and Mexico City, Mumbai and São Paulo, each with around 21 million inhabitants. Several decades ago, most of the world's largest urban agglomerations were found in the more developed regions, but today's large cities are becoming concentrated in the global South. Ninety-five per cent of urban expansion in the next decades will take place in the developing world. By 2030, the world is projected to have 41 mega-cities (defined as having more than 10 million inhabitants). By 2050, the projection is for well over 6 billion people to be living in cities. Three countries together – India, China and Nigeria – are expected to account for 37 per cent of the projected growth of the world's urban population between 2014 and 2050. (Currently, Asia and Africa are the most rural continents.) (These figures come from the United Nations unit which makes regular 'projections' on population size gathered from each country in the world.)

Many big cities are seen as global cities – the term global city is usually seen to be defined as big business investment hubs, as defined by the Global Finance Index. On the surface, cities often look like fine places to live with their fancy skyscrapers, big business and art worlds. Yet many of these cities harbour the world's great slums: 828 million people live in slums today, and the number keeps rising. Mike Davis, a political sociologist, writes of the world now becoming a *Planet of Slums* – a world of shanty towns and *favelas* well depicted in films like Danny Boyle's Oscar-winning film *Slumdog Millionaire* (2008) or Fernando Meirelles and Kátia Lund's *City of God* (2002). Here the stories of Mumbai and Rio de Janeiro are told against backdrops of massive poverty, violence, drugs, crime and overcrowding where life is hard – stories which depict the daily struggle to survive. (A documentary on a similar theme is Mark Volker's *The Fourth World* (2011).) Worse still, while the world's cities occupy just 2 per cent of the earth's land, they account for some 60 to 80 per cent of energy consumption and 75 per cent of carbon emissions. They are a driving force behind the environmental crisis, which is discussed below. Rapid urbanization is exerting pressure on the living environment – on water, supplies, sewage and so on. Sociologists have long taken a keen interest in how cities develop new forms of social life and often generate damaged lives.

CAPITALISM, LABOUR AND ECONOMIES:
NEO-LIBERALISM AND ITS BREAKDOWNS

The modern world has essentially become a capitalist world. **Capitalism** comes in many forms but usually brings three key features: private individuals own wealth-producing property; money is invested to make profit; and markets operate with (supposed) minimal state intervention. We can find evidence of early capitalism with merchants making money through investing in goods throughout recent history – for example, in Genoa and Venice in the twelfth century. But the arrival of distinctively modern capitalism is usually linked to the rise of the industrial world, first in the cotton mills in England at the turn of the eighteenth century, then throughout Europe and the United States, and ultimately the rest of the world. In this earlier factory-based capitalism, workers sold their labour for (low) wages and in the process capitalist owners made profits.

The eighteenth-century thinker Adam Smith (1723–1790) maintained in *The Wealth of Nations* that the market system is dominated by consumers who select goods and services that offer the greatest value. He developed ideas around what some call market capitalism. Producers compete with one another by providing the highest-quality goods and services at the lowest possible price. Thus, while entrepreneurs are motivated by personal gain, it is claimed that everyone benefits from more efficient production and ever-increasing value. In Smith's famous phrase, from narrow self-interest comes the 'greatest good for the greatest number of people'. This *laissez-faire*, 'trickle down' approach claimed that a free market and competitive economy would regulate itself by the 'invisible hand' of the laws of supply and demand. Government control of an economy would inevitably upset the complex market system, reducing producer motivation, diminishing the quantity and quality of goods produced, and short-changing consumers.

Early sociologists such as Marx and Weber (and later ones such as Polyani, Wallerstein and Harvey) disagreed. The system was less of a rational market than a site of the 'battle of man against man . . . to attain control over opportunities and advantages' (see Max Weber's *Economy and Society*, 1978). One of Karl Marx's major contributions to social thinking was his scathing indictment of the workings of capital. For him, capitalism generated inequalities, exploitation and the poverty and pauperization of workers as they found themselves disadvantaged in markets, forced to sell their labour power at less than its value (so that the owners could make more profits for themselves) and driven ultimately into conflicts with the owners of capital. Capitalism here is not the benevolent system of Adam Smith but an inherently unstable and conflictual one driven by the ever-increasing need for more and more profits, which works in favour of the few and against the majority.

These models of capitalism are somewhat abstract, and pure ideal capitalism is non-existent. Capitalism takes many forms, has been through many phases, faces routine crises and keeps adapting and changing. In the early and middle nineteenth century, *liberal capitalism* involved a free market with a supportive government and legal framework to help maintain it. But by the start of the twentieth century, mass assembly line production had emerged (often called *Fordism*), with ever-increasing profits, investments and scale as work became more and more monotonous for the masses. After the Second World War, a pattern of *organized capitalism* emerged which involved an administered market and a more 'directive state'. There was, for example, in the UK between 1946 and 1979 much more 'state' intervention as governments often shaped economic policies. But during the 1970s and 1980s, a **neo-liberalism** was ushered in by Thatcher in the UK and Reagan in the US. Here state intervention was decreased and the centrality of markets grew with more global and dispersed operations. In the UK it was marked by the end of nationalized industry, the decline in welfare state provisions, an increase in the service sector, a massive increase in consumption and a breakdown of a stable labour market with job security. Each one of these phases is marked by crisis and breakdown, and right now we may be entering a new phase and form linked to digitalism.

The United States is usually seen as the purest form of capitalism – private markets are more extensive than in Europe – but even here the government does play a role in economic affairs. For example, the entire US military is government-operated, and in 2008–09, the government had to intervene to prevent the collapse of businesses and banks in the 'bailout' of the financial crises.

For much of the twentieth century, industrial capitalism was in a 'cold war' with the East, especially China and the USSR (Russia), both of whom came to adopt and then 'drop' communist systems. After the crises of 1989 – the revolutions of Eastern Europe which heralded the end of the Soviet Union and the protests by Chinese students in Tiananmen Square – the triumph of capitalism has seemed assured for a while. Eastern Europe (including the German Democratic Republic, Czechoslovakia, Hungary, Poland, Romania and Bulgaria) moved towards market-led or capitalist systems. Only North Korea, Laos and Cuba maintain full communist regimes. In 1992, the Soviet Union itself dissolved. Ten years later, three-quarters of state enterprises were partly or entirely under private ownership. These market reforms in Eastern Europe have been very uneven, however. Some countries (Slovakia, the Czech Republic) are faring well; others (such as the Russian Federation itself) have brought out many of the weakest points of capitalism, with growing poverty and inequality, high competitiveness and social decline. Along the Pacific Rim, Japan, South Korea and Singapore, yet another blend of capitalism and socialism is found. During this century, China has also conspicuously opened itself to the market system – whilst still keeping central state control. Indeed, with deep irony, China has become a world leading capitalist system, even as it opposes democracy and liberal ideas in favour of totalitarianism.

So capitalism is diverse, adapts and is constantly on the move. We live more and more in a global network capitalism where markets cross countries, crisis in one reverberates in all and local capitalisms take on different forms. There is neo-liberal capitalism, state capitalism, Chinese capitalism, Islamic capitalism, Arab Gulf capitalism – and all have been the topic of sociological investigations. Riding above them all is a kind of global network capitalism (dominated by a small group and excluding the vast majority of the world's population) where social instability, social inequalities and economic unpredictability become the norm. In the 'credit crunch' and worldwide economic crises of 2008–09, the banks had to be assisted to loans totalling trillions and trillions of dollars. This marked an end point for the capitalist system as it was. Governments across the world had to intervene in order to restore some kind of stability, and the neo-liberal dream bubble of total free enterprise was (for a while) burst. In the long run of world history, contemporary capitalism's future is very uncertain, but right now, its changing fortunes have to be central to any analysis of the social world. We live in a profoundly – if wobbly – capitalist world. But it is surely changing.

CRITICAL ECONOMICS: IS CAPITALISM HARMING OUR WORLD?

Capitalism is a system of permanent *crisis* in pursuit of more and more profit. The deregulation and lack of control of the neo-liberalism of the 1990s resulted in the fall of the investment bank Lehman Brothers and a worldwide crash in September 2008. Yet the major response to it was to support the financial world while developing a system of austerity for others. But 'austerity economics' (with reduced spending and increased frugality by governments) brings its own problems. More crises can be expected. Sociologists have long debated the nature of capitalism, highlighting critical issues which include:

1   **Widening inequalities:** In 2015, the richest 62 people in the world own as much as the poorest 3.6 billion, and 1 per cent of the population own 46 per cent of the world's wealth. A tiny number of rich and powerful people are cut off from the mass of poor – many of whom are now more or less excluded from social life. A catalogue of health problems and human vulnerability flow from this. *What are the limits of this inequality?* (Dorling, 2015; Sayer, 2015; Sassen, 2014; see Chapter 7)

2   **Engulfing marketization:** In the twenty-first century, everything is up for sale, even water. What was once thought to be for the general good and the government's responsibility (like prisons, education, health, good transport systems, good energy systems, good communication) are now put into the market place (privatized). *Is there*

anything money can't buy? What are the moral limits of markets? (Sandel, 2012)

3 **Growing financialization:** Modern capitalism is a world of fictional money and profits, with people getting very rich on it: 'profiting without producing'. With little production and work involved, what matters is people investing for profits, then taking profits and reinvesting for more profits. There are different kinds of profit and wealth under capitalism, and the question becomes: *what is the use of money for money's sake and who gets this money?* (Lapavistas, 2013)

4 **Increasing debt:** Capitalism depends upon investments that are usually bound up with debt. One man's investment is often another man's debt. We have become the 'indebted man'. Capitalism generates a very widespread system of debt – public and personal, from student loans to mortgages and credit cards. In 2015, the average UK household was in debt by over £54,000. *How do people live in debt? What are the limits of debt?* (Lazzarata, 2007)

5 **Pervasive cultures of financialization:** The central values of the world become money, materialism, markets and consumption: a logic based entirely on finance. It displaces other more human values like care, justice and human flourishing. *Are market values the best human values for a society?* (Haiven, 2014; Brown, 2015)

6 **Emerging precariat:** A new social class is emerging where more and more people live lives of greater insecurity and precariousness, usually through their very low wages and poor, unstable work situations. *How can we prevent more and more people from becoming precariats?* (Standing, 2015)

7 **Hiding offshoring:** A powerful 'offshore rich' secretly conceal their income, wealth and profits in tax havens and private islands, weakening democracies. *How can offshoring be reduced?* (Urry, 2014)

8 **Spreading corruption:** A widespread abuse of power for private gain (corporate theft, financial service frauds, the ever-revolving doors between Big Government and Big Business). *How widespread is corruption under capitalism?*

9 **Damaging the environment:** It is Big Business across the world who are the top emitters of carbon dioxide (China (over 8 million tonnes, 23 per cent), United States (over 5.5 million, 19 per cent), EU (13 per cent) and Japan (over 1 million, 4 per cent)). *How does capitalism damage the environment?*

See also Harvey (2015); Walby (2015).

DIGITAL SOCIETY, MEDIATIZATION AND THE TRANS-HUMANIZATION OF LIFE

We can trace four revolutions in the development of modern media: printing, visual, electronic and digital. Printing has been developing since Gutenberg, and newspapers and journalism have been around since 1700. New communication technologies started to radically change things when they began to appear in the early nineteenth century. Thus the camera arrived around 1839, setting in train a new visual world of reproduction never possible before and leading to the ubiquity of recorded images – from camcorders to digital photography. The telephone arrived around 1876, bridging remarkable distances and heralding the mobile phone and a dramatic reordering of human communications. The phonograph arrived around 1877, anticipating the Walkman and the iPod a hundred years later. Nowadays, iMusic and Spotify let us have music wherever we go – a far cry from the live, local musics of the silent past. In the 1890s, film arrived, leading to the twentieth century being called 'the century of the film and cinema'. Where these new forms became an everyday experience for large numbers of people around the world, now they can be streamed directly into our homes. Radio and television started to appear in the 1920s and

1930s and became commonplace in most Western homes by the late 1950s. All this changed the world.

But then the new **digitalism** brought computing, social networking and 'the internet of things', arriving at the turn of the third millennium and now embedded firmly in all the major social institutions and everyday life of most people around the world. By 2015, well over 40 per cent of the world used the internet (in 1995, it was less than 1 per cent). Its penetration was uneven, though, with Asia, 48 per cent; the Americas, 21 per cent; Europe, 29 per cent; and Africa, 10 per cent. The average internet user spent around four hours and twenty-five minutes using the net each day, with Southeast Asians registering the highest average daily use. **Digitization** and **mediatization** have become key features of the twenty-first-century world, radically changing it. Friendships and families now live life through smart phones, Facebook and Twitter. Schools, hospitals and workplaces foster the 'e-revolution' in education and cyberhealth, breaking down when computers are hacked or fail. Crime shifts into identity theft and computer hacking, whilst policing creates the new surveillance society. There is the cyberchurch, the online social movement, digital democracy, the digital city and, of course, the digital divide and the digital self. We are witnessing the making of a new digital information economy that is changing, if not superseding, capitalism (see Castells, Mason, Rifkin). And modern terrorism has created 'the digital caliphate' in ISIS (the Islamic State of Iraq and Syria) (Atwan, 2015). No social institution has been untouched by it, profoundly shifting our communities, relations and structures of feeling, marking out major transformations as the new media sweeps through social life and changes all in its wake. With this has also come a growing *Digital Sociology,* which I will draw on throughout the book.

Overall, we live in the digital. New media have now become an inescapable part of human experience. There is little we can do in society that stands apart. Yet even as these digital processes have become embedded in everyday life and institutions, they have brought their fair share of troubles and worries. What are these 'digital troubles'? The box below explains.

CRITICAL DIGITALISM: FUTURE CHALLENGES FOR A DIGITAL WORLD

The digital world has brought many well-known benefits (information, data, access, efficiency, speed, productivity, creativity, 'choice' and so forth) and has become an indispensible part of twenty-first-century life. It is not going away. But it has also brought the potential for a wide array of *'digital troubles'*. Here are some of the critical and challenging questions that sociologists need to keep asking.

1   *Digital surveillance and democratic failure*: As 'every click is registered somewhere', critical digitalism has to keep asking: who gets to know what about our digital lives? Through the sensational cases of Edward Snowden and Julian Assange, much has been revealed about the ways governments are already accessing our internet and phone activities, and much more is to come. Digitalism raises enormous issues of privacy and freedom, and democracies may well be threatened by it. Indeed, we may have already gone well beyond the predictions of George Orwell's *1984*. (See 'Think On: A Surveillance Society', pp. 76–7.)

2   *Digital crime and abuse*: Why and how does digitalism feed into so much contemporary crime? From hacking, phishing and copyright infringements to financial fraud, drug dealing and terrorism, the digital is at the forefront of rising crime. And for many, the internet has become a very scary place indeed: the home of abuse, threats, harassment, bullying, violence, vigilantism and widespread misogyny, homophobia and **racism**.

3   *Digital dehumanization, impersonality and the collapse of the private*: How does digitalism shape our interpersonal face-to-face personal life as human contact is replaced by

machines and we 'overshare' our personal lives with others? Where people were, so machines now arrive. Privacy goes public as a 'selfie' generation is created of public narcissism and celebrity. We are now 'alone together' and in need of 'reclaiming conversation' (to use the terms of Sherri Turkle, who has been studying human computer interaction for over thirty years). For many, we are arriving in the world of the 'post human' and a world of diminished relating and communicating.

4   *Digital worklessness*: How does the new digitalism shape the future of work? Increasingly, robots and digital machines take over the work of shops, restaurants, libraries, education, offices, accountants, businesses – everything! We find the accelerating destruction of much conventional work, creating new problems of mass unemployment and the growth of a more provisional and tentative labour force (often called the **precariat**).

5   *Digital social inequalities*: How are new forms of inequalities being created for those without access to digital life? The internet embodies free-market individualism and brings with it new elites and masses, extending digital divides across countries, social groups and people.

6   *Digital capitalist concentration:* How does digital capitalism work to shape 'mega platforms' that 'rule the world'? Nowadays global digital corporations like Google, Amazon, YouTube, Facebook and Twitter make the largest profits and form a major concentration that regulate and transform our lives into market consuming/prosuming lives. Only a few, like Wikipedia, seem to be open and democratic.

7   *Digital complexity and overload*: How can we live with a 'catastrophe of abundance' (Andrew Keen's term)? Nowadays we face worlds of complexity and speed hitherto unconceivable – a land of petabytes, where we are daily confronted with information overload and proliferating, excessive choices. We have too much information to handle and the speed of life is becoming too fast.

8 *Digital dumbing*: Are our brains being rewired into a new mode of thinking? As we move from the depth of close and linear narratives and reading to skimming, scanning, hyperlinking and 'Big Data', there may come a loss of intellectual depth, sustained thought, logical argument and creativity. Is there a digital death of narrative and human agency?

9 *Digital takeover*: How are artificial intelligence (AI), robots and sensor networks taking human life beyond human control? A nightmare world hitherto only depicted in science fiction becomes a reality.

There is a lot of critical writing on digitalism. For examples, see Sherry Turkle's *Alone Together* (2013) and *Reclaiming Conversation* (2015) as well as Nicolas Carr's *The Shallows* (2011) and Andrew Keen's *The Internet Is Not the Answer* (2015).

ENVIRONMENT AND SUSTAINABILITY:
AN IMMINENT WORLD CATASTROPHE

In the grandest scheme of things, civilizations – and even the human species – will come and go. But whereas in the past, the numbers on Planet Earth ('Gaia' as some leading environmentalists like James Lovelock call it) were very small and relatively little damage could be done to it by human activity, now, as populations expand (to repeat: by three billion in the past thirty years), the planet comes under siege. A major climate catastrophe is likely to happen if we allow global temperatures to rise more than two degrees Celsius above pre-industrial levels, and it has been widely claimed that we will indeed do this by 2050 or much earlier. There are already signs of this through a major increase in global weather disasters – the Indian Ocean tsunami in 2004, Hurricane Katrina in 2005, the Haiti earthquake in 2010, etc. Today we hear much talk of *The Next Catastrophe* (Charles Perrow, 2011), *World at Risk* (Ulrich Beck, 2009) and 'the new catastrophism' (John Urry, 2011).

Discussions about 'the environment' are usually seen to be the province of economists, scientists and politicians. In fact, they are very much the concern of sociologists too. After all, the 'crisis' about our environment is social – surely it is social behaviour that is damaging the world? There are many key questions for sociologists to ask: *How do changing social conditions (like consumerism, capitalism and policies of perpetual economic growth) shape our world environments? How do different social responses (like media, social movements and government policies) emerge towards the 'environment' and shape the perception of an 'environmental crisis'? What are the consequences (and risks) of human actions for the future environment, especially how is environmental damage distributed unequally? What if any are the likely pathways into our sustainable environmental futures? And how can we understand how people respond to disasters – a sociology of disasters.* Sociologists need to understand 'the drama of the environment' as an escalating sphere of contested politics unfolds.

This is surely an urgent sociological agenda for research. Ultimately, the broadest challenge for a sociologist is to understand how our 'environmental practices', of people and institutions, are changing the environment. How we endanger wildlife, overhunt and overfish, destroying the rich biodiversity of species and plant life and damaging ecosystems. How we degrade the land through chopping down forests and eroding soil – the vanishing rainforest in an age of deforestation. How we threaten the water supply, pollute the air, overpopulate our cities and produce too much waste. How our transport systems have produced too many cars, planes and cruise liners tipping waste into the environment. All this is most surely of our own human social making! The larger economies are the ones creating the greater problems. (Just ninety major corporations have produced nearly two-thirds of gas emissions since the dawn of the industrial age!) As capitalism gets greedy for more and more profit, and governments seek more and more economic growth with ever-spiraling consumption, sociologists are forced to ask: what are the limits to all this growth and consumption? Is there to be no end to it? How might we envisage human activities that lead to **sustainable development**, a low-carbon society and the importance of building a shared sense of a common world that needs our care and protection – the '**commons**'.

All these developments have led some sociologists to claim that the human world has never been more at risk. A key book in discussing much of this has been *Risk Society* (1986/1992) by the late German sociologist Ulrich Beck (1945–2015), who introduced the idea of the **risk society**. Here global technological changes are shown to have unforeseen consequences that we cannot easily predict. From genetic engineering to nuclear weapons, the massive spread of networks of cars and planes, the development of genetically modified crops, the cloning of animals, the deforestation of the planet, 'designer children and surrogate mothering', all have consequences which may be far reaching. Often the smallest of acts can have the most unpredictable dire consequences.

RATIONALIZING SOCIAL LIFE: ARE WE BECOMING TRANSHUMAN?

A key to much of this change is the way it is now pervasively shaped by science, rationality and research (along with the technologies that accompany them). Science has a long history (Arabic–Islamic science was very advanced up until the thirteenth century; Chinese technology was displayed in the Great Wall of China in 200 BCE), but over the past 400 years or so, it has become an increasingly defining feature of the West. A *Quantum Revolution* brought us new understandings of matter, outer space and energy: putting a man on the moon and exploring the possibilities of space travel and satellite surveillance (along with the dropping of a bomb on Hiroshima/ Nagasaki that killed an estimated (and much-contested) 150,000 to 300,000 people). A *Biomolecular Revolution* mapped our life and genes in the Human Genome Project – making possible cloning, designer babies, racial eugenics and the extension of human life. And an *Information (computer) Revolution* generated unparalleled communication possibilities through mobile phones and the internet – as well the potential for a robotic, surveillance society.

Modern science is omnipresent in the world we live in, and it has generated technological organizational societies cultivating 'organizational people', even 'transhumans'. Many lives are now spent in large-scale hierarchical bureaucracies regulated by systems of rules, rationalities and responsibilities; many bodies now become subject to new technological interventions. Noticed and described famously by Max Weber in his idea of the Iron Cage at the turn of the nineteenth century (and well illustrated in the novels of Franz Kafka such as *The Trial*), by the start of the twenty-first century, we can find an all-pervasive regulation running through government, education, health, research, workplace, media: nothing seems untouched by it. It is the world of 'quality assurance', 'health and safety', 'audits', 'accountability', 'form filling', 'the audit culture', the 'surveillance society', and what George Ritzer has called *The McDonaldization of Society* (1993), which as we have seen (Chapter 2) suggests that the rules which govern the running of the McDonald's food chains have come to organize much of social life globally. Although this all brings many problems, without it much of the world as we know it would not work: superstores would collapse, colleges would break down, medical records would not be available and air travel would grind to a disastrous end!

But this rationality goes even further: we are now witnessing a new kind of human being in the making. This 'transhuman' (or for some 'post human') being finds its body, behaviour, subjectivity transformed by machines. This is a world of 'biotechnology'; artificial intelligence; pharmaceutical markets; drug control; stem cell research; genetic screening; genetic therapy; EEGs; PET, CAT and MRI scans; reproductive technologies; 'cyborgs'; digital sex; digital 'second life'; genetically modified food; advanced prosthetics; robotics; body part donation; transplantations; and the market in body parts. Modern science and rationality is eating into our bodies, making us something different from what we once were and raising a multitude of political and ethical issues along the way.

THINK ON: A SURVEILLANCE SOCIETY

With the growth of rationalization, digitalism and information, human life has potentially become more and more monitored. Think of the many areas where your own life is under inspection with public surveillance like CCTV, IDs, evaluations of all sorts, passports, etc. Some of it we do not mind, but as it extends further, deeper and wider we find surveillance extending its tentacles into everyday life. Think of *'biometrics'* (where physical characteristics like fingerprints, body, brain and eyes are scanned); *'dataveillance'* (where a person's digital life gets systematically coded through 'electronic footprints', credit transactions, bar codes, emails, internet searches, mobile phones – all waiting to be 'scraped and harvested' for Big Data); *genetic screening* (like the Human Genome Project (HGP); and *geographic information systems* (GIS), which bring geo-location devices like radio frequency identification tagging (RFID), global positioning system (GPS), and satellite monitoring and drones to monitor everyday life. It seems George Orwell's *1984* has been reached and surpassed.

The task for sociologists is to map out this surveillance society, trace its various histories and examine its consequences for people and society – both positive (a secure, efficient society) and negative (loss of freedom, vulnerability and generation of fear and suspicion). Edward Snowden, the North American privacy activist and whistleblower, and Julian Assange, founder of WikiLeaks, raise very public debates about the trade off between liberty and security: just how much needs to be known about us by the state to make our society secure? The central problem is the balance between public security and safety and personal freedom and privacy. These are big and important issues for the future – especially for democracies.

Multiple books and films have been produced about this surveillance world. Popular films include *The Net* (1995), *Gattaca* (1997), *The Lives of Others* (2006), *Minority Report* (2002) and *The Truman Show* (1998). A good source of academic studies is *The Routledge Handbook of Surveillance Studies* (Ball, Lyon and Haggerty (eds.), 2012). See also the websites for Surveillance Studies Net (www.surveillance-studies.net) and State Watch (www.statewatch.org).

'THE RETURN OF THE GODS' IN A 'DESECULARIZING'
WORLD: HOW TO LIVE WITH MULTIPLE FAITHS

Yet, science and rationality are not the only belief systems of the modern world. Religion (and spirituality) plays a key role in all societies, and there are thousands of idiosyncratic religions across the world, with seven major ones, alongside huge numbers of non-believers. Christianity has over two billion followers and is projected to grow to nearly three billion by 2050. (The growth will mainly be in Africa with four out of every ten Christians in the world living in Sub-Saharan Africa.) Islam has over 1.5 billion followers and is the most rapidly expanding; by 2050, 'the number of Muslims will nearly equal the number of Christians around the world' (Pew Research Center, 2015). Hinduism has around one billion, and Buddhists come in at about 7 per cent of humanity at 488 million. There are some twenty-seven million Sikhs. Judaism is relatively small with only fourteen million adherents worldwide (six million being in the United States). Two other belief systems are not strictly religions. Much of China has been shaped by Confucianism (ancestor worship) and latterly communism, the anti-religion. There are also approximately one billion people who are non-believers (in Europe around forty million).

Sociologists have long been claiming that the world is becoming more and more secularized – the Gods are in decline as the world becomes more rationalized. 'God is dead' was the famous remark by Nietzsche, and certainly atheism is on the rise in some mainly Western countries in the world. But in general, the secular sociologists are being proved wrong. The post-9/11 world has brought an end to any straightforward secularization view of the past, putting Islam and the full orbit of world religions with their multiple schisms back into sharp focus. We have now entered the 'post-secular' age, with its 'return of the gods'. Secularism now is under attack; new violent Islamic, Hindu and Christian religious organizations, often 'terrorist', are on the increase; and both the Muslim faith and Christianity are globally becoming stronger and more radically conservative. In Africa alone, Christians grew from less than ten million in 1900 to more than 540 million by 2015.

The world is currently 'bubbling with religious passions', to quote a leading sociologist of religion, Peter Berger, himself a Catholic. And what is really striking about this change is the way these expanding religions are becoming more fundamentalist – traditional, morally conservative, living by the Holy Books, and evangelical. By 2050, it is estimated that 72 per cent of Christians will live in Africa, Asia and Latin America. They are often Pentecostal. Many are inclined to deal with faith-healing, exorcism and mysticism. Frequently, they raise huge funds from the relatively poor. This new 'Christendom' arriving in the poorer world is often the proselytized product of the West, as religious crusades failing in the West have turned their attentions elsewhere. And likewise there has been a major growth in the politicalization of Islam across the globe and the rise of the Jihad or holy religious war. As I write, ISIS has become a major world threat with its violent killings (see Atwan, 2015).

This new global (and often digital) religious order is struggling to come to terms both with the presence of a new *modern* world – and often it can't – alongside the need to learn to live with the *variety* of religious experiences now publicly visible in the world. There has been a strong development in multifaith dialogue over the past century, but at the same time there has been a distinctive rise in fundamentalisms. Many growing religious movements seek a return to a more absolutist past. Making serious, even violent, demands to reinstate traditional gender roles and traditional sexualities, they set the ground for an increasingly contested world under multiple modernities.

New religious worlds (like their older counterparts) bring a simultaneous potential for good alongside enormous harm and violence. It has led the sociologist Ulrich Beck to ask just how we are to civilize the global potential for conflict between the monotheistic world religions and bring about 'the cosmopolitanization of religions' with a new type of goal: 'not truth but peace' (Beck, 2010). The rise of global faith movements has been one key response. Sociology, which once proclaimed the inevitability of secularization, has had to rethink.

SOCIAL MOVEMENTS AND IDENTITY POLITICS: IS DIGITAL ACTIVISM CHANGING THE WORLD?

Mass mobilization and social movements began to take shape in Western countries during the later eighteenth century – symbolized massively by the French Revolution. During the nineteenth century, a durable set of elements started to appear that moved through the world (through colonization, migration and trade) whereby more and more groups and populations engaged in new forms of political actions. Charles Tilley (1929–2008) was a sociologist who spent much of his life showing the rise of social movements in parallel with the development of the ballot box. In his book *Social Movements, 1768–2004*, he suggests that these new social movements (NSMs) combine three things. They develop public campaigns, getting organized to make collective claims on targeted audiences. They combine whole repertoires of political actions ranging from public meetings, processions and rallies through to demonstrations, petitions and the creation of special purpose associations. Ultimately, they display and present themselves to the public as good causes and worthy people. They are united, with large numbers of committed supporters.

Social movements have become a key feature of modern political life. Not only do they provide the momentum for political change, they also provide a sense of meaning in life. Very often people build their sense of who they are (their identities) from these very movements. Sociologists claim that often '**identity**' becomes a key basis for social action and change. The list of such organizational movements and identities is very long and very striking. Amongst them are the women's movement; gay, lesbian, bisexual and transgender (LGBT) movements; environmental movements; student movements; anti-globalization movements; the right to life movement; the animal rights movement; the landless people's movement; the indigenous people's movements; the human rights and civil rights movements; the disability movement; the AIDS movement; the Austerity movement; and rights of all kinds. All these have been studied by sociologists and often made central to a grasp of contemporary political life.

Since the arrival of the digital age, such movements have changed and become even more prominent through what the sociologist Manuel Castells has called *Networks of Outrage and Hope*. We now have web activism (Dartnell), 'online activism' (McCaughey), 'cyberprotest' (Pickerill), 'liberation technology' (Diamond), 'digital rebellion' (Wolfson), the *People's Platform* (A. Taylor) and 'information politics' (Jordan). Smart phones and social networking like Facebook and Twitter are a key to a more fluid, leaderless, participatory activism that arises more spontaneously. Amongst many recent examples are those of the Occupy Movement, the Arab Spring in Egypt, the Umbrella Movement in Hong Kong, the Gezi Park Movement in Turkey and the Pussy Riots in Russia. While some suggest that these new politics are enhancing democracy, others maintain that they do not really challenge the dominant power groups.

GLOBAL PERPETUAL VIOLENCE: A PROBLEM OF MASCULINITY?

Violence, in its many varieties, has been found across most societies throughout history. Since 3600 BCE, it has been estimated that some 14,500 major wars have been waged, killing some four billion people. Violence takes many forms: interpersonal (homicide, abuse, rape, bullying) or collective (gangs, genocide); legitimate and state-sanctioned (wars, capital punishment) or illegitimate (terrorism); instrumental or ritualistic. Sociology is charged with examining how rates of violence differ across social groups and societies. (Anocracies – with a mix of democratic and autocratic features – appear to be much more violent than democracies.)

In the twenty-first century, violence has been marked by 'new wars', 'terrorism', 'genocides', 'interpersonal violence', 'sexual violence' and the continuing 'global brutalization of women'. Since the extraordinary atrocities of the First World War, Holocaust and Soviet Purges, we have generated more and more 'extreme' modes of violence – beyond humanity. There is a lot of violence, but overall, as a percentage of numbers of past violence, some (like psychologist Steven Pinker) claim it is in decline even as others (like historian Robert Bessel) claim it has become 'a modern obsession' that makes it more and more unacceptable. Ironically, even if violence has become less acceptable, it has also become routinized and normalized in media and games playing.

A short litany of modern violence in 2015 would show about a fifth of the world was in conflict (there were some thirty wars being conducted around the world). Many of these are within states: they are 'new wars' – 'degenerate wars' (Martin Shaw, 2003) – attacking people at local levels, with rape and genocide commonplace. Some key areas of conflict in 2015 included Syria, Iraq (ISIS), Ukraine, South Sudan, Nigeria (Boko Haram insurgency), Somalia, Democratic Republic of Congo, Afghanistan, Yemen, Libya and Venezuela. There is also much sexual violence. (Nicole Westmarland traces fifteen types of violence against women: in relationships, families, the public sphere and institutions.) Global statistics have their problems, but routinely it has been claimed that one in every three women in the world has been beaten, coerced into sex or abused – usually by someone she knows; that as many as 5,000 women and girls are killed annually in so-called 'honour' killings (many of them for the dishonour of being raped!); that worldwide some 140 million girls and young women have undergone female genital mutilation (FGM); that an estimated four million women and girls are bought and sold worldwide each year, either into marriage, prostitution or slavery; that some sixty-four million women and girls become child brides; and that each year, women undergo an estimated fifty million abortions, twenty million of which are unsafe, and some 78,000 women die and millions suffer.

Much violence is often bound up with 'honour' and masculinity. It is overwhelmingly men who initiate and fight wars; men who commit and are convicted of homicide – as much as 90 per cent (they are also most likely to be the victims). It is men who commit suicide (often 75 per cent), men who rape, men who abuse, men who join gangs, men who become violent terrorists. It is epitomized in fraternity gang rape and war rape. This world of violence often suggests that masculinity in the modern world is under crisis.

UNDERSTANDING TERRORISM IN THE TWENTY-FIRST CENTURY: MAKING A SOCIOLOGICAL AGENDA

Since the suicide bombings of the World Trade Center in New York and the Pentagon in Washington on 11 September 2001 (with around 3,000 people killed), terrorism has moved centre stage in world politics. Sociologists are building an agenda for 'a sociology of terrorism'. Here are some of the questions they ask:

1. What is meant by 'terrorism'? (One study suggests over 100 definitions in use (McDonald, 2013).) How to define it, and whose definition? Make sense of the truism that 'one man's terrorist is another man's liberator'? Is it political violence not legitimated by a state?

2. What is its *historical* context? Consider the history of specific terrorism, probably starting with the struggles of the French Revolution (1789–99), and go on to ask about the histories of 'modern terrorism'. Are there key differences between old and new violence, fears and technologies?

3. Examine the *varieties and types* of terrorism: from faith-based revolutionaries and Jihads to environmental activists, from old (tight, local) to new (loose, global, etc.). An empirical listing on the web shows over 150 clickable entries to terrorist groups, with al-Qaeda, Boko Haram, ISIS, Taliban and Hamas being only the iceberg tip.

4. What are the *causes* of terrorism? How do terrorist groups emerge and work? Examine the world/social conditions that generate them (alongside, perhaps, the more psychological question of what makes a person a terrorist).

5. Are terrorist organizations *social movements*? Can the old models of social movements discussed by sociologists – usually involving issues of 'strain, identity, claims making, resource mobilization' – make sense of these movements?

6. What are the different kinds of *responses* to terrorism by governments, media, populations and victims – and what are their consequences? How does resistance to terrorism (counter terrorism) through international policing and 'homeland security' work? What are its intended and unintended consequences? This might also include an examination of some films and books and poems that have been written about it.

7   How does terrorism work as a form of social *control*; the creation of cultures of fear by both terrorism and opposing governments?

8   What role does terrorism play in *social change* – shifting moral boundaries and public awareness of issues, fear, etc.?

9   How does terrorism have an *impact* on wider issues of human rights, freedoms, violence, conflict resolutions and the flourishing and denial of human life?

10 How does terrorism link to *inequalities*?

A range of ideas around terrorism are discussed in Caroline Kennedy-Pipe, *Terrorism and Political Violence* (2015), and Kevin McDonald, *Our Violent World: Terrorism in Society* (2013).

THE GROWTH OF NATION-STATES: THE CRISIS OF MIGRATION

Most people living on the earth today live in nation-states. This is a new phenomenon, far from typical of the past, where land masses have been ruled diversely by tribal chiefs, kings, emperors and sultans – despots who ruled by force and theocracies held together by religion. Ethnic groups made claims to their territories, and right up to the sixteenth century, people lived with these territorial limits set through land stewardship. But starting with the Treaty of Westphalia (1648), criteria start to be set out to demarcate local domestic territories and recognize independent nations. Old empires – the Russian Empire, the Ottoman Empire, the British Empire – continued until the early twentieth century, when they started to collapse and new nation-states started to appear. Modern nation-states subsequently became the core of the systems of catastrophic wars built around nationalism in the twentieth century.

A nation-state sounds like a contradiction. A **state** is a political organization with effective rule, sovereignty and governance over a limited geographic area – claiming a monopoly on authority, controlling armies and civil service and believing it can use violence 'legitimately'. By contrast, a **nation** suggests a human and cultural community – connected often with religions, languages, ethnicities and a shared way of life. It is something to make a sacrifice for, even lay one's life down for. It is linked to nationalism and usually generates strong identities. (I am German; I am Thai; I am a Maori.) Often these are less real than imagined. The idea of imagined communities – an influential term developed by Benedict Anderson – suggests how nationalism is linked to the emergence of a 'print-capitalism' and the growing rejection of ideas of the monarchy and divine rule. (There has been much recent sociological research on the nation-state and its workings by Michael Mann, Anthony Smith and Saskia Sassen, along with a concern about the democratization or not of these states.) Nationalism and nation-states raise the issue of migration as people move across states. 'Think On: Crisis Migration' discusses just how much movement there is in the world today.

THINK ON: CRISIS MIGRATION

There has always been worldwide migration, and in 2015, approximately one billion of the world's seven billion people are migrants. A major feature of twenty-first-century life, however, has become 'crisis' and 'forced' migration where people are trapped, flee their 'homes', require relocation and find there is no option but to leave their country. We are now dealing with a large and growing number of people who are fleeing conflicts, persecutions, wars, violence, human rights violations, floods, famines, earthquakes and political instability on a scale not known in recent times. It is deeply bound up with inequalities: the rich can move around the world much more easily.

At the start of 2015, nearly 60 million individuals had been displaced worldwide: 19.5 million refugees, 38 million displaced people and 1.8 million asylum seekers. More than half of all these refugees came from just three countries: Afghanistan, Syria and Somalia. Poor and developing countries received the majority of migrants. Turkey, Pakistan and Lebanon were the major refugee hosting countries, with Turkey alone hosting more than two million. Sociologists ask questions about the social conditions that generate these migration crises, examine how people face such situations, ask why some move and others do not, and question how they settle or fail to settle. They ask how different social groups face problems: migrants at sea, migrants in camps, migrants trapped in war zones, children, older people, women, young men. While all this suffering is happening, a new industry – the 'migration business', both legal (border control) and illegal (trafficking) – has emerged. Overall, major global humanitarian issues are being generated by all this as both governments and international organizations fail to deal with it.

Take a look at:

UN, *UNHCR Global Trends 2014: World at War* (2015)
Katy Long, *The Huddled Masses: Immigration and Inequality* (2015)
Internal Displacement Monitoring Centre, www.internal-dis placement.org

THE HYBRIDIC DIASPORA: TOWARDS COSMOPOLITANISM

Linked to the problem of nations (suggesting unity) is the growing awareness of the differences of peoples in the twenty-first century. There are some 200 nations and several thousand indigenous peoples and local tribes speaking some 7,000 languages with different religions, values, politics and ways of life. Over history, there have been multiple mass migrations within and across countries, creating a global **diaspora** as people move and disperse around the world. A truly cacophonous din of voices can be heard. Such diversity can be found both *between* different cultures like India or Zimbabwe but also *within* a country: Indonesia has more than 700 languages, Russia has over 150 cultures, many Arab cultures are riddled with internal schisms over the true nature of their Muslim beliefs. The deep complexities of these differences is an issue we are only beginning to take very seriously and often with much controversy. To start with, we might see all societies usefully as **hybrids**, revealing a blending and mixing of all these differences: there is no simple society or unified nation, political ideologues notwithstanding. Hence they all also pose questions of **multiculturalism** (the mixing of different cultures, often ethnic, in a society) raising issues of immigration policy, social cohesion and fears of 'outsiders'. National identities can be challenged. The ability to handle such issues depends on government policies of assimilation, accommodation, integration, separatism, etc. All this leads to the modern interest in an old idea: **cosmopolitanism**, which proposes a kind of openness and tolerance to these differences. It suggests both developing social structures of tolerance and attitudes of empathy for others. It involves a willingness to engage with others. At its best it leads to a world with fewer borders and boundaries, less stigmatizing of the 'other', and a wider, more sympathetic global moral community of human differences.

At the broadest level, as people become more aware of differences, we enter a society that has been called *postmodern*. Originally, **postmodernism** was a major twentieth-century movement in architecture and the arts which recognized that uniformity, linear coherence, unitary wholes or absolute truths were at an end (if indeed they had ever existed). We live increasingly in a fragmented world overrun with multiplicities and complexities, where all we can do, as the French philosopher Jean-François Lyotard (1924–1998) put it, is 'play with the pieces'. The term subsequently became a buzz word of the 1980s and helped shape the ways in which we now see different cultures as fragmented.

MONITORING THE TWENTY-FIRST-CENTURY WORLD THROUGH THE INTERNET

Sociologists need to keep the big picture of the state of the world in mind. And they can do this with the help of websites. Here is a small selection of key words to search to add to your 'favourites' list and which will help you keep up to date. This way, you can regularly check up the state of the world and know what is going on. Always be aware, though, that *all statistics bring problems* and need thinking about critically (see Chapter 6).

- **Societies**: search *The World Bank; The CIA Factbook; United Nations; NationMaster; New Internationalist; Human Millennium Development Reports*
- **Populations**: search *United Nations World Population Reports (UNFPA); World Population Prospects and Projections*
- **Cities**: search *UNhabitat; World Urbanization Prospects; State of the World*
- **Economic development**: search *United Nations; OECD*
- **Poverty**: search *World Bank Poverty Net; Global Issues*
- **Environment**: search *World Watch Institute; World Resources Institute: IPCC (Intergovernmental Panel on Climate Change); UNEP (United Nations Environmental Panel); Defra UK (Department for Environment, Food and Rural Affairs); People & Planet (student activism)*
- **Human rights**: search *Amnesty International; Human Rights Watch; Map of United Nations Indicators on Rights; ILGA (International Lesbian and Gay Rights)*
- **Violence, war, terrorism and genocides**: search *Global Peace Index; Terrorism Index; Vision of Humanity; Genocide Watch; Stockholm Peace Research Institute*
- **Migrations, refugees and displaced people**: search *United Nations High Commissioner for Refugees (UNHCR); Refugee International*
- **Political freedom and democracy**: search *Global Democracy Ranking; Freedom House*
- **Religions**: search *Adherents*
- **Languages**: search *Ethnologue*
- **Values**: search *World Values Survey*
- **Maps**: search *World Atlas; Google Maps; mapsoftheworld.com*
- **Human Flourishing**: search *UN Human Development Index; World Happiness Report; Human Security Index*

A quick guide to all this is *The Economist Pocket World in Figures* (2015, twenty-fifth edition).

The most serious challenge to all these positions, of course, comes from the development of **fundamentalisms** – views which assert there is only one way and usually provide an authority (often religious) from a voice lodged somewhere in the past. It is here in this divide that we find much of the conflict of the contemporary world.

FUTURE SOCIAL IMAGINARIES AND THE DIAGNOSIS OF CHANGING TIMES

Sociologists study a wide range of social changes in the contemporary world, and I have just given a few examples. Many more could be added: there are changing families (new forms of living together like gay marriages, global families and new reproductive care), health (AIDS and the new global pandemics), education (the world growth of both primary and higher education) and so on. To end this chapter, it helps to ask where this all takes us. Can we make an overall assessment of change? Clearly, sociologists are not fortune tellers or futurologists; they are not charged with predicting where we are heading. But they can construct future **social imaginaries** and diagnose the trends of the times. Table 3.3 shows that they are harbingers of very mixed messages.

BAD NEWS

On the one hand, the bad news just gets worse and worse, and this chapter provides my pessimistic sociological friends with further ammunition. We live in a time of environmental catastrophe. There are slum megacities, digital dehumanization and religious wars. Violence is ubiquitous, terrorism is on the rise, slavery is still prevalent and women's lives are severely brutalized. Inequality is increasing and racism runs deep. For many, it is a risk world of fears and loss of control. There is a migration catastrophe with growing numbers of desperate displaced people in need of help. Democracies are collapsing with growing marketization and surveillance. Crisis capitalism is corrupted and generates growing mass global inequality: half of the world's riches lie in the hands of a mere 1 per cent of the population who more or less rule the world. All these problems are

Table 3.3   Diagnosis of our times: future social imaginaries

Towards dystopia: darkness and visions of tragic worlds	*Towards utopia: hope and visions of better worlds for all*
Growing inequalities	Narrowing inequalities: the fair society
Environmental breakdown	Sustainability, the low-carbon society and the 'commons'
Violence, terrorism and war	Peace-making and a society at peace
Perpetual capitalist crisis	New economic orders
Religious intolerance and ethnic conflict	Empathy, multifaith, multiculturalism and the cosmopolitanism society
Wasted life without dignity or rights	Civility, **citizenship** and the human rights society
Technological dehumanization and surveillance	Humanized digitalism: the humane society
Exclusion and expulsion: the exclusive society	Inclusion: the inclusive society

compounded and amplified by the sheer rise in population numbers we now confront.

There is a significant library of sociological scholarship analyzing all this, and we can document much more. For example, more than seventy countries have laws which criminalize homosexual acts, and a number of these – Iran, Afghanistan, Saudi Arabia and Chechnya amongst them – have the death penalty for gay sex. Torture is common to extract confessions of 'deviance', gays are raped to 'cure them of it' and they are sometimes killed by death squads. The rights of women, children and homosexuals are violated everywhere.

GOOD NEWS

And yet the good news is that there has been some progress on a number of fronts. Some now suggest there may have been a growing civility (Elias), compassion (Sznaider) and empathy (Rifkin) alongside a steady decline in violence (Pinker). There are now many organizations devoted to making the world a better place, creating websites and providing regular reports that help monitor the state of the world. A good example is *Worldwatch*, which has produced an annual report, *The State of the World*, since 1984. Issues of human rights are now raised universally, as are concerns over care, justice, welfare, security and 'the environment' in ways that were simply not on the agenda 200 years ago. Even as billions suffer, there have indeed been documented improvements in the lives of many.

To take one, admittedly controversial, example. In 1990, the United Nations instigated the Millennium Development Goals (MDG) with eight aims to change such things as world poverty, infant mortality, world illiteracy and the situation of women. Although it was far from being wholly successful, and it was very costly, it brought about many significant changes. In 2015, at the end of this project, it could claim that world poverty had significantly fallen: globally, the number of people living in extreme poverty had declined by more than half, from 1.9 billion in 1990 to 836 million in 2015. It seems there might have been more success in the war against poverty over the past fifty years than in the preceding 500 years! Likewise, the numbers of starving and chronically undernourished in low-income societies has declined from around 40 per cent in 1960 to 12.9 percent in 2013. There is also more access to drinking water in 2015 (more than 90 per cent) and more reasonable sanitary conditions (open defecation has fallen by half since 1990). In low-income societies, there has been clear improvement in child mortality: from 165 deaths per 1,000 live births in 1960 to about 43 in 2015. Literacy has increased from around 16 per cent in 1960 to about 91 per cent by 2015, and education at all levels is recognized and significantly on the increase, especially for girls. Indeed there has been growing global concern about the situation of women, and there has been more gender equality in employment and in political institutions.

In 2015, this project was widened to become the Sustainable Development Goals (SDG), now with some seventeen goals and 169 targets! The goals could direct at least US$700 billion in foreign aid towards positive change between 2015 and 2030. Amongst the seventeen goals are such things as 'end poverty in all its forms everywhere'; 'ensure healthy lives and promote well-being for all at all ages';

'achieve gender equality and empower all women and girls'; 'reduce inequality within and among countries'; 'promote peaceful and inclusive societies for **sustainable development**'; 'provide access to justice for all'; and 'take urgent action to combat climate change and its impacts'. So here is a major new project for sociology: to understand how these goals come to be constructed, modeled and ultimately – maybe – achieved.

We could go on. Over the past 500 years, the struggle and gaining of freedoms and justice for the ordinary person have been placed so firmly on the agenda in ways that simply weren't imaginable in the longer past. Some also now claim that perhaps 46 per cent of the world are now more 'free' – living in democracies – though there are real problems about what this means. Looking at the many technical developments over the past century or so also cannot fail to impress. It is probably fair to say that the last 200 years have brought both more knowledge and artistic creativity than all the previous centuries and that the past fifty years have made all this more accessible to more people than ever before in history. The world history of art, culture, music, sport and human creativity is a wonderful topic for sociological study.

Recently, alongside all this 'advance', there has also been a growing interest in what might be called *a sociology of happiness, well-being and flourishing*. Theoretical sociologists build arguments about human capabilities and flourishing whilst more empirical researchers attempt to measure 'happiness'. For many years now, the Human Development Index has gone beyond economic indicators to include measurements of education and environment. More recently, the Happy Planet Index combines ecological footprint, life satisfaction and life expectancy to measure happiness and well-being. (An appendix to this chapter samples some countries on the Human Development Index for 2015.)

In sum, a balance sheet on the state of the world now brings very mixed stories indeed. Sociologists are embedded in all these changes, study them and try along the way to make the world a little more of a better place for all. On some issues – life expectancy, literacy, internet use, etc. – life may be getting a little better; on others –

environment, terrorism, corruption, etc. – it is getting worse (see UN Millennium Project, *2015–16 State of the Future*). The future is ambivalent.

SUMMARY

A major challenge for sociology is to make some sense of our ever-changing world. This chapter illustrates some of the key issues that sociologists now research and debate across the world. Its themes have been big and wide-ranging: the changing nature of capitalism; the digital world; the growth of population and cities; the development of science and rationality; the environmental crises; the 'secularizing' and fundamentalizing of religions, modern terrorism and violence; the emergence of nation-states; the migration crisis; the changing nature of social movements. Every one of them is a subsphere of sociological study, and sociologists analyze them with an eye on the future: just where might we be headed?

EXPLORING FURTHER

MORE THINKING

1 Start your own website called 'Monitoring the Twenty-first-century World through the Internet'. Use the guideline links suggested in the chapter, p. 88.

2 Take each of the topics discussed and think how they relate to your life now. For example, look at the box on 'digital troubles'. Can any of these troubles be found in your place of study, your workplace or amongst your friends? (Indeed, who are your friends these days – are they all online?) Look at the environmental issue and consider how you experience this crisis: think about some of your own actions and gather up some 'data'. Remember, it is human social activity which helps pollute, degrade and even destroy our land, our water and our air.

3 Think about some of the people you know and consider what kinds of social groups they belong to. How do they differ? What do they have in common?

A good general introduction is Goran Therborn's *The World: A Beginner's Guide* (2010). A brief history of the modern Western world is Mary Evans's *A Short History of Society* (2006). Patrick Nolan and Gerhard Lenski's textbook *Human Societies: An Introduction to Macrosociology* (2014, twelfth edition) discusses different types of society. Robin Cohen and Paul Kennedy's *Global Sociology* (2013, third edition) is an excellent introduction covering a wide range of fields. *The Economist's Pocket World in Figures* (2015, twenty-fifth edition) provides a simple annual guide to basic world statistics.

Many books on social change are cited in the chapter. The shortest and easiest read is Anthony Gidden's *Runaway World* (1999); more comprehensive is Manuel Castells's *The Information Age* (originally published in three volumes; revised edition 2009). Three texts will help guide you through the voluminous writings on globalization and glocalization: Jan Nederveen Pieterse, *Globalization and Culture* (2015, third edition); George Ritzer, *Globalization: A Basic Text* (2015, second edition); and Luke Martell, *The Sociology of Globalization* (2010). More specifically, see the works of Ulrich Beck (1986, 2000, 2006, 2008, 2009, 2013).

On particular issues, see: demography, Danny Dorling, *Population 10 Billion* (2013); capitalism, Geoffrey Ingham, *Capitalism* (2008) and James Fulcher, *Capitalism: A Very Short Introduction* (2015, second edition); environment, John Urry, *Climate Change and Society* (2011): terrorism, Kevin McDonald, *Our Violent World: Terrorism in Society* (2013); social movements, Imogen Taylor, *Revolting Subjects* (2013); digital and media sociology, Deborah Lupton, *Digital Sociology* (2015) and Christian Fuchs, *Social Media: A Critical Introduction* (2013); religion, Ulrich Beck, *A God of One's Own* (2008/2010) and Mark Juergensberger, *God in the Tumult of the Global Square: Religion in the Global Civil Sphere* (2015); the new rationality and the transhuman, Nikolas Rose, *The Politics of Life Itself* (2007) and Rosi Braidotti, *The Posthuman* (2013); surveillance, Thomas Mathiesen,

Towards a Surveillant Society: The Rise of Surveillance Systems in Europe (2013) and Zygmunt Bauman and David Lyon, *Liquid Surveillance* (2013); cosmopolitanism, Robert Holman, *Cosmopolitanisms* (2009) and Robert Fine, *Cosmopolitanism* (2007); nations, Sinisa Malesevic, *Nation-States and Nationalisms* (2013); and cities, Saskia Sassen, *Cities in a World Economy* (2006).

Table 3.4 Appendix: Global development: a select sample of countries from the Human Development Index, 2015

Rank Country	HDI	Rank Country	HDI	Rank Country	HDI
Highest				to Lowest	
1 Norway	0.944	39 Saudi Arabia	0.837	147 Pakistan	0.538
2 Australia	0.935	40 Argentina	0.836	152 Nigeria	0.514
3 Switzerland	0.930	41 United Arab Emirates	0.835	171 Afghanistan	0.462
4 Denmark	0.923	42 Chile	0.832	176 Democratic Republic of the Congo	0.433
5 Netherlands	0.922	43 Portugal	0.830	180 Mozambique	0.416
6 Germany	0.916	50 Russia	0.789	181 Sierra Leone	0.413
6 Ireland	0.916	67 Cuba	0.769	182 Guinea	0.411
8 United States	0.915	74 Mexico	0.756	183 Burkina Faso	0.402
14 United Kingdom	0.907	75 Brazil	0.755	184 Burundi	0.400
20 Japan	0.891	90 China	0.727	185 Chad	0.392
26 Spain	0.876	93 Thailand	0.726	186 Eritrea	0.391
29 Greece	0.865	110 Indonesia	0.684	187 Central African Republic	0.350
36 Poland	0.843	130 India	0.609	188 Niger	0.348

HDI refers to the United Nations Human Development Index, which has been measured annually since 1990. It is a composite measure of three concerns: *longevity* – life expectancy at birth; *knowledge* – adult literacy and enrollment in schooling; and decent *standards of living* – income per head. You can easily access the full tables online at Human Development Index, 2015.

HISTORY: STANDING ON THE SHOULDERS OF GIANTS

> To be ignorant of what has occurred before you were born is to remain always a child. For what is the worth of human life, unless it is woven into the life of our ancestors by the records of history.
> Marcus Tullius Cicero, 106–43 BCE, Oration xxxiv

Throughout the world's history, many people have puzzled about the nature of the social world they have lived in: how did their world come into being, what was their place in it and what might be the great thread that holds it together? In all societies, there are people who think about the nature of their society. In the past, this social thinking has often taken on a religious or spiritual turn: the social is examined and explained as the creations of various gods (there are an awful lot of them and often significant enough to kill for), and the place of humans in it is located within this religious canopy or arc. Sometimes this social thinking takes a political turn: people explain societies as the creations of powerful people or groups (key tyrants or emperors, or groups like the exploiters and the exploited). Often people explain social things in biological terms: as evolution, as hormonally driven or as the result of individual brains and wills. There is then a long history of diverse ways of thinking about the social world we live in.

I have no space here to trace a world history of the more formal thinking about the nature of society discussed by many great thinkers and artists throughout history: in the East, the significance of the Chinese philosopher Confucius (551–479 BCE); in the Arab countries, the ideas of the fourteenth-century Muslim Ibn Khaldun (1332–1406); in Africa, the long history of poets and folk storytellers. Ideas about the social have developed throughout the world and its history. 'Sociology', in a sense, is just the most recent – and most Western. We stand on the shoulders of giants who have thought long and hard about the world we live in; our past is full of creative and artistic endeavours struggling to make sense of the social. There are significant histories not to be forgotten. But I ask simply how sociology has developed over the past 200 years, mainly in the West.

A VERY SHORT HISTORY OF WESTERN SOCIOLOGY

As societies have grown in scale and as scientific thinking has developed, so it is not surprising that 'sociology' should have emerged slowly as a new intellectual discipline. Since the 'great transformations' of the early nineteenth century, it has progressively entered the Western world as a university-based research discipline, and now in the twenty-first century, it is to be found in most countries of the world. The complexities of the modern global life almost demand that we cultivate serious (even 'academic') thinking about society and that in the grand divisions of labours of life that the modern world brings, many people should now devote their time, talents and intellectual energy to providing this. At the same time, always remember that modern sociology is Western, which means that the whole of sociology is drenched with Western assumptions and values. This, as we shall see, is about to change.

THE ANTECEDENTS OF MODERN WESTERN SOCIOLOGY: THE ENLIGHTENMENT PUZZLES

It has been claimed that the thinking, intellectual world emerged between 800 and 200 BCE, with what the philosopher Karl Jaspers, in his *Way to Wisdom* (1951), called the Axial Age. It is a time that we find Confucius in China, the Buddha in India, Zarathustra in Iran, Isaiah in Palestine and Homer, Plato and Archimedes in Greece.

Here we find the early development of 'great thoughts and great thinkers' about society and the human condition, and many others have followed this sweeping trajectory of humanity's intellectual history. Yet the distinctly modern Western world takes much of its intellectual shape much later, between the fifteenth and eighteenth centuries, during the long search for emancipation from religious and absolutist dogmatism and terrorism through the pursuit of science and the struggle for human 'freedoms and rights'. Here we see the breaking away from the rule of superstition, magic, religion, the church and the various monarchies and aristocracies. Here too we find the horrors of the long history of the Spanish Inquisition, the witchcraft hunts, the Thirty Years War and the English Civil War and the ultimate revolutions in France and America – side by side with the growth of slavery and then ultimate emancipation. This period also saw the gradual rise of mercantile capitalism and the massive colonization (and oppression) of much of the world by Europe. Simultaneously, it also saw the gradual emergence of emancipation movements fighting for their freedoms – of women, of slaves and of minorities of all kinds.

The Enlightenment – associated with many, including Diderot, Hobbes, Hogarth, Hume, Kant, Locke, Mozart, Newton, Pope, Rousseau, Voltaire and others – made claims for the world to be rational, scientific and progressive. The Enlightenment engaged diverse strands of radical thinking, but there was hope of making progress through rational thinking. Often looking back to the ancient Greeks, they posed some very major questions about society, which still haunt sociology today. The 'Think On: Perpetual Puzzles of Enlightenment Thinking' box outlines some of these big questions.

THINK ON: PERPETUAL PUZZLES OF ENLIGHTENMENT THINKING

The foundation of sociology is usually claimed to lie in the **Enlightenment**. This was a time for rational reflection, scientific development and the breaking free from religious and traditional 'myths'. It puzzled over a series of critical questions. Amongst these were:

1 What might be human nature? Is there such a thing, and if so, is it universal? (The debates between Locke, Hobbes, Hume and others.)
2 How should we live our lives? (The moral and ethical questions posed by Voltaire, Rousseau, Kant and others.)
3 How does society exist, what kinds are there and how are they changing and developing? How is human order – and human progress – possible? Is there a move from 'savage' and 'barbaric' to 'civilized'? Gradually, a classification of types of society emerges. How can societies be studied? (The sociological questions posed by Comte and others.)
4 How are societies to be ruled? Should power lie in the hands of a God, a ruler (the Leviathan) or the people? Is democratic rule possible or desirable? (Often called The Hobbesian question, after Thomas Hobbes.)
5 Can diverse religions be tolerated and accepted – a freedom of religion? How much terrorism should religion be allowed in maintaining its supremacy? Can religious diversity be accepted without society falling apart? (The religious question, discussed fully in Charles Taylor's *A Secular Age*, 2007.)
6 Who and what is a person? What is the emerging self like and who is the modern individual? Closely linked, are people selfish? Is the basis of society a collective concern for others or a rather more basic self-interest? (What might be called the Adam Smith question.)
7 What is knowledge, truth, morality? (The Cartesian, Kantian and Humean questions.)

Again, in a small book like this, I cannot follow up these ideas. Many, like Adorno and Horkheimer in their *Dialectic of Enlightenment* (1944), have been very critical of this seemingly rational, optimistic and Western-centred view of the world. They suggest that it has led to a world that is far too instrumental, technical, controlling – the harbingers of the modern surveillance society, rationality, disenchantment and even the Holocaust. Despite this, a great many more have seen it as a critical advance in the development of science and rationality as tools for trying to develop a critical understanding of the world – and changing it for the better. Sociology was born of this moment.

1800–1920: EARLY MODERN SOCIOLOGY

Sociology as a grand and general 'scientific discipline' is often told as a story that emerged out of **Enlightenment** thinking and the great revolutions of the eighteenth and nineteenth centuries. It is seen as a discipline born out of 'the shock of the new'. Social life had seemingly never been in such turmoil. It was now confronted with the French Revolution, the Industrial Revolution, the newly emerging nation-states, the independence of the US and the growth of ideas of democracy, as well as the escalation of populations across the world and the rise of new cities and the slums that accompanied them. We often think today that we are in periods of extraordinary social change, but a little history shows that this change has been unfolding for several centuries. There was undoubtedly something in the air at this time in the Western world that saw a new world in the making, a time of rapid and even revolutionary change. The old order seemed to be (indeed was) in serious decline: a traditional life was being swept asunder.

It was in this climate that sociology was born to appraise just what was happening: to analyze the sheer complexity and scale of the new modern society arriving before its eyes. What were the key features of this new world? Why was this change taking place? How might social order be maintained in the midst of such change? And just how could this new social order be studied? Was a science of society actually possible, and if so, what should it look like? Many of the founders of sociology who were engaged in a mapping of these differences thought of sociology as a mission to make the world a better place.

Two of the earliest pioneers of this Western sociology were the eccentric Auguste Comte (1798–1857) and the odd and solitary Herbert Spencer (1820–1903). Comte, growing up in the wake of the French Revolution, is usually claimed to be the founder of sociology, coining the term sociology in 1838. For him, societies moved from being religious to philosophical to scientific societies. The earliest era, right through the medieval period in Europe, was the *theological stage* – a world guided by religion, a society as God's will. With the Renaissance, the theological approach to society gradually gave way to the *metaphysical stage* – a world understood as a natural, rather than a supernatural, one. The modern world, however, brought a *scientific stage* and the development of technology, propelled by scientists such as Copernicus (1473–1543), Galileo (1564–1642) and Isaac Newton (1642–1727). Comte claimed that society followed invariable laws. Much as the physical world operated according to gravity and other laws of nature, so the task of sociology was to uncover the laws of society. This new approach of science was what he called **positivism**. Today, the word is still widely used to refer to the scientific method.

Herbert Spencer, writing a little later and with Darwin's discoveries firmly in sight, also saw societies as inevitably evolving – this time from the less complex or simple towards the massively, multiply complex. Militant society, structured around relationships of hierarchy and obedience, was simple and undifferentiated; industrial society, based on voluntary, contractually assumed social obligations, was complex and differentiated. As we have seen in Chapter 2 (p. 36), Spencer conceptualized society as functioning like a 'social organism' (parallel to a human body), which evolved from the simpler state to the more complex according to the universal law of evolution. He saw progress as 'the survival of the fittest' (this was his phrase, not Darwin's). He was one of a growing number of thinkers who were trying to classify and understand the emergence of different types of society. A summary of some of these positions is given in Table 4.1 (and look too at Table 3: pp. 53–4).

THE MAKING OF CLASSICAL SOCIOLOGY IN THE NINETEENTH CENTURY

The nineteenth and early twentieth centuries saw an enormous flurry of intellectual activity around the nature of society – much of it now long forgotten. Reading the historical documents now leaves the feeling of a large group of white genteel gentlemen struggling to look across the world to make sense of rapid change whilst dealing with the shock of evolutionary theory. They compare world societies and try to make some sense of where we have come from and are now heading. Remember, evolutionary theory was influential but also shocking. It was challenging many orthodox views of the

Table 4.1 Rapid social change: the evolutionary typological tradition of Western thinkers

'Sociologist'	Earlier societies	Newer societies arriving	Explanatory dynamic
Adam Smith (1723–1790)	Hunting, herding, agricultural	Commercial	Rise of free markets
Auguste Comte (1798–1857)	Theological, metaphysical	Scientific, positivist	Growth of science
Henry Maine (1822–1888)	Status	Contract	Changes in law
Herbert Spencer (1820–1903)	Homogeneous – simple, militant	Heterogeneous – complex, industrial	Changes in population
Ferdinand Tönnies (1855–1936)	**Gemeinschaft** – community based	**Gesellschaft** – association based	Community shifts
Karl Marx (1818–1883)	Primitive communism, slavery, feudalism	Capitalism (but leading to socialism)	Economic exploitation
Émile Durkheim (1858–1917)	Mechanical solidarity	Organic solidarity	Population density and division of labour
Max Weber (1864–1920)	Traditional	Rational – bureaucratic, secular	Changes in religion (Protestant) and economy (capitalism)
Georg Simmel (1858–1918)	Primitive production	Money and modernity	Circulation of money; group size grows

world – especially religious ones. Although they were all Western, they all had their eye on a wider, if colonial, global world.

There are hundreds of thinkers during this period, but the now orthodox account of the history of sociology came to be written in the 1950s and saw three key figures as symbolic of classical sociology. We have met them all already: Karl Marx, Émile Durkheim and Max Weber. They are the holy trinity of sociology and are usually taught religiously in all sociology degrees for the simple reason that they do 'open up' some major debates of their time which are still alive today. Marx analyzes the growth of capitalism, the significance of the economy and the material world, the importance of class, exploitation and inequality – and the possibility of a socialist society. Weber finds the growth of mass rationality, the bureaucratic state and a disenchanted world. Durkheim shows the significance of the social bond, examining changes in religion and the division of labour. All articulate the role of religion.

We have encountered the key work of Karl Marx before (and will meet him more later) as he examined the impoverished lives of the masses under the exploitations of industrial **capitalism** and analyzed the **class** struggles of societies. His earliest writings were philosophical and often called humanist, whilst his later works developed the material conception of history and the scientific analysis of the **mode of production** (see Chapter 6). In the 1850s, he produced historical studies of the working class movement and analyzed the relationship between the economic base and the ideological superstructure. He saw the role of historical actors and social class, as people lived in the squalor produced by the Industrial Revolution, as central to human understanding, and he marked out the role of the economic inequality and social class as key factors in social change. Alone amongst the early sociologists (and indeed the later ones), his work played a crucial role in the development and shaping of the twentieth-century communist societies. (At one point, probably over a third of the globe had been inspired by his work, including Russia, China and much of Africa and Latin America.) He wrote the texts that subsequently led to the major Marxist revolutions (and failures) of the twentieth century (Russia in 1918, and China in 1949).

Émile Durkheim was professor of education at the Sorbonne between 1887 and 1902 and wrote four studies of lasting significance. *The Division of Labour in Society* (1893) traced the development of society from 'mechanical' to 'organic'. *The Rules of Sociological Method* (1895) analyzed the very nature of 'social facts' and how they should be studied. *Suicide* (1897) took a highly individualistic phenomenon – killing yourself – to demonstrate through the analysis of suicide rates just how socially patterned it was. *The Elementary Forms of*

Religious Life (1912) demonstrated through a case study of the Aborigines how 'religion is something eminently social'. Durkheim leads us into key debates about the massive growth of human populations and the shifting moral order of societies. For him, the growth of dense population shifted the nature of the human bond. As society moved from mechanical to organic solidarity – from traditional similarity and bonding community to the new industrial societies based on huge scale, difference and changing patterns of divisions of labour – they became much more prone to a breakdown of norms (**anomie**) and a weakening of social bonds. As old forms of bonding weakened, new ways of building solidarity and community were needed.

Max Weber was more concerned with human actions and their meanings. He told us that 'ideas have consequences'. The new rationality helped shape capitalism and the emergent bureaucratic world. For Weber, transformations taking place were more connected to shifts in ideas and religious belief: the modern capitalist world had a close affinity to the rise of Protestant Christianity (or as he put it, 'The Protestant Ethic'). He can be seen as the sociological counterpart of Franz Kafka; for him, the modern world led to the growth of the cold, impersonal bureaucracy and ultimately to a massive disenchantment with the world.

A CAUTIONARY WORD: CONCEALED AND SUBTERRANEAN TRADITIONS

I have so far described a rather orthodox and straightforward history that is the tale commonly told. But no histories are ever quite like they are told. Randall Collins' magnificent study of ideas throughout history suggests that intellectuals work through networks that promote some ideas yet exclude others. There are always hidden histories waiting to be excavated. Although there are key figures, sociology was a young discipline and being developed on all sides with many disparate struggles as to its nature. Often now this is hard to see. Here were fermenting yet concealed traditions trying to grasp the social through a wide range of tools; many of the earliest writers were novelists, political tract writers, reformers, politicians, photographers, journalists, historians, priests and researchers. A motley crew indeed. There are now, for example, histories of feminist and black sociologists being written out of the history, even as they made great contributions (see Morris (2015) on Du Bois and Deegan (1990) on Addams). So do remember as I rehearse this 'short history' that there was no unity in the origins of the discipline. As we shall see, there still is not – but that is to jump ahead of my tale . . .

EARLY TWENTIETH-CENTURY SOCIOLOGY: PROFESSIONALIZATION

Whatever the undercurrents, by the twentieth century sociology was fast becoming 'fixed' and 'professionalized' into an academic discipline. Albion Small (1854–1926) founded the Department of Sociology at the University of Chicago in 1892, and it remained the key institution until the mid-1930s when challenged by Pitrim Sorokin (1889–1968), who established the Sociology Department at Harvard in 1931. Durkheim founded the first European Department of Sociology at the University of Bordeaux in 1895, publishing *The Rules of Sociological Method* as a kind of manifesto stating what sociology is and what it should do. In the UK, sociology as an academic subject began life at the London School of Economics in 1907 when L. T. Hobhouse (1864–1929) became its first Professor of Sociology. London remained the centre – indeed was the only place (apart from Liverpool University) until the middle of the twentieth century. In Germany, the first chair of sociology was created in 1918, and in 1923, the influential Institute of Social Research was established. In 1919, the first Indian Department of Sociology was established at the University of Bombay (Mumbai). But in many countries round the world, sociology hardly developed at all throughout much of the twentieth century, and in some countries, sociology was more or less banned.

Although much of the foundational work of Western sociology came from Europe, at the start of the twentieth century, a new 'American' sociology started to develop where the United States (believing in its own exceptional position in the world – of democratic government and economic opportunity) would assume a prime role. Indeed, it would not be too wrong to say that the first half of the twentieth century belonged to American sociology, marking a (sad) move from a global awareness of societies across the world to one that increasingly focused on the workings of one: the United States. Bit by bit, the model of social analysis becomes North American – based on North-American thinking with the United States taken as the normative core of social life in the world. Life in America was social life. Capitalism and individualism became core assumptions.

The foundations of this sociology are usually seen to be the **Chicago sociology** – though the story is much more complex than this. Chicago has to have the credit for popularizing the discipline – with its key focus on urban research and the problems generated by the city, its textbook (*The Green Bible* of Park and Burgess) and its new, well-published graduate school. For the Chicago sociologists, the city became the key feature of the newly arriving world – more and more people found themselves in the city as 'urbanism' became 'a way of life'. A key influence here had been the German Georg Simmel (1858–1918), who we have met before and who saw the city characterized by secondary rather than primary contacts. The contacts of the city may indeed be face-to-face, but they have now become impersonal, superficial, transitory and segmental. The reserve, the indifference and the blasé outlook of people in the city help immune themselves from the expectations of others. It also leads to the sophistication and the rationality generally ascribed to city-dwellers. The city gave rise to new forms of social life.

This period also marked the first great African American sociologist, W. E. B. Du Bois (1868–1963). From the 1920s onwards, he demonstrated the impact of modern capitalism on the structuring of race and social differences. In his *The Souls of Black Folk* (1903), he outlined his theory of double consciousness: 'One ever feels his twoness – an American, a Negro: two souls, two thoughts, two unreconciled strivings; two warring ideals in one dark body, whose dogged strength alone keeps it from being torn asunder'. Here is 'the negro's' sense of always looking at one's self through the eyes of others. Du Bois believed in the possibilities of racial progress and conducted major empirical research in Philadelphia on the lives of city-dwelling blacks. Subsequently, there has been a major strand of US work that takes the 'race divide' very seriously.

SOCIOLOGY IN THE WAR TIMES

This 'short' twentieth century was confronting new problems: the horrors of two major world wars, two major world revolutions (China and Russia – along with many others), a coming to terms with the ravages of the colonial past, and the damage and immiseration caused by much of the ruthless earlier industrialization. Human suffering and death were enormous. A different set of social conditions thus started to bring different analyses. In Germany, there was a creeping rise of fascism, watched as it developed by a group of thinkers who developed **critical theory** and came to be known as the Frankfurt School (where they were based). Theodor Adorno (1903–1969), Herbert Marcuse (1898–1979), Marie Jahoda (1907–2001), Eric Fromm (1900–1980), Walter Benjamin (1892–1940) and Max Horkheimer (1895–1973) have left major legacies as social and cultural critics.

Their core concerns were the application of broadly Marxist (and often Freudian) ideas to the workings of culture as they examined the arrival of mass society, the proliferating of technology and bureaucracy, and the growth of what Adorno called 'the Culture Industry' – often regulating and trivializing our lives. Karl Mannheim (1893–1947), who developed the sociology of knowledge, and Norbert Elias (1897–1990), with his theory of 'civilizing process', were also at some time based at Frankfurt. But all in the end fled the rise of Nazism, most finding a home in the US, either in California (Adorno and Marcuse) or New York (at the New School), or England (Elias and Mannheim). Their writings – often hard to understand – have been crucial in shaping contemporary analyses of culture. (Today, probably the most significant development of this position can be found in the work of Jürgen Habermas.) During this period, sociology more or less disappeared under both Stalinism and Maoism – two vast continents for whom sociology was an unacceptable discipline.

SOCIOLOGY AFTER THE SECOND WORLD WAR: FROM CONSENSUS TO A MULTI-PARADIGM DISCIPLINE

In the period after the Second World War, a new age of 'professional sociology' appeared to bring a maturity, and for a short while, a kind of consensus appeared – 'the end of ideology' (claiming the exhaustion of political ideas). It was especially associated with the work of **functionalist** theorists like Kingsley Davis, Robert King Merton and Talcott Parsons. Indeed, in the mid-twentieth century, no sociologist was more well-known than Talcott Parsons (1902–1979). Like all sociologists, his ideas changed over time, but in 1951 he published *The Social System*. This heralded the search for developing a grand, overarching explanation of how social orders worked, and here he outlined the pre-requisites for the functioning of societies in a series of elaborate typologies and boxes. For Parsons, all societies must perform certain key functions: they have to *A*dapt, achieve their *G*oals, become *I*ntegrated and ultimately maintain themselves (which he called *L*atency) – a framework often abbreviated to *AGIL*. This highly abstract systematic depiction of certain social necessities, which every society must meet to be able to maintain stable social life, led to a typology and table of approaching 100 boxes – a map of the social system and its interconnected functions, from biological systems to world systems. His work can be applied to many areas of social life – how do schools work, hospitals run, prisons function as systems? They can all be seen as systems striving to achieve certain goals, socializing their members to their cultures and adapting along the way. Grand systems of society – an almost utopian order – were a key theme.

But not for long. Whilst Parsons was developing this abstract model of society, others became critical. As sociology became more and more formally organized in universities and professions, by the end of the 1950s, sociology had become obviously divided and suffered a number of major internal critiques about the directions it was heading. The publication in 1959 by the North American Marxist C. Wright Mills (1916–1962) of *The Sociological Imagination* has come to be identified as a kind of landmark publication (even though Mills himself was author of only a few books and died young, he gained a maverick reputation). The book opens with an amusing – if unfair – attack on Parsons and his jargon, and is famed for its critique of the state of sociology at this time, which he saw as being dominated by three main misleading trends: grand abstraction, empirical triviality and methodological fussiness. For Mills, sociology had lost its critical way. Likewise, the Russian émigré to the US Pitrim Sorokin – fleeing imprisonment in the Czarist regime of the Russian Empire – suggested that sociological work had now become a 'jungle of diverse and often discordant theories', spoiled by the tendency towards 'fads and foibles' (the title of one of his many books). It seems Sorokin was right – for the discipline has continued so ever since. Although professional sociologists often try to create a semblance of underlying theoretical cohesion and order in understanding society, in

Table 4.2   From Comte to Beck: twenty-one landmark male Western texts, 1824–1992

A landmark provides a marker by indicating the arrival of something that breaks with the past and generates new work for the future. There are thousands of studies which could be placed on a list like this, but here is a small 'sampler' selection. To get on this list, you have to be dead! I have not included texts that developed from feminist work here, as I do this in Table 4.3. It would be odd for a professional sociologist to not at least know about most of the following:

1. 1824: August Comte, *System of Positive Politics* – introduced the term sociology

2. 1846: Marx and Engels, *The German Ideology* – the theory of materialist history outlined

3. 1886: Charles Booth, *Life and Labour of the People in London* – measuring poverty in the city with a very large survey

4. 1897: Émile Durkheim, *Suicide* – suicide statistics show just how suicide varies socially

5. 1889: W. E. B. Du Bois, *The Philadelphia Negro* – first major study of the American Negro

6. 1904: Max Weber, *The Protestant Ethic and the Spirit of Capitalism* – ideas shape history, and here religion shapes capitalism

7. 1900: Georg Simmel, *The Philosophy of Money* – changes in organization of money shift human relations

8. 1921: Robert Park and Ernest Burgess, *Introduction to the Science of Sociology* – first major textbook from a major new sociology department at the University of Chicago with a stress on city conflict

9. 1918–20: W. I. Thomas and Florian Znaniecki, *The Polish Peasant in Europe and America* – highly regarded five volumes of innovative method, theory and data on migrants and city life

10. 1929: Robert and Helen Lynd, *Middletown* – small town community life (Muncie) in the US observed closely and especially through its class system

11. 1934: George Herbert Mead, *Mind, Self and Society* – philosophical foundations for bridging individual and society

12. 1944: Theodore Adorno and Max Horkheimer, *Dialectic of Enlightenment* – asks 'why mankind, instead of entering into a truly human condition, is sinking into a new kind of barbarism'

13. 1949: Robert King Merton, *Social Theory and Social Structure* – major statement of mid-twentieth-century functionalism

14. 1950: David Riesman, Nathan Glazer and Reuel Denney, *The Lonely Crowd* – society has moved from tradition-directed to outer-directed

15. 1951: Talcott Parsons, *The Social System* – theoretical treatise about the integrated social order.

16. 1959: C. Wright Mills, *The Sociological Imagination* – left critique of grand theory and overworked methodology in sociology

17. 1956/59: Erving Goffman, *The Presentation of Self in Everyday Life* – micro-sociological argument about social life as drama

18. 1970: Alvin Gouldner, *The Coming Crisis of Western Sociology* – another substantial and left-based critique of mainstream sociological theory

19. 1975: Michel Foucault, *Discipline and Punish* – popular discourse theory of prison and crime

20. 1984: Pierre Bourdieu, *Distinction* – key late-twentieth-century analysis of social class

21. 1986/92: Ulrich Beck, *Risk Society* – influential account of 'modernity' and its risks

---

practice, sociology was and continues to grow into a fractured, fragmented and **multi-paradigmatic** discipline that is often guilty of following trends and fashions of the time.

1968 AND ALL THAT: A SYMBOLIC YEAR

Let's move on. After the war, sociology expanded in major ways, developing momentum, status and a certain kind of fashionability as it entered both the universities and the schools in a mass way. The discipline became more and more popular – almost fashionable and trendy till the mid-1970s – and the field expanded rapidly. Its expansion is often linked to the radical global student politics of 1968, a symbolic year that came to be a watershed signalling:

- The start of a massive expansion of higher education throughout the world.
- The coming of age of the baby boomers, born just after the Holocaust and the Second World War. Like each generation,

it was different – but this was the one that became the first major, self-designated 'youth culture'.

- A sense was 'in the air' that 'a new social order' was coming, creating quite a lot of hope and optimism. The world was about to change.
- So with this, the new times (postmodern) were in the making: of individualism – the 'impulsive self' and the 'Me decade'; of consumption – of new markets; and of informalism.
- The development of human rights since the United Nations declarations of 1948 – from the civil rights movement and the women's movement.
- Continuing war and international conflict, notably in Vietnam.
- The dawn of the spiritual 'Age of Aquarius' and the growth of countercultural movements.
- The simultaneous rebirth and slow death of the Marxist world.
- The spread of global awareness largely through the mass media. More and more, as Todd Gitlin put it, 'the whole world was watching'. Symbols had gone global.

These are very big themes. '1968' signified not a year but a whole period (roughly the late 1950s to the early 1980s) when significant social changes were settling in. And the significant growth of sociology was bound up with this period. Sociology now became a popular university discipline (and the butt of many jokes!). This period really marks the rapid development of professional sociology and the arrival of sociology's widespread incorporation into university syllabuses. A key mid-twentieth-century UK sociologist, A. H. Halsey, has provided a detailed (if very traditional) account of British sociology and marvels that whereas there could have been no more than 200 undergraduates in the 1940s, by the year 2000, there were 'as many as 2,000 sociologists teaching and 24,000 students in the universities of the United Kingdom' (Halsey, 2004). In the UK, sociology was introduced in to the school curriculum in the mid-1960s; and throughout the Western world, sociology became a growing and popular area of study in the universities.

The sociology that started to flourish in this time became much more critical of the traditional canon or orthodoxies of sociology – indeed became much more influenced by the work of Marx than that of Durkheim and Weber. One sociologist, Alvin Gouldner (1920–1980), wrote of *The Coming Crisis of Western Sociology* (1970), and it seemed a new era was being ushered in. Gouldner argued for a greater reflexivity in sociology – that sociology needed to see itself in the same ways as it saw society. Sociology was always bound up with the contexts of its times, and these needed to be fully incorporated into sociological thinking. This meant the serious analysis of capitalism which structured sociology as much as everything else.

WIDENING THE BASE OF SOCIOLOGICAL THINKING: BREAKING DISCIPLINARY BOUNDARIES

One of the striking features of post-1968 sociological thinking has been the gradual widening of its intellectual base and the questioning of its traditional assumptions. Some sociologists have buried their heads very deeply in the sand about such developments; others have been very critical and condemnatory of such trends. But like it or not, the study of the social has broadened out: no longer is it simply in the hands of sociologists. There are now other pathways and scholars outside the mainstream of sociology that have challenged the supremacy of the sociological profession in looking at the social. Amongst these new inquiries are cultural studies, feminism and gender studies, media and communication studies, post-colonial studies, multiculturalism, race and anti-racism studies, queer and LGBT (lesbian, gay, bisexual and trans) studies, global studies, digital studies and human rights studies. Quite a lot of challenges then. Bridges have also been made to many linked disciplines – geography has become 'space studies', history has engaged with the new cultural and social histories as well as oral history, and anthropologists have been developing 'cultural anthropology'. You can soon see these shifts in major book shops: the old sections on sociology have become somewhat smaller whilst these new sections have developed into sections all of their own – and often overtaken and even replaced those of sociology. Although professional sociologists have tried to hold on to their traditional claims over the field of the social, in practice it has now significantly diversified. Scholars now study the social from within a wide range of fields. Sociology has dispersed and become less 'pure'.

ENTER POSTMODERNISM, MULTICULTURALISM AND FOUCAULT

There are many influences on this diversification. As we have seen in Chapter 3, **postmodernism** became a buzz word in sociology by the mid-1980s for a transforming world where the search for one grand truth is over. Likewise, **multiculturalism** also arrived during the 1980s – most significantly in the US, though it spread everywhere – and critiqued the idea of a monologic culture, i.e. one that speaks with only one voice. From the discovery of a black history and a women's history in the heady days of 1968, it soon became clear that there had been a tremendous bias in academic life in favour of white, middle-class Western men. The voices of many had been silenced. It could be seen simply by looking at the people who taught and ran the universities and schools – women and women's views of the world were rare, black voices very few, non-Western voices lost, queer voices silenced. One path here was the direct recruitment of more women and more ethnic groups to the universities to teach. But the content of study and academic disciplines also changed, leading to much conflict on the campus over what should be taught – the so-called 'culture wars'. The challenge over the syllabus and what constituted knowledge was on. And it influenced sociology. Certain new writers appeared who started to have a major impact on social thinking but who were not sociologists. Michel Foucault (1926–1984), who we met in Chapter 2, has had a major impact on all of the humanities and social sciences, and the philosopher Judith Butler's (1956–) work has developed almost a cult-like status.

FEMINISM UNBOUND

A good and prime example of this broadening out is the arrival of **feminism** in the academy. In the 1970s, sociology was roundly criticized for overwhelmingly being *by men, about men and for men*. The hidden agenda of much early sociology was 'masculinist'. Not only had there been few women sociologists (and those there had been were 'hidden from herstory'), the subject matters (and many assumptions) had been tacitly largely about men: men and industry, men and class, men and education, men and power were its themes. It was time to bring women in. And we can see this shift over the past fifty years or so. Many old topics have been given new slants – religion (why are gods and priests overwhelmingly male?)

or criminology (why are so many criminals men?). Methodologies and theories have been scrutinized for their male slant on objectivity. And there has been a major revisiting of past theories to see why women have been ignored. Indeed, it has led to a discovery of many women sociologists who have been written out of history. Harriet Martineau (1802–1876), Jane Addams (1860–1935), Charlotte Perkins Gilman (1860–1935), Marianne Weber (1870–1954), Anna Julia Copper (1858–1964) and Beatrice Potter Webb (1858–1943) are examples. Their stories are slowly being recovered. But above all, feminism has brought many new concerns to the sociological agenda: care, emotions, sexual violence, domestic violence, childbirth and reproduction, housework/domestic labour – as Table 4.3 illustrates. These were simply 'off' the sociological agenda before feminists highlighted them.

Table 4.3 Expanding the concerns of sociology: the impact of feminism

Feminism expands sociology to look at	*Illustrative author and book*
Domestic labour	Ann Oakley, *Sociology of Housework* (1974)
Emotional work	Arlie Hochschild, *The Managed Heart: The Commercialization of Human Feeling* (1983)
Caring	Selma Sevenhuijsen, *Citizenship and the Ethics of Care* (1998)
Sexuality	Gayle Rubin, 'Thinking Sex' (1984)
Sexual violence	Liz Kelly, *Surviving Sexual Violence* (1988)
Mothering	Nancy Chodorow, *The Reproduction of Mothering* (1979)
Young women and girls	Angela McRobbie, *Feminism and Youth Culture* (2000)
Gender	Judith Butler, *Gender Trouble* (1990)
Women and crime	Carol Smart, *Women, Crime and Criminology* (1976)
Rethinking masculinity	Raewyn Connell, *Masculinities* (2005, second edition)
The state and women	Sylvia Walby, *Theorizing Patriarchy* (1990)

continued

Table 4.3 continued

Feminism expands sociology to look at	Illustrative author and book
Lesbian life	Arlene Stein, *Sex and Sensibility: Stories of a Lesbian Generation* (1997)
Rethinking race	Patricia Hill Collins, *Black Feminist Thought* (1990)
Belonging	Nira Yuval-Davis, *The Politics of Belonging* (2011)
Feminist methods	Liz Stanley and Sue Wise, *Breaking Out Again* (1993, second edition)
Colonialism	Chandra Mohanty, *Feminism Without Borders* (2003)
Feminist epistemology	Sandra Harding, *The Science Question in Feminism* (1968)

THE RISE OF CULTURAL STUDIES

The last decades of the twentieth century saw an unmistakable 'cultural turn' in the social sciences. In Europe, its inspiration came from Gramsci (1860–1937), Foucault, Bourdieu, Habermas and others – all of whom we will briefly meet in this book. In the UK, an interest grew out of a literary socialism associated with Richard Hoggart (1918–2014) and Raymond Williams (1921–1988) and leading to the work of the Marxist Stuart Hall (1932–2014) and the so-called Birmingham Centre of Cultural Studies (BCCS), prominent in the 1970s for its research on cultures, identities, class, post-colonialism, media, race and gender. In the US, a more mainstream focus on culture – its symbols, language and civil society – started to develop in the work of Jeffrey Alexander (1947–), Steven Seidman, Ann Swidler and others. Different as they all were, understanding the conflicts and changes found in the workings of culture became more and more a core concern.

ASCENDANT POST-COLONIAL VISIONS

Post-colonial theory is another example. Post-colonialism looks at countries that were once colonized by others – notably the invasion or influence of Britain, France and Spain over many countries in the eighteenth and nineteenth centuries. In this process, indigenous peoples lost their own sense of who they were along with their own histories in the wake of the dominance of these colonizing thinkers. Shaped heavily by Edward Said's book *Orientalism* (1978), **post-colonialism** shows how the knowledge of colonized (subordinated, subjugated) peoples is often shaped by the colonizer. Very often in the past, the sociologist's own approach had legitimated the colonizer's position, indeed even masking the assumptions of the ruler. Now, coming from many traditions, post-colonialism highlighted the voice of the neglected ('**subaltern**') others. Much sociology, it has argued, has been complicit in this earlier science – indeed, Enlightenment thinking itself may well have been a central tool of the colonizers, holding as they did to the Western view of science, rationality and progress as the key to future thought. Sociology itself then may here become a tool not of scientific advance but of complicit, colonial oppression. Taking this seriously, in effect, means a much more careful listening to other voices from other cultures.

COMING OUT OF THE CLOSET IN SOCIOLOGY: GOING A LITTLE QUEER

During most of sociology's 200-year history, sociology paid no attention to the complexities of sexuality and took for granted the punitive polarity between homosexuality and heterosexuality, in which homosexuals were presumed sad, sick, sinning criminals. Homosexuals – a term invented in the 1870s – had been a classic case of the stigmatized outsider we met in Chapter 1, even within sociology itself. But with the new wave of sociology since 1968, the arrival of the Gay Liberation Front in 1969 and the Queer Movement in the 1990s eventually started to change this. As with women, blacks and post-colonial groups, gays and lesbians started to find a voice in many countries around the world. This also challenged the blatant **homophobia** and **heteronormativity** of much sociological writing. From the late 1980s onwards, queer theory entered the academy and questioned the stability of both gender and sexual categories. An international sphere of critical sexualities studies has become more and more prominent and it has now become a major area of interest.

SOCIOLOGICAL IMAGINATIONS AND
THE FUTURE OF SOCIOLOGY

Sociology is (and always has been) a fragmented discipline. It can hardly be otherwise. Looking closely, you will find hundreds of different theories, methods and areas of interest. Textbooks try to simplify this into various schools of thought, but the point really is that *sociology is a very messy discipline*. At the very least, we can say it is **multi-paradigmatic**. A number of new developments from feminism through cultural studies to digital analysis have made it even more fragmented. Does the future of sociology lie in more and more specialisms, fragmentations and new 'disciplines'? Almost certainly.

A caution is now in order. We can see this chapter as a short introduction to a history of mainstream Western sociology. Shaped by the Enlightenment and the modern industrial–capitalist world, it is a world where white, Christian (and often Jewish) men held all the prominent positions. It kept its baseline as the Western world focused overwhelmingly on only a limited number of societies associated with the rich – often colonizing – West. It left most other countries to be studied either by 'anthropology' or to specialist areas like 'development studies'. To put it bluntly, *over three-quarters of the world – China, the Islamic countries, Africa, much of Asia and Latin America – go missing from much of the mainstream Western sociological account of the world.* For much of the twentieth century, the arrogance of much Western sociology is really rather surprising. Today, some changes are in sight: you can often find people looking away from the West to a more global world. Sociology is starting to flourish in many non-Western countries, and at their best, they are finding their own way without drawing too much on the biases of the West. There are lessons to be learnt from the West, of course, but what is now needed are home-grown sociologies of different countries – the sociologies of China, Indonesia and Korea, for example – that look themselves outwards to a twenty-first-century global sociology.

Ultimately, though, for all its multiple varieties and voices, sociology is held together by a common critical awareness of the significance of the social. Sociology is an imagination, a way of thinking, a critical consciousness. And as such, it is always needed globally. What the rest of this book tries to show is that despite all the variations, disagreements and cultural contrasts, doing sociology always means the development of this common critical consciousness about the social. The next three chapters aim to tell you what to look for in developing this sociological imagination. Areas of interest, theoretical tendencies and methodological skills may come and go: there will always be trends and fashions. But the essential wisdoms of sociology will always be needed.

THINK ON: SOCIOLOGY IN THE TWENTY-FIRST CENTURY

Sociology is now at least 200 years old, and it keeps changing. Here are some of the possible current trends that will shape it in the twenty-first century.

1   Globalization: Increasingly, sociology will move from the 'hegemony of the West' and recognize three perspectives: national or local (studying just one place), comparative (contrasting different countries and states) and global (examining the world's interconnections). Future students will develop a transnational sociology that will increasingly require them to be multilingual and be mobile across cultures.

2   Digitalism: Increasingly, sociology will be digital. Some key trends are discussed in Chapter 6, and problems are raised in Chapter 3. Future students will be expected to develop a critical digitalism that moves beyond the many problems that a banal everyday digitalism poses.

3   Multidisciplinarity: Increasingly, students will have to cope with growing awareness of complexity in academic work and thinking. A worrying trend of recent sociology has been the narrowing of its focus and interests. It will continue with this at its peril. Future students will be

expected to become aware of a wider range of areas of study that feed into critical sociological analysis and handle a much wider range of intellectual interests and thinking than at present.

4 Value awareness: Increasingly, sociology will become aware of its value base. Although sociology will continue to pursue objectivity and value neutrality, it will need to take a stance on values and become more aware of its biases. Future students will increasingly be expected to be self-reflexive and reflective, understand the role of values in social life and their own lives, and build a sociology that makes more of a public contribution towards a 'better' world for all.

5 Beyond the universities: Increasingly, sociology is being subjected to 'management, money and metrics' model found in modern universities. If this continues and universities become places where only sterile work can be done, future sociologists will look more and more to wider communities and worlds where they can be more creative in their work.

SUMMARY

Thinking about the social goes a long way back, but modern Western sociology was born of the Enlightenment and industrialization in its 'professional form' some 200 years ago. This chapter provides a quick history. But, like society, sociology is in constant change. Some recent social trends (such as digitalism) and critical trends (like multiculturalism, feminism and queer theory) are changing the discipline. Many recent world developments increasingly challenge much of 'Western' sociology (dominated in the past by Europe and the US). We can expect in the near future that this history will be reworked when a proper focus is given to all countries, regions and groups of the world.

EXPLORING FURTHER

MORE THINKING

1 Construct your own 'time line' on the history of sociology. (You could do it online; there are programmes to help you.) Think of key theorists, countries, ideas and historical phasings.

2 What is meant by the 'Axial Age' and the 'Enlightenment'? Discuss some of their ideas and consider if this was early sociology.

3 There are some 220 countries in the world. Consider one or two of them that interest you and attempt to show how their sociological history may be different from the one I have given above. In some countries, it may be nonexistent; in some, very new; and in others, have a distinctively different path. Consider, for example, the histories of Japanese sociology, Indonesian sociology, Portuguese sociology and Chinese sociology. What do they look like? (Raewyn Connell's *Southern Theory* may give you an impetus; online searches will be necessary.)

FURTHER READING

On the wide history of intellectual thought, see Karl Jaspers, *Way to Wisdom: An Introduction to Philosophy* (1951); Randall Collins, *The Sociology of Philosophies: A Global Theory of Intellectual Change* (1998); and Yuval Harari, *Sapiens* (2015). On the Enlightenment tradition, see Anthony Pagden, *The Enlightenment and Why It Still Matters* (2013). On the history of sociological theory, see Alan Swingewood's *A Short History of Sociological Thought* (2000, third edition). A. H. Halsey's *A History of Sociology in Britain* (2004) is a very valuable account of the whole of British sociology; Jennifer Platt's *A Sociological History of the British Sociological Association* (2003) provides the history of a key organization. John Holmwood and John Scott (eds.) review the state of UK sociology now in *The Palgrave Handbook of Sociology in Britain* (2014); and my own study, *Imaginations: Fifty Years of Essex Sociology* (Plummer, 2014) looks at one department. For the

US, the major recent commentaries can be found in Craig Calhoun (ed.), *Sociology in America* (2007). For a history of early women in sociology, see Patricia Madoo Lengermann and Jill Niebrugge-Brantley, *The Women Founders* (1998). See also Rosemarie Tong, *Feminist Thought* (2015, fourth edition). On sexuality, see Jeffrey Weeks's *Sexuality* (2009, third edition) and Ken Plummer's 'Critical Humanism and Queer Theory' (2011) and 'Critical Sexualities Studies' (2012). On race and racism, see *Theories of Race and Racism: A Reader* (2007), edited by Les Back and John Solomos.

Critical commentaries on the biased development of Western sociology and new directions include Raewyn Connell, *Southern Theory: The Global Dynamics of Knowledge in Social Science* (2007); Patricia Hill Collins, *Black Feminist Thought* (1990); and Gurminder K. Bhambra, *Rethinking Modernity: Postcolonialism and the Sociological Imagination* (2007).

QUESTIONS: CULTIVATING
SOCIOLOGICAL IMAGINATIONS

> The sociological imagination enables us to grasp history and biography and the relations between the two within society. That is its task and its promise.
>
> C. Wright Mills, *The Sociological Imagination*, 1959

So now we reach the search for the Holy Grail: the sociological imagination. Just how are we to develop ways to think and understand and make sense of this enormously complex, ever changing, politically laden flow of human social life – or at least some parts of it? What 'frames of mind' need to be developed and what critical questions posed? C. Wright Mills's influential book *The Sociological Imagination* has inspired several generations of sociologists, and I use his idea to frame this chapter, widening it ultimately to raise twelve critical challenges (see pp. 176–7).

This discussion leads us to core features of how sociology is studied and taught – generally through three concerns: **methodology**, **theory** and **empiricism**. *Methodologists* give their intellectual energies to rendering the tools and statistics of social research ever more sophisticated: 'good measurement and sophisticated research design' – that's what is needed, they say. *Theorists* are often devoted to the beautiful intricacies of human thought and elegant thinking – of making our thinking as precise, logical and clear as possible: to establish the general and abstract principles of social thought. And *empiricists* are often obsessed with researching the minutiae of social life and seek to describe as much as they can in great detail. 'The truth of the story lies in the detail of the research'. This divide is an old, old story between those more comfortable with facts and those happier with abstractions. Studying sociology will almost inevitably mean doing a course or two in 'methodology' (often run by the 'empiricists' and the 'methodologists') and a course or three in 'sociological theory' (usually run by the male 'theorists' – and they usually are male). Methodologists will tell you how to do research in an ideal world, theorists will tell you how to search for more general laws and understanding and empiricists will give you the 'facts'.

MAPPING SOCIOLOGICAL QUESTIONS

In the next two chapters, I look at the basics of these approaches. But here I also want to argue *against* the fetishes of methodology and abstract theorizing. Of course, 'methods' and 'theory' are always significant in serious research in *any* field or discipline – from physics to music. But they can be overstated: *theory and methods are simply our tools, a means to an end*. The challenge for sociology is to develop a deep understanding of the **empirical** social world we live in, through whatever routes this can be achieved best, and to keep it accessible. In this chapter, then, I suggest some simple guidelines for cultivating ways of thinking about the social; in the next, I suggest some basic skills to be developed in both doing research and thinking about the adequacy of research you read. As always, these are just starting points: the basics. The box summarizes these.

1 SEARCH FOR STRUCTURES: WHAT ARE THE UNDERLYING PATTERNS OF SOCIAL LIFE?

The first ingrained habit of the sociological mind is to keep looking for social patterns. Social life has many random and chance factors, but if we look hard enough we can usually find a sense of order beneath much of it. Terms sensitizing us to this include **social structures**, **institutions**, **social forms**, **habits** and **habitus**.

THINK ON: QUESTIONS FOR CREATING A SOCIOLOGICAL IMAGINATION

Sociology is an acquired form of consciousness, a critical imagination. Put simply, here are twelve key tips for developing good habits to foster such an imagination.

1   Search for underlying structures and social patterns.
2   Understand social actions and meanings.
3   Bridge micro/actions and macro/structures.
4   Empathize with lived cultures.
5   Interrogate the material world.
6   Develop an awareness of time and history.
7   Keep moving on: look at contingency, change and flow.
8   Locate social life in place and space.
9   Connect with biography.
10   Take power seriously.
11   Think complexity, multiplicity and contradiction.
12   Analyze the matrix of inequalities. *(This twelfth issue is not discussed in this chapter, but Chapter 7 is devoted exclusively to it.)*

For the moment, let's simply see them as the underlying patterns of social life.

THE DAY AND ITS HABITS

The simplest start is to think about a typical day in your own life – or anyone else's for that matter. It is not usually a completely chaotic mess, even if it sometimes seems like that. Indeed, some people can be very tight and rigid about their day. In the film *Stranger than Fiction* (2006), the hero, Harold Crick – a dull auditor for the tax office – is shown as a man ruled by his clock (and one who hears the narrative of his life). He counts the number of times he brushes his teeth in the morning (38!) and knows the precise time he should leave each day for the bus, which he catches every day for the office and has never missed. At work, every event is timed and structured by time. He is a man dominated by ritual, time and narrative. Likewise, the film *Groundhog Day* (1993) shows a man who gets up every day to do exactly the same things. He is – as the tag goes – 'having the worst day of his life – over and over'. The hero, the meteorologist Phil Connors, awakens each day to find it is again February 2: it starts each morning at 6:00 a.m. with his waking up to the same song, Sonny and Cher's 'I Got You Babe', on his alarm clock radio. His memories of the 'previous' day intact, he seems to be trapped in a seemingly endless 'time loop' to repeat the same day in the same way in the same small town.

Now look at your own day, your own environment and chart its own patterns or structures. Even if you party every night, get up very late and spend most days just lazing and grazing around, you are probably caught in a pattern. Most Western people most days follow the same daily routines: getting out of beds, stumbling to bathrooms, having some kind of breakfast, setting out on some kind of work or the day's 'schedule of events' – seeing friends, going to work, dropping the children off, cooking the meals. The influential late-nineteenth-century pragmatic social philosopher William James called this the flywheel of habit. He suggests that most of our lives are lived in habits and routines and that this is indeed what makes social life work.

THE STREET AND ITS SOCIAL ORDER

Now go a little beyond your own life – but not far. Look around your neighbourhood. Sociologists have long strolled around cities and streets looking at the patterns of life that appear before their eyes. And what becomes clear is that the spaces we move in develop definite ways of life.

Elijah Anderson is an African American Professor of Sociology and author of *Code of the Street* (1999). His study looks at the rituals, values and social etiquette to be found in the multicultural neighbourhoods along Philadelphia's Germantown Avenue, a major artery of the city which reflects the vast social and economic difficulties confronting many urban centres throughout the world. In the opening chapter, Anderson invites the reader to take a stroll with him along this road. It is a long road, and as he moves along, it changes its shape and culture from the richest of the posh folk to the poorest of the poor. As he moves, the social patterns of the street – which groups go where, their shifting values, their street codes – change. He looks at the differences between the 'decent' families and the rougher 'street' families – the smart areas and the parts shaped by urban decay. Anderson's study belongs to a tradition of urban sociology which has long been mapping out the shapes and structures of city life for the past century and a half. In a way you will already know this intuitively: some parts of the city are no-go areas; others are stinking rich! Streets tell you what is expected of you. Strolling around Mayfair in London, you will meet very different people to when you are strolling around Brixton. Sociologists have long mapped the features of many cities. Thus, the pioneering Charles Booth (1840–1916) mapped out poverty in London, and the Chicago sociologists became famous for their analysis of 'zones' during the 1920s and the 1930s. And these days, there is also a whole industry devoted to mapping out lifestyles attached to postal areas and zip codes.

THE WORLD AS A PRISON

Having gone so far, we can now take our mapping of social orders much further. We can look at all of society as a flow of social orders and patterns constantly being generated and regenerated around certain 'problems' – in families, schools, workplaces, churches, governments, stock exchanges and prisons. What is the pattern here?

Consider, for example, families. All societies have structures which help organize the raising of children, the regulation of sexuality, and the organization of identities and generations, etc.; but, as is well documented, the variety of family organization across different times and places is considerable. People enter marriages, for example, by contract, coercion, force, choice. They marry opposite-sex and same-sex partners. They have many partners (polygamy) or one (monogamy); they marry within the same category (endogamy) or outside of it; they have large families and small families, raise them on their own or with the aid of all kinds of others. And they may be close to the wider family (extended family) or not. Nevertheless, within all this variety, there will always be patterns and structures.

And it goes yet further than this: all societies across the world develop definite identifiable patterns. French society is not Thai society is not Australian society. **Social structures** are the patterns of predictable human actions that cluster around key problems in living, and they vary across societies.

2 EXAMINE SOCIAL ACTIONS AND MEANINGS: HOW DO PEOPLE MAKE SENSE OF ACTING TOWARDS OTHERS?

Sociology's first task is to excavate these broad patterns of social structure and ultimately attempt to understand how they work. But if we just stayed with this question all the time, it would not get us very far – for people would soon object to the way society is seen as a prison in which they are trapped and patterned. People are much more *active* than this. Human beings engage continually in social action and interaction with others – changing their own lives and others, challenging what they find around them. Human lives are never passive but always in perpetual motion. And, indeed, they are often enabled to act because of this structure.

In this sense, a basic unit of sociology to think about is human social action and interactions. People act in the world towards others, they create social worlds with others; they are not the mere passive recipients of presenting social orders, structures, prisons or patterns. Indeed, their actions keep changing the world and keep social life in perpetual motion as they engage with others. We are historical actors, never solitary individuals, and always depend on others for a sense of who we are. Sociologists work hard on examining **social actions, selves, subjectivities** and **habitus**.

SOCIAL ACTIONS

The most celebrated account of **social action** was provided over a century ago by Max Weber. Put simply, he claimed that 'social actions' refers to human life when it takes into account the meanings people have of other people. It is linked to what is sometimes called '**inter-subjectivity**', whereby people make sense of social life through entering the minds of others they interact with. Charles Cooley saw this too when he claimed that 'we dwell in the minds of others'.

So, one task of the sociologist is to investigate the different kinds of social actions, which have their own reality and properties. A quick listing of such social actions might include (the list is not exhaustive):

- Rational actions, where our actions are shaped by ends and means (e.g. science; some – especially economists – also say that following paths to maximize our own self-interests is rational).
- Value actions, where our actions are shaped by (often personal) values (e.g. when we take moral or ethical positions).
- Practical actions, where our actions are guided by solving daily problems.
- Instrumental actions, where our actions are shaped by pursuing one's own ends (e.g. we use a teacher as a means for getting access to knowledge or learning).
- Emotional actions, where our actions are shaped by feelings (e.g. when we cry at funerals).
- Traditional actions, where our actions are shaped by habits (e.g. cleaning our teeth, driving a car).
- Embodied actions, where our actions are closely linked to the functioning, movement and projects of our bodies (e.g. washing activities, sex play, the clothes we adorn ourselves with; see Chapter 2, pp. 30–1).
- Innovative actions, where our actions are guided by creativity (e.g. art, music, much writing).
- Technological/digital action, where our actions are bound up with machines of various kinds (e.g. computing, smart phones).

Of course, such a list is just a start, and these areas often overlap. You may like to note the sheer range of these actions – they include feelings, bodies, creativities, values, practicalities. Much social science has a tendency to focus on rational actions, but very often much of social life is not shaped by this at all. Note too that these days we are increasingly engaging in what I have called digital actions – using smart phones, for example. These are different kinds of sections bringing different kinds of relationships and meanings. Sociologists have to study these actions – in science, in the gym, in schools, in street behaviour, in love and conflicts – but this is not psychology. The psychologist would study the individual's motives. The sociologists look at the creation of social actions and how people orientate life to others. You may like to review some of the 'social actions' you encounter during an afternoon or evening. How do people orientate themselves to others and how does meaning arise? Remember: you are never alone in a social action.

PRACTICES AND HABITUS

Indeed, taking these actions further, we might also see them as clustering into patterns themselves. Here, some sociologists speak of the logics of practice (Pierre Bourdieu is a key figure here; see also p. 188; pp. 191–3), and again, these emphasize the importance of the body and **practices** within the social world. This view stands against the rather naïve view that people simply act in rational and coherent ways. Just ask yourself if you do. Instead, social actions are usually practical – they operate according to an implicit, habitual, practical logic for them. We engage practically with certain bodily dispositions and feelings which become experienced routinely in different environments with different people. Sociologists often speak here of **habitus** to indicate a system of habits acquired through social life which we carry around with us. We develop rituals, a sense, a 'feel for the game' of whatever we are doing. This idea gets us beyond the simple notion of *individual* habits and on to a wider sense that we dwell all the time within our *social* habits. One major task of sociology is to understand the workings of these everyday logics, these common sense forms of social action – because this indeed is what we live with all the time. They are, in a sense, what makes the world go around. They are linked to other ideas like subjectivities and personhood. Most sociological studies focus on the meanings people build up in their activities, and we will look a little at how this is done in the next chapter.

3 BRIDGE ACTIONS AND STRUCTURES: HOW DO WE CONNECT MICRO WITH MACRO, INDIVIDUALS WITH SOCIETY?

We have seen that sociologists look at 'social structures' and the big patterns which organize social life deeply whilst at the same time examining 'social actions', active human orientations to others which keep changing and challenging the structures. The interests of sociologists are dual: there is the *collective, the broad, the wide* concern with how societies work and the concern with *concrete lives lived by individuals*. This leads us to one of the major recurrent problems of all sociological thinking: *how to cope simultaneously with both constraining structures and creative actions*. This is the action/structure tension (sometimes called the micro/macro issue), and it is sociology's abiding tension.

INDIVIDUALISM AND THE SOCIAL

The problem appears in many ways in sociology: it is never far away. How can a society develop a cohesion and a collectivity whilst fostering an individuality and cultivating a unique humanity? How can there be individuals within society and a society with individuals? How can we have freedom yet constraint? How can the individual dwell in the social and the social dwell in the individual? How can we have communities and bonding which do not overreach themselves into totalitarianisms and despotism? How can we have creative and caring individuals who do not overreach themselves into selfish, narcissistic egoists? How, in short, can we develop and maintain *a balance of individuality and sociality in life and society*? Too much focus on individuals leads to accusations of *individualism and reductionism*; too much focus on structures will lead to accusations of *determinism, holism and abstraction*.

It would be hard to find any sociologist (or indeed any thinker about the social from any discipline) who does not in the end have to deal with this question. Although discussions take many forms and may be partially resolved in many ways, it is the big social question. If 'individuals' triumph, we can so often sense a crumbling anarchy of egoism and selfishness taking over; if the 'social' triumphs, we can so often sense a painful loss of individuality as we are stalked by collective terrors. The roll call of thinkers on this issue is enormous: Plato, Aristotle, Hobbes, Rousseau, Montesquieu, Adam Smith, Kant, Goethe, de Tocqueville, Marx, Durkheim, Weber, Simmel, Dewey, Mead and on to major contemporary sociological works such as David Riesman's *The Lonely Crowd* (1950), Robert Bellah *et al.*'s *Habits of the Heart* (1985), Robert Putnam's *Bowling Alone* (2000) and Elliott & Lemert's *The New Individualism* (2009). Welcome to the club!

THINK ON: SIX OPENING WAYS INTO THE ACTION–STRUCTURE PUZZLE

The action–structure debate is a complex one and has produced many major and often dense theoretical studies dealing with it. Here are a few of the ways sociologists try to resolve this puzzle. Look out for them.

1 *Biographical life history*: start studying human biography and work out the ways in which social structure constrains you (see Mitch Dunier, *Slim's Table*).

2 *Structural analysis*: start with external social facts of structure but then work down to real people and see how their lives are shaped (see Raewyn Connell, especially in her book *Masculinities*).

3 *Cultural configurations*: look simultaneously at cultural meaning and individual meaning and move between them (see Norbert Elias in *The Civilizing Process*).

4 **Structuration** *theory*: see the *duality of structure* in motion: social structures make social action possible, and at the same time, that social action creates those very structures (see Anthony Giddens, *The Constitution of Society*).

5 *Positions and relations*: study relationships and practices in their habitus (as in the work of Bourdieu; see Beverley Skeggs, *Formations of Class and Gender*).

6 *Ethnographies*: get close to what you want to study and see both action and structure at work in the real situation (see Paul Willis, *Learning to Labour*).

4 EMPATHIZE WITH LIVED CULTURES: HOW CAN WE GRASP MEANINGFUL SYMBOLIC WORLDS?

Over and over again we see through this book that social life for humans is invariably bound up with 'meaning'. Whether we are looking at the societies of the Aztecs, the Romans or the Enlightenment, in the largest cities of the world or the smallest tribes on a Peruvian hilltop, humans – from birth to death – are engaged in a constant search to make sense of the world around them. Crucial to grasping this meaningful world is the idea of **culture** (revisit Chapter 2). Culture is uniquely human. Every other form of life – from ants to zebras – behaves in a more uniform, species-specific way. It is culture that makes us truly distinct from most other animals. *We are the meaning-making animal.* And meanings have consequences. How people give meaning to their lives becomes a key reality for them.

Cultures might be seen as 'ways of life' and 'designs for living', as 'tool kits' for assembling 'webs of significant meanings', as 'the scraps, patches and rags of daily life'. They can be seen as a set of creative tools and responses, lived daily in a flow and a flux to try and help us resolve our daily problems of living. At the heart of cultures are such things as the languages, symbols, narratives, stories, rituals, values, roles, identities, myths, beliefs, practices and material objects which make up any people's way of life – the recipes for us to make sense of it all. Never tight, fixed or agreed upon, it is dangerous to think of cultures as unities, wholes or fixed in any way. They never are. Instead, they are always alive and changing – contested, debated, modified, supported and rejected by their members in a vast stream of practical actions. They are always messy, multilayered and multiple mosaics and are bridges to the past as well as guides to the future.

Cultures suggest innumerable social worlds that are constantly contradictory and full of tension. When we are looking *across* cultures, we should never be at all surprised to find their enormous differences. But this is so also when we look *inside* specific cultures. Cultures do not speak to consensus and uniformity; by their natures, they cannot. Thus, to speak of cultures as harmonious well-ordered consensual wholes is sheer nonsense. Shorthand talk of 'Muslim culture', 'working-class culture', 'women's culture', 'British culture' or even 'gay or queer culture' is, in truth, to construct a lie. Immediately sociologists can recognize that human social worlds are stuffed full of massive ambiguities, contradictions, tensions – never worlds of agreed-upon consensus. Social life as lived by all peoples at all times grows out of these tensions. It is extremely important to grasp this because views of cultures which flatten them, homogenize them and turn them into monologic, monolithic and mono-moral overly stable forms are very dangerous to sociological thinking – they foster the stereotypes of much everyday thought.

One of the most striking features of human cultures is the sheer range of things that people come to believe in at different places and times. The religions we encountered in Chapter 2 are a good example. Sociologists are not in the business of making value judgements about what people come to believe and how they make sense of social life. Rather, their concerns are with showing how such beliefs come to arise (historical questions), with the ways in which they have come to be learnt and organized into people's lives (socialization questions) and the overall roles and tasks that they play (functional questions).

These cultures are everywhere. As well as attempting to capture mainstream and dominant cultures, sociologists have paid much attention to studying a mass of different cultures. Basically, they enter these worlds and try to understand the language, the stories, the rituals, the identities within them. This task is often called **ethnography** – literally describing ways of life. Think of the ways of life with which you are familiar. Here are some that sociologists have studied:

> astrology cultures; cyber cultures; drug cultures of all kinds (dope cultures, heroin cultures, LSD cultures, etc.); ethnic cultures (black, Asian, Muslim, etc.); environmental groups; feminist groups; flying saucer cults; gay, lesbian and queer cultures; gun rights cultures; leisure cultures; music cultures (rock groups, jazz bands, orchestras, opera, etc.); political cultures (right, left and middle); racial supremacists (Nazis, Ku Klux Klan, skinheads, Black Panthers, British National Front, etc.); religious and spiritual cultures of all sorts; school cultures; sports cultures (boxing, football, running, swimming, etc.); and youth cultures (teddy boys, mods and rockers, punks, goths, heavy metal, raves, etc.).

The list could go on and on. And this is what many sociologists do – they study little social worlds and their ways of life. They employ the method of **Verstehen**. They get close to people, live in their worlds and understand what is going on. Such attempts to analyze the cultural then requires thinking about language, symbols, stories, role-taking, feelings, bodies, identities and values. Ideally, a sociologist always works to understand these contested meanings that drench all of life: in signs, gestures, languages, narratives and the stories that people give to their lives, as illustrated in Table 5.1.

Table 5.1 Doing a cultural analysis

Think about	Question	Discipline linkage
Language	What are the words, the slang, the special meanings of terms in this culture?	Linguistics
Signs and symbols	Examine key symbols, look at the chain of signs and the process of signification.	**Semiotics**
Stories and narrative	Listen to the stories (narratives, myths, accounts, etc.) that people tell.	**Narrative** theory
Verstehen and role-taking	Understand the ways people come to see others; see the world through others' eyes.	Max Weber used the term '**Verstehen**'; G. H. Mead developed the idea of role-taking
Emotions and empathy	Appreciate what others are feeling.	Sociology of emotions – Cooley, Hochschild
Identities and roles	How do people come to see themselves (who are they?) and what roles do they perform?	**Dramaturgy** – see Goffman; and role/performance theory; modern identity theory
Bodies	What are the key projects in which people use their bodies?	Mind/body dualism debates; **embodiment** and 'body theory'
Values	Know the values that guide lives.	Studies of attitudes and values

5 INTERROGATE THE MATERIAL WORLD: JUST HOW ARE WE CONSTRAINED BY OUR BODIES, THE ECONOMY AND THE ENVIRONMENT?

Sociology is fascinated by human social worlds being cultural and symbolic. But this is *never* enough. For we also live in worlds that are undeniably material and have a brutish, physical reality about them – 'red in tooth and claw', as the poet Tennyson put it. Think of your own life and social world. You know that you are a physically biological-bounded animal with definite needs to be met like food, water, shelter, safety and health. You live on the land in a universe shaped by vast physical forces: evolution, environments and economies (including your 'land', the intense population, your 'property' and 'technologies', the digital world about you and ultimately the power of law and governments). Here too are deep human capabilities waiting to be cultivated or not. Here are things you most certainly cannot lightly wish or think away. They will exist independently of us giving them meaning. This is the material social world: a 'kickable world', a really real world, one which exists beyond our own wishes, beyond the realm of ideas and culture, a physical world not of our making. We confront these material conditions of our existence every day. Two modern thinkers (of many) who have played a major role in sensing this world have been Darwin and Marx.

At its most general level, **materialism** (and its often linked pal, **realism**) is a philosophical stance that explains the nature of reality – in all its aspects – in terms of matter. The world is first and foremost material, physical, tangible: a world of bodies and resources. The earliest material philosophers (like Democritus, around 460–370 BCE) were atomists who thought that universe and matter are only made up of atoms assembled in a purely mechanical way. The formation of world and life are explained by the associations of these atoms that are the only reality. Here the social world is an external world with an absolute existence independent of ideas and consciousness. At its extreme, it stands in opposition to any kind of **idealism** – or any theory that gives primacy to meaning. At this point, sociology enters one of the oldest debates in philosophy – the controversy between idealists (who give attention to the world of ideas and ideals) and materialists (who give attention to matter and materialism). By contrast, the earliest idealist philosophers from Plato through to Kant argued that social reality is based on mind or ideas. As we shall see, this also helps to generate another one of sociology's continuing tensions: the realist–idealist debate.

Never mind all this. At the most direct and concrete level, the material world directs sociologists to study the evolutionary, the economic and the environmental (the three 'E's as I like to call them).

Evolutionary thinking directs us to see our bodily tensions and limitations. Economic thinking directs us to the resources we work for and live through (the minerals, the oil, the land, our housing) and the technologies of production that are generated. Environmental analysis makes us aware of the wider universe and the severe limits it places upon our actions, as well as the competition for land and scarce resources on the earth now. All these forces work largely over and beyond our own control. We cannot (usually) control our own brain functioning and hormones – our animal-like nature. We do not control the wealth and work situations we initially find ourselves in, whether our technologies are ploughs, computers or everyday things turned into sellable commodities (commodification, as it is often called). And as we know these days, the environment and its four key elements of air, fire, earth and water may rage into human disaster and environmental degradation. Every day we hear of another catastrophe – a tsunami, a fire, an earthquake. (There is, of course, a sociology of disasters.)

6 DEVELOP AN AWARENESS OF HISTORY AND TIME: HOW CAN WE CONNECT THE PASTS, PRESENTS AND FUTURES OF HUMAN SOCIAL LIFE IN THE FLOW OF TIME?

The social always has a past, a present and a future and it is always on the move. Whether studying migration, music or mass movements, sociologists will want to understand their histories, the way they are lived dynamically in the here and now, and ultimately sense their movements and where they might be heading (though they are not futurologists – the future can never be known). 'The social' is always on the go!

All social things have a past, and sociology has to examine their history, archaeology and genealogy. More than this, the past is plural and ever present in the moment – there is the perpetual haunting of all social things in their multiplicities. Avery Gordon's *Ghostly Matters* (2008) shows how centuries of racial oppression in the US live on as ghosts in the present. More, this history is both big and bold and small and trickling. Major studies have been done on the histories of nation-states (in the work, for example, of Michael Mann on genocide and Charles Tilley on social movements) but also in the smaller histories of every damned thing – the social histories of toilets, telephones and tomatoes! Look at the social things of the present and examine how they are haunted by the past. The past itself is always constructed in the present moment, which then itself turns back into a lost past, even as both anticipate a future.

And this raises the complexity of time. There is, as we would expect, a sociology of time which looks at the whole shaping of 'the temporal order'. Time is not simply 'natural' and given but a very problematical humanly produced thing too. We have not always had clocks, and they are not all the same across the world. Yet once they were invented, they arguably changed the way we live in a significant way. (Yes, there is a sociology of the clock and time maps too; see Zerubavel, 2003.) A sociology of time looks at the ways in which we construct our sense of time: *objectively* through clocks and various measures, but also *subjectively* – how we experience the daily flow of time (the phenomenology of time, as we say) and indeed construct our memories (social memories) of the past. Memory in sociology cannot be seen as simply an individual psychological trait but rather as something that is partially structured by the groups we are moving in. Memory is collective.

Part of this time movement is organized through the idea of 'generations'. All lives are organized through specific age cohorts: those born in the Thatcher/Reagan years, or who lived through the Rwandan genocide, or who grew up during the Chinese Revolution, or who were survivors of the Holocaust: all share common experiences which bond them together. And these are unique to their lives, anchoring their lives as they move through them. Generational lives are the escalators of our lives: whole groups of people are in perpetual motion (Baby Boomers, the X generation, the Millennials), moving onwards together within a particular generational cohort or set of experiences, common to them and them alone, bonding them with each other, but also creating major differences with others who are not part of this generation. Moving further and further along this escalator, they become more and more distant from those at the other end who are just alighting upon it. And along this journey, a whole series of issues arise. (See, for example, Arlene Stein's research on the problems faced by 'third-generation holocaust survivors' (Stein, 2014).)

7 KEEP MOVING ON: HOW TO EXAMINE THE CONTINGENCIES, MOBILITIES AND FLOWS OF SOCIAL LIFE?

Closely linked to the above is the need to always view human social life (and sociology) as a process, as mobilities: everything changes, life flows and nothing stays. Whether we are analyzing harassment, homicides or health systems, all change by the moment as they are shaped by contingencies. Sociology's subject matter – even its very categories – is *never* fixed or stable. A comment made in one moment can be changed the next. A group formed in one hour changes in the next. A situation moves on. A biographical life is transformed from second to second. Societies are bubbling cauldrons of never-ending change. Nothing stays the same. Every sociological finding is out of date the minute it is done. All 'findings' are short-lived – they last for the moment they are found. In this sense, sociology is permanently out of date as the world moves on. Hence, a major challenge often arises: what in the midst of the vast flow and flux can just be of stable and recurrent value? Where is the permanence in all this perpetual change? How do we live in continual permutations of social actions?

Like most of what I am saying, this is not a simple idea. Life is a flow moving through all manner of chancy, unforeseen events that can have enormous social consequences. Even as life is determined by major biological, personal and social forces, it often is much less determined than some science likes to suggests. Small chance factors can have huge causal power. And equally, many contingencies can pile up into regular sequences and patterns to become almost unnoticed. Oddly this idea of contingency – deserving surely of a full-blown sociological theory and philosophical account – lacks one. Humans are vulnerable, life is precarious and we *suffer from contingencies*. Chance happenstances are the stuff of our everyday lives, and the sociologist has to grasp this.

This central role of contingency is a popular theme in history, literature and art. Consider Peter Howitt's film *Sliding Doors* (1998), which stars Gwyneth Paltrow and John Hannah. Here, the central character Helen is sacked from her job; returning home at an unusual hour, she rushes to catch the Tube train. In one moment, the film depicts one reality in which she just manages to squeeze through the sliding doors and get on the train; in another depiction, a second moment or reality shows her missing the train. But it is a decisive moment. With the first moment, she meets James on the Tube but gets home to find her boyfriend, Gerry, cheating on her with his ex-girlfriend. Following the other moment, Helen misses the Tube train, gets mugged, goes to hospital and eventually arrives home to find her partner all alone! At that one moment – that one contingency – her life is full of different possibilities. And in the film, the two moments – shaping two realities – move forward in parallel with radically different outcomes. The first moment means that Helen leaves Gerry and forms a positive, delightful, loving relationship with James; the other shows Helen's life taking bad turns as her boyfriend continues to cheat on her. A moment in life makes a huge difference. Classically, it is that moment when we cheerfully leave the front door of our house and are then run down by a passing lorry. You can never tell; anything could happen. Moments really do matter. Possibilities are everywhere for things to be different from what they are.

There are many films and stories which tell similar tales. And yet most of the time – most days of our life – we stave off the wider possibilities of our existence and their shaping through chance occurrences because of our persistent tendency to make social habits. The huge potential and risk of human existence is persistently narrowed by the flywheel of habit. The buzzing booming confusion of the world is persistently narrowed down so that most of our lives – most of our days – we follow well-patterned habits. We cannot stand too much life, and we have to narrow and restrict our daily potentials into well-formed routines in behaviour, in thoughts, in feelings. Crudely, we become zombie-like. But this does not stop the many precarious moments harbouring full-scale chance possibilities of change.

8 LOCATE SOCIAL LIFE IN PLACE AND SPACE: HOW IS HUMAN SOCIAL LIFE SHAPED BY THE SITUATIONAL, THE GLOBAL AND THE PUBLIC?

All of social life flows and moves with places and spaces. There is a geography – and a geometry – of social things. Nothing happens

THINKING IN THE PLURAL: ON THE VARIETIES OF MUSLIM EXPERIENCE

The philosophers William James and Hannah Arendt highlight both a pluralistic world and the need to take seriously how every human being is different. Indeed, a major lesson for all sociologists is to *avoid the single and see things in their variety and multiplicity*. Look for the varieties of anything you study. To talk, for example, of 'Muslim' requires recognizing diversities: there are multiple Muslims. There are over 1.5 billion Muslims, with a majority population in around fifty different countries, each with its own culture: there are Indonesian Muslims, Malaysian Muslims, Pakistani Muslims, New York Muslims and the rest. They divide between the Sunni (the largest and most orthodox) and the Shi'at Ali. Some women veil, others do not, and there is a wide range of veiling practices. Female genital mutilation is common in some Muslim societies (Egypt, Somalia, Sudan, the Gambia) but not others. Honour killings are found in some (Pakistan, Arabia) but not others. Bedouin tribes are worlds apart from the oil-rich Gulf-State capitalists. In Indonesia there are *tombois* who act as masculine females identified as men who desire women, while their girlfriends view themselves as normal women who desire men. In Iran, transgender is common. There are queer/gay Muslims and 'new Arab men'. And there are varieties of radical groups fighting the Jihad (or holy war) across the world: the Muslim Brotherhoood in Egypt, the Islamic Revolution Front in Algeria, Hezbollah in Lebanon, Hamas in the West Bank, al-Qaeda in Afghanistan, and ISIS in Syria and Iraq. These more militant paths all have their own distinctive cultures – language, worldviews, identities and knowledge. The Arab in the Arab world is very conservative and different from the Muslim in Southeast Asia, where things are changing.

Sociologists always have to recognize and look for differences – a golden rule of social life.

outside of the flow of situations or context, and sociology is always asking questions about the construction, organization and impact of these spaces. We have already seen something of this when we were looking at the habits of the street and in the mappings of cities earlier. Well over a century ago, Charles Booth mapped out the streets and life of the London poor, whilst in the US, a strong classical tradition of sociology – known as the Chicago ecological school – documented the importance of city zones in our lives, making major contrasts with the spaces and lives conducted in rural areas. It matters whether you live in cities or the countryside – and as we know, more and more people have now come to dwell in the space of 'the global city'. Today we live in the postcode society where regions, city, province, street become clues to lifestyles. We have also seen how the roles people play differ across various settings. And we have sensed the ways in which the world is moving from being a local place to a global one (see Chapter 3).

To start thinking about space and the social, it might help for a moment for you to do an exercise. Consider yourself, your body and your mind as a kind of vehicle driving gently through – and at the same time, constructing – different social spaces, situations and settings. You might encounter five spaces moving out from your body. First, there is the phenomenology of space – this is the mental map you make of the world you live in. If you think about the area you live and move around in, you will find you have your own sense of space which is not one that anyone else has. Second, as you move into any social situation – a school classroom, a street corner, a workplace, a church, a public toilet – you will find that awaiting you there are some expectations of how you should behave; that you may not behave that way is another matter. What is certain is that some general ways of behaving are tied up with almost all spaces. There is a sociology of situations and co-presence. Broaden this out and we can find that people often connect with each other through various groups – social worlds and their perspectives. In this sense, a society can be mapped out as different kinds of worlds, a bit like the different cultures I have outlined above. Society is not a homogenous whole but a series of intermeshed social worlds. It is also a network – a chain of relations through which we live. With the arrival of the internet, more and more people live their lives through virtual spaces that can only be called the network society. Finally, we can sense that social life moves from being located within specific social worlds to a much wider sense of the global world (see Chapter 3). Now much of your life can be seen as part of a chain which connects to others round the world. Spaces have become more and more globalized – and sociology has to search out these connections.

9 CONNECT WITH BIOGRAPHY: HOW TO MAKE SENSE OF REAL, EMBODIED, EMOTIONAL PEOPLE?

The billions of people on Planet Earth cannot all be studied by sociologists (perish the thought!). But if we lose sight of real, lived, biographically fleshy, feeling lives, then we easily can get lost in abstractions divorced from social life. Sociologists can never afford to forget that *the web of human life is biographically grounded*. Hence whatever else they do, sociologists have to return regularly to real bodily lives, observe their experiences and listen to what they have to say. Connecting to life histories, with their wider links to actions, structures and histories, is the necessary corrective to prevent sociology from becoming far removed from social life (as it often does). A wonderful display of this can be found in Pierre Bourdieu's *The Weight of the World* (*La misère du monde*) (1993), a study made up entirely of interviews with downcast Parisians telling of the sufferings and contradictions of their lives.

Studying human life stories closely reveals many features of the social world. The unemployed life story reveals not personal failure but the workings of the wider economy; homosexuality is not a personal pathology but something deeply shaped by laws and the social meanings of gender; our bodies are not simple biology but connect to the body projects and emotional structures of our time (see Chapter 2 again). A central tool for sociology is hence always the life narrative – listening with empathy to the stories that people tell of their lives. However broad-ranging your study may be and however many people may be studied (often in the thousands), sociology always needs the in-depth study of one concrete life to remind itself of the actual impossibility of grasping the whole situation.

10 TAKE POWER SERIOUSLY: WHO IS CONTROLLING WHAT'S GOING ON HERE?

How does power touch your social life? Sociology sees power as a prominent – if contested – feature of the social. Loosely defined as the process by which people are able to influence and exert control over their own lives and resist the control of others, **power** comes in many forms and spawns many debates raising matters of domination and subordination.

BIG POWER, LITTLE POWER; VISIBLE POWER, INVISIBLE POWER

Power is identifiable in a big sense – most societies have governments that exert different kinds of power (and come in different forms such as authoritarian, monarchic, theocratic, totalitarian and democratic states). It is also present in myriad little ways – in the choices, rules and regulations that face us in everyday life (at school and work, between men and women, in the family, amongst friends or in the fields of discrimination like race and sexuality). The former is generally the topic of 'the sociology of power' whilst the latter is often seen as the 'micro-politics' of everyday life. Either way, power is omnipresent and ubiquitous in the study of social life. It asks the question: *who is controlling what's going on here, and how?*

Some forms of power are highly visible, and we can see them at work straight away. Think of the despotic ruler and tyrant, slavery or even the prisoner and his guard. It is upheld through coercion, physical control and ultimately brutal violence over others' bodies. Some forms of power are given over to others. We concede power to a democratic government that is chosen initially by us and that is supposed to act on our behalf; children concede power to their parents, who are supposed to act in the best interests of the child. And some forms of power come to work in hidden ways – we consent to others regulating our lives without really realizing we are doing this. Very frequently, the workings of power is the key feature to grasp behind the workings of stratification.

The most apparent account of power is that which highlights a dominant group over another, and it probably gets the most attention in sociology – maybe too much attention. With a long history of theorization stretching back (via Plato and Machiavelli through to Pareto, Mosca, Weber and Marx), this 'elite theory of power' holds that in every society there must be a minority who rules over others (a political class or governing elite), though just what nature of this minority is in question. It could be an economic group (Marx's ruling class), or a religious leader (as in Iran, a theocracy), or intellectuals (in China under the rule of the *literati*), or a combination of groups (C. Wright Mills's famous study of the US power system in 1956, *The Power Elite*, distinguished three major elites: the corporation heads, the political leaders and the military chiefs). These are the people who occupy the 'command posts'. Marxist sociologists of various persuasions ultimately connect these ruling groups back to a class – the ruling class is the dominant economic class (in writings such as Ralph Miliband's *The State in Capitalist Society*). Others have argued for a long time that power is more dispersed than this and is connected to a much wider range of groups. (This was for a long time called the pluralist theory of power and was identified with Ronald Dahl's *Who Governs?* (1961).)

A key problem in thinking about power is the ways in which people dwell in systems of domination and subordinations *without really thinking about them*. It has been called 'non-decision making' (how people do *not* make decisions about their lives). How are some issues organized into politics whilst others are organized out? A key concept developed here has been that of **hegemony** – an idea developed (from the Greeks) by the Italian Marxist Antonio Gramsci (1891–1937) in his *Prison Notebooks* (1929–35) to suggest the way in which people come to accept the coercive roles of the state unthinkingly and uncritically. How do people come to consent to governments that act against their interests? For many political theorists, there comes a crucial wider turn to culture and the workings of what the French Marxist Louis Althusser (1918–90) called 'the ideological state apparatuses' – those crucial mechanisms such as the media, organized religion, the schools (educational curricula) and the commercialized popular arts (cinema, music, etc.) which work to influence the citizens to be subordinate to the state and accept its dominant values – hence maintaining the **hegemonic** *status quo*. This kind of approach means that sociology needs to focus a great deal upon these media as a way of understanding the workings of power and ponder when consent might cease.

And we ask what stops people rebelling? A long list of reasons can be provided: inertia and habit hold it all in place; ideological manipulations by the media prevent people from seeing their true interests; people get sufficient satisfaction from the government to go along with it much of the time; rebellions of an extreme kind are just too damn costly for people's lives (think of the tragic consequences of most revolutions where thousands, sometimes millions, die). And, perhaps most intriguingly, many people do indeed resist their governments and others' power every day – there is a permanent grumble and resistance in society. In all societies there are subterranean traditions of resistance and fighting back in myriad little ways. Once we start analyzing this, we can see that power permeates through the everyday life of a society. It is everywhere (and nowhere)! It was Foucault who puts power right at the centre of his theory, and power is for some sociologists the central feature of social life.

So back to your own social life. It might help to think of how power is ubiquitous in your own social relations – pervasive and circulating through all situations. Even more, it may actually enter your body and mind: how is your everyday life organized through power relations (in families, with friends, in schools, at work)? This is not a matter of brute force or simple repression but a matter of the way in which society saturates our being with a host of minor regulatory forms and practices. From childhood onwards, we are, so to speak, made out of this power: all our ideas, our bodies, our behaviours are inside a system of power that regulates us. We find it operating in families and schools, in prisons and hospitals, in streets and media, in our knowledge and daily encounters. Power is diffused everywhere. And of course we resist it: 'where there is power, there is resistance' says Foucault. But even as we resist, we enter new fields of power and control: our social movements have their own regulations. It seems we are trapped. And it is another sociological challenge to grasp it.

11 LIVE WITH COMPLEXITY AND CONTRADICTIONS: HOW ARE THE CONTESTATIONS AND CONUNDRUMS OF SOCIAL LIFE TO BE LIVED WITH?

One of the most irritating myths about sociology is that it is an easy subject! If you take seriously the ten little points I have suggested as guidelines for studying sociology seriously, then I think you will by now be feeling very intellectually challenged – even threatened. Sociology raises endless conundrums and intellectual puzzles – in a sense it struggles with the meaning of life! And there are problems with everything I have said above. You will not travel far in sociology – or society – without sensing that life is a series of conundrums. Everything seems to harbour its opposite. Life is a paradox. Amongst the most common tensions we face are:

- Are societies free or determined? They are both.
- Are societies material or ideational? They are both.
- Do societies progress or regress? They do both.
- Are societies whole or individualist? They are both.
- Is the social unique or general? It is both.

We can continue. Human social life – including sociological thinking – is incorrigibly contradictory and contested. All social things seem to be contested. We have *Contested Cities*, *Contested Nature*, *Contested Communities*, *Contested Identities*, *The Contested Self*, *Contested Environment*, *Contested Meanings*, *Contested Histories*, *Contested Citizenship*, *Contested Knowledge*, *Contested Space*, *Contested Futures*, *Contested Justice* and *Contested Values* (all these are recent book titles!). Such tensions are ubiquitous in sociology, and indeed you will find whole books built around them – classically in Robert Nisbet's *The Sociological Tradition* (1966), where it sets out major tensions such as secular versus sacred and authority versus power; more recently, Chris Jenks's edited collection *Core Sociological Dichotomies* (1998) discusses over twenty of these major tensions. We will find contestation at the heart of Marx's theory of materialism and class conflict; it is there when Durkheim claims that the normal seems to be inextricably bound up with the abnormal or pathological – you can't have one without the other. Opposites and tension seem to thrive on each other.

Again, there is nothing new here. A long history in world philosophies recognizes these contradictions and tensions. For Heraclitus, a perceived object is a harmony between two fundamental units of change, a waxing and a waning. For Plato (*c.* 424–348 BCE), it was the spectre of idealism and materialism. In Chinese thought, the notions of yin and yang (or earth and heaven) describe two opposing aspects of reality which then complement each other, or create a unity. And in the work of the German philosopher G. W. F. Hegel (1770–1831), ideas and societies can be seen as inevitably moving through contradictions or opposing tendencies. He speaks of these as dialectics – when two opposites clash (thesis and counter thesis) and a new form emerges (synthesis). He analyzes, for example, how an event like the French Revolution brought both great ideas of equality and a major upsurge of violence (the Reign of Terror), but these clashes could ultimately lead to the possibility of a new constitutional government (which then itself becomes the next part of an endless **dialectical** process).

So here comes the big difference between these theoretical and philosophical debates and the sociological project: *sociologists always have to return to the empirical world in order to see what is happening in lived human social life. They look at contradictions as lived.* Sociology is an empirical discipline, and sociologists always have to come back to ground from the theoretical heavens. And in that sense they find they have to show how people in societies live with these contradictions – philosophers may, in their heads, sort them out, but daily practical social life is not so easy. We live in a pluralistic universe, and human social life is incorrigibly stuffed full of contradiction, difference, tension and ambiguity. Sociologists have to recognize this sooner or later. They have to observe these tensions, think them through, negotiate and struggle between opposing paths, and learn ultimately the hard trick of dealing with them in their thinking. They are ever-present – it is a fine balancing act – we have to live with them. It is some of the ways of doing this that will be our concern in the next chapter.

Living with these tensions is not easy, but doing sociology necessarily means the recognition that social life is a paradoxical affair. There are rarely easy answers, and although we may take sides, in the end, life is everywhere flushed full of tension, contradiction and paradox. Sociology is charged with thinking through – and living with – this continuous, contradictory and contingent social world we live in. Like life, sociology is a conundrum.

SUMMARY

Sociology is a form of imagination, and this chapter maps some of its complexities and contradictions. Sociologists need to look at action, structures and the tensions and bridges between them.

MACRO

GLOBAL WORLD
Globalization, glocalization, interconnections, flows
Located in POWER AND COMPLEXITY

SOCIETIES
('The land' – used to be communities, now commonly nation-states)
(with their **INSTITUTIONS AND STRUCTURES**
e.g. states, economies, families, religions, communications, law, etc.)

↕

CULTURES ←——————→ **MATERIAL WORLDS**
(and their meanings and   (and their resources:
languages, dominant and   economies, environment
subterranean)   evolution, the land and
                                                    population, technology)

↕

MESO

 FIELDS, SPHERES, ARENAS OF SOCIAL LIFE
(instituting and habitualizing social relations)

↕

**organizations and networks of relations
habitus, fields and life worlds
social worlds, etc.**

MICRO

↕

SOCIAL ACTIONS, INTERACTIONS AND PRACTICES
Human energy, capabilities and goals
(enabling and determined)

↕

EMBODIED LIVES, HUMAN SUBJECTIVITIES AND NARRATIVES
(bodies, brains, emotions, talk, inner worlds, etc.)

TIME   **organized in**   **SPACE**
Emergence: past, present and future   *the interaction order; rural/urban,*
Synchronic *(simultaneous)*   *globalization/local and situational*
Diachronic *(phases, development)*   *public/private*

Figure 5.1   Putting it together: mapping out the flows of 'the social'

They simultaneously examine material and cultural worlds. They see social life as located in time (history) and space (geography) and the flows and movements between them. They search for the power relations behind the social – asking who is shaping what. And they try to connect all this to the grounded connections of lived lives, biographies and the stories that people tell of them. It is hard for any sociology study to do all this, but the more you can examine in any study, the better. In this chapter are a number of the key entrance points to thinking about the social. Figure 5.1 suggests some of the key elements for any sociological analysis.

EXPLORING FURTHER

MORE THINKING

1 Examine the idea that sociology is a way of thinking and a form of consciousness. If so, what does this 'way of thinking' look like? (Hint: look at the conclusion of this book, Twenty-one Theses.)

2 In this chapter, I have suggested a road map with twelve sign-posts to help develop a sociological imagination. You should think a little about each, but you will find some more inter-esting and suited to you than others. Try and apply them all initially to your sociological work and thinking, and then develop those which interest you most. Nobody can do it all!

3 Write a short essay entitled 'The Varieties of . . .', choosing a topic that interests you (see the Box: Thinking in the plural, p. 141).

FURTHER READING

A valuable introduction to many of the puzzles posed in this chapter can be found in Chris Jenks (ed.), *Core Sociological Dichotomies* (1998). Here are just a few suggestions to take you further on some of the issues raised: on structure and system, see Talcott Parsons, *The Social System* (1951); on meaning, see Paul Ricoeur, *Hermeneutics and the Human Sciences* (1981); on structure/action, see Anthony Giddens, *The Constitution of Society* (1986). On time, see Barbara Adam, *Time* (2004), and on generations, see Ken Plummer, 'Generational sexualities' (2010). On power, see Steven Lukes, *Power* (2004) and C. W. Mills, *The Power Elite* (1956). Some classic books of sociology to read could include Elijah Anderson, *Code of the Street: Decency, Violence and the Moral Life of the Inner City* (1999), which looks at race and inner-city trouble, and Stanley Cohen, *States of Denial: Knowing About Atrocities and Suffering* (2001), which looks at the ways we ignore the atrocities of the world. Clifford Shaw's *The Jack-Roller: A Delinquent Boy's Own Story* (revised edition, 1966) is the life story of one boy, a classic Chicago study. Arlie Hochschild's *The Managed Heart* (1983) introduces the significance of emotion through a study of flight attendants. In *The Weight of the World* (1999/1993), Pierre Bourdieu's important theoretical work is 'fleshed out' with interviews. Arthur W. Frank's *The Wounded Storyteller* (1995) draws on his own illness to develop an account of the stories we tell of our illnesses. See also: Jürgen Habermas, *The Structural Transformation of the Public Sphere* (1989); Jeffrey C. Alexander, *The Civil Sphere* (2006); Roberto Mangabeira Unger, *The Self Awakened: Pragmatism Unbound* (2007). Finally, see Ken Plummer, 'A Manifesto for Critical Humanism in Sociology' (2013).

RESEARCH: CRITICALLY ENGAGING WITH THE EMPIRICAL

> Be a good craftsman. Avoid any rigid set of procedures. Above all, seek to develop and to use the sociological imagination. Avoid the fetishism of method and technique. Urge the rehabilitation of the unpretentious intellectual craftsman, and try to become such a craftsman yourself. Let every person be their own methodologist; let every person be their own theorist; let theory and method again become the practice of a craft.
>
> C. Wright Mills, *The Sociological Imagination*, 1959

Sociologists are often seen as people who do interviews, conduct social surveys or design questionnaires. Maybe. But they are hardly alone in this: many other groups use such research tools. What make sociologists distinctive are their 'questions' and 'perspectives'. From these they select any and all methods that empower them to engage critically with a wide range of data. Practically, sociologists always need to develop a close awareness of the empirical world we live in – looking and listening carefully, engaging with people and their plights and thinking deeply. We observe the world in many different ways, come to appreciate its multiplicities, complexities and inner meanings and engage with it through all our senses. In doing this lies the excitement and challenge of sociological method. We match our methods with our problems and research topics. In doing all this, the aim is ultimately to tell the truth with an 'adequate objectivity', a fair enough neutrality. But all this is simple to say and so much harder to do: there is much controversy between sociologists as to just exactly how this can or should be done. This is the focus of this chapter, dealing again with introductory, but difficult, matters.

THE PRACTICE OF SOCIOLOGY: THE TRICKS OF THE TRADE

To understand the world sociologically is like any skill: it requires practice, and it means learning some of the 'tricks of the trade', Howard Becker's term, from others who have been there before. Sociologists (like all scientists, artists and intellectuals) need to cultivate certain crafts, imaginations and ways of thinking to be critical, dialogic and reflexive. We need to attend to complex human biographies and actions in emerging times and spaces, to grasp human subjectivities embedded in power relations and material worlds, and we need a calm distance – struggling for adequate objectivity – whilst maintaining a personal passion. Some parts of doing sociology are a bit like learning to play the piano or a new language or like acquiring the tools (and subsequent knowledge) of a biologist or chemist. There are layers of skill involved in all of these from the novice to the expert: at the start, there is much to be learnt and many skills to acquire. Bit by bit, levels of competences are acquired. Ultimately, a fresh flair and creativity are required to make it all work well.

One difference with sociology from other skills lies in the fact that we are all already 'novice sociologists' by virtue of us living in society: to navigate our ways around the social world every day requires some modicum of knowledge about how the society works. We can, though, mistake this early and basic knowledge as being enough to say we are sociologists. In fact, becoming a sociologist is a slow process of acquiring a sociological imagination. It is the difference between a pianist who can vamp out a simple tune on two or three notes and distinguish a crotchet from a quaver and someone who can read music, appreciate scale and chord complexities and play concerts.

There are hundreds of books and courses on all aspects of sociological research methodology, and this book cannot serve as an introduction to much of this (but see the reading suggestions at the end of this chapter). What I propose instead is to provide a very basic schema to guide you through some of the big issues. Broadly, doing sociology means cultivating some of the following kinds of skills:

1 Epistemological work: *asking questions about the kinds of truths* social science can produce, its **paradigms**.
2 Empirical work: *developing an intimate familiarity* with your topic in all its 'sources' and 'forms' – learning about tools and methods that enable you to get close to data that shows you what is going on in the world.
3 Analytic work: *making good critical sense of it all* – learning how to dissect social life (a bit like a zoologist might an animal!), build good concepts and theories and develop intelligent, thoughtful observations.

EPISTEMOLOGICAL WORK: THE FRAMING OF SOCIOLOGICAL KNOWLEDGE

As with all intellectual work, sociology requires serious thinking. Earlier chapters have suggested the many pathways into sociological thinking. The previous chapter alone suggested eleven key areas to scrutinize. At every stage of study, sociology asks you questions about the very nature of the kind of knowledge being assembled (**epistemological** questions), puzzles your sense of what is really real in the social world (**ontological** questions) and examines your own personal location in the research process (known in the trade as '**reflexivity**').

SOCIOLOGY AS A HISTORICAL, SCIENTIFIC ART

For 200 years of its history, sociology has struggled to define itself as the science of society. Yet since its inception, there have always been long and heated debates as to just what is meant by this very idea. This 'debate on methodology' (sometimes called – in German – the *Methodenstreit*) between the human and natural

sciences (*Geistwissenschaften* and *Naturwissenschaften*) arose significantly in Germany between the philosopher and cultural historian Wilhelm Dilthey (1833–1911) and the neo-Kantian Heinrich
Rickert (1863–1936) and Wilhelm Windelband (1848–1915) in the
late nineteenth century. What an intellectual buzz there must have
been in those days as they debated the true nature of social science,
history and human knowledge. These were modern rehearsals of
old philosophical debates. But they influenced all who followed
them (including Max Weber). And such debates have not gone away
in the twenty-first century.

THINK ON: WHAT IS KNOWLEDGE?

Epistemology is the branch of philosophy which studies the
nature of knowledge and its various versions of truth. There are
major debates on epistemology within sociology, and four can
be listed here:

1 **Positivism**: The classical and traditional view of science:
   measurements of observables, as in classifying animals or
   doing laboratory experiments. Common tools are surveys
   and statistical data.
2 **Interpretivism**: Human life differs because of meaning and
   hence a key task is to understand these meanings through
   '*Verstehen*', empathy and intimate familiarity. Common
   tools are life stories; in-depth interviews; and field work,
   participant observation and ethnographic work (these last
   three terms are often interchangeable).
3 **Standpoints** and perspectives: Recognizes that all science
   and serious analysis is conducted from a socially grounded
   point of view and we need to be clear what this standpoint
   is. Common standpoints are 'feminist', 'queer', 'anti-racist'
   and 'post-colonial'.
4 **Realism**: Stronger and more theoretical view of science.
   Claims that science does not depend simply on observation and measurement but seeks deep, underlying causal

> processes. A physicist may observe planets, but a theory is then needed to explain them; a biologist may observe plant and animal life but then needs to explain them. Realist accounts include Darwin's evolutionary theory or Marx's theory of materialism: both are grounded in observations but also develop much grander and wider explanatory tools.
>
> (For a good collection of background readings on all this, see Gerard Delanty and Piet Strydom, *Philosophies of Social Science: The Classic and Contemporary Readings* (2003).)

Dilthey wanted to produce what might be called a cultural science, and he aimed to show that the knowledge of the world of humans could only be gained through close inspection of lived experiences (*Erlebnis*) and gaining understanding (*Verstehen*) of them, rather than through mere observations of the external observable world. As we have seen before, a central data for sociology is human meaning, and Dilthey claimed that we need to develop good ways to grasp the meanings and spirit of the times and place we are studying. Sociology must definitely *not* be the same as the natural sciences since cultural sciences always needed to understand these experiences through re-experiencing (*Nacherleben*) the meanings carried by historical actors or cultural objects. These world views (*Weltanschauungen*) are relative to cultures. Windelband and Rickert agreed with much of Dilthey, but they argued that real distinctions did need to be drawn between those who wanted to establish universal laws and uniformities (the so-called nomothetic sciences) and those who thought that history could only give specific, probably unique constellations of action (the idiographic sciences). Following Kant, they argued that the human sciences should indeed look for universal laws (leaving history to look at the unique cases).

Now this is a complicated debate of the kind in which many sociologists revel. Be warned, if you want to study sociology to any advanced level, these are the kinds of questions that are constantly addressed. But let me be simple: sociologists are always busy pondering questions like:

- Are the social sciences really like the physical sciences? (This in turn raises the issue of what the physical sciences are.)
- Does the subject matter of social science differ so much from that of the physical sciences that it requires a very different method? Do human meanings make a big difference?
- Should the social sciences really be a branch of history and hence idiographic, focusing upon unique and specific instances?
- Should social sciences seek out universals and be capable of making generalizations? Is abstract theory a good way of doing this?

I can tell you now: there are no simple answers to these questions, much ink has been spilt on them and academics take very different stands on them today. But to start out in your own thinking, it might help if you go back to your own experience (probably in school) of three things: science, art and history. Science – be it biology, physics or chemistry – always involves some kind of *observations* of what is going on in the world. Personally, I always think of David Attenborough's many television series of nature watching – of the scientist watching carefully his animals and their behaviour. But usually they go beyond simple observations and classify, conceptualize and attempt a few generalizations. Nowhere is this clearer than in the astonishing theories of the origins of the universe. Physics may have created the Hubble Space Telescope to observe the heavens, but it has not observed the famous 'Big Bang' theory. Drawing from evidence, there is a lot of imaginative speculation in science too. Sometimes sociologists invent a rather simple-minded view of science as observation and testing when it is always so much more than this.

So now consider history. Again, at school, you always learn a lot of very specific facts about the past. But – if you were taught well – you will soon also know that a lot of these facts pose very real problems of interpretation. These days, with a lot of history programmes on TV, the problems here really do become much clearer: how do historians get their facts? Often historians are manifestly opinion-ated people telling a good yarn, trying to persuade us how the world is alongside the truth of what they have found. Think how the history is bound up with the presenter (at the present time in the UK: think of some of the most famous tele-historians, Simon Sharma, David Starkey, Lucy Worsley and Mary Beard and how different their styles and approaches are). There is so much more to history than a straightforward presentation of the facts.

Finally, think of art – a piece of music, a painting, a play or poem. What do you learn from this? At the very least, I hope, something about human imagination and creativity, and more – just maybe something about humanity and its lot? So much literary writing (Shakespeare, Tolstoy), visual art (Hogarth, Warhol) and music (Mozart, Mahler) address the great social themes of their times and our times. And this can shift imaginations, perhaps more than sci-ence. As Keats waxed lyrically: 'Do not all charms fly at the mere touch of cold philosophy?' ('Lamia', 1820).

So there is art, history and science. If we want to understand what is going on in the world, is one better than the other? Should we junk art in favour of science? Favour history over science? See art as the supreme entrance to the condition of humanity? Science as the gateway to the stars? Well that is your choice, but for me, we need all three equally. They are not incompatible, and each is there to check the worst excesses of each other.

All of which is why I think it is best to see sociology as engaging with multiple methodologies and as a historical, scientific art which aims to understand what is going on in the human social world. *We struggle with understanding our unique pasts (history); we seek to make con-nections and generalizations from observations of the world in order to under-stand what is taking place in the empirical world (science); and we need our imaginations to make sense of it all (art)*. Of course, individuals might specialize in one or other styles of doing sociology, but ultimately to grasp a depth of understanding of society, we will always need the three bubbling around: a science for objectivity, a history for unique understanding and an art for critical imagination.

Sadly, contemporary knowledge is often divided into what the scientist and novelist C. P. Snow – back in the 1950s – called 'the two cultures': the arts (humanities, arts, history) versus the sciences.

You can see this in the ways in which contemporary universities award degrees (Bachelors of *Arts*, Bachelors of *Sciences*) and organize their faculties (The Faculty of *Science*, The Faculty of *Arts*). Even in schools, students are often asked to choose a scientific or artistic path at ridiculously early ages. Indeed, in modern times, it has become almost a divide – societies get organized on this split. You can see it in an omnipresent tension between 'philistine scientists' and overly 'romantic artists'! But it has not always been so. If you look, for example, at the work of Leonardo da Vinci (1452–1519), you will find his work was variously that of a painter, a sculptor, a musician, an architect, a scientist, a mathematician, an engineer, an anatomist, a botanist – the list goes on and on. He was not concerned with the petty divides that modernity has made for their convenience. There were no mutually exclusive polarities between the sciences and the arts. His studies of science and engineering

Table 6.1 'Only Connect': bringing together micro and macro, science and art

	The artistic pole	Mediating forces	The science pole
Task	Interpret and understand	←——————→	Measure and find causes
Focus	Worlds of inner meaning, feeling and experiences	←——————→	Outer structures, objective causes
Tools	Empathy, imagination, familiarity	←——————→	Trained research skills
Values and politics	Everywhere	←——————→	Neutral and value-free
Presentation	Film, novels, drama, art, music	←——————→	Data papers, reports, tables

Caution: I have dangerously oversimplified these positions of the research process, which is much more complex than this simple schema. Both approaches are often combined, and there are many other stances. But as an opening way of thinking about the choices available in social research, this does suggest some key, and very different, pathways. In an ideal world, they should complement each other, not compete.

fused with art and philosophy and filled some 13,000 pages of notes and drawings. He is, of course, the classic Renaissance Man. But he shows, so vividly, that the worlds of science and art need not be kept as apart as the modern world tries to do. Table 6.1 suggests some of the false splits that need bridging.

EMPIRICAL WORK: GETTING INTIMATE WITH DATA

All good sociology is **empirical** in the sense that it engages closely with what is going on in the social world (if it does not, then it becomes something else). But there are multiple ways of pursuing these common goals. Another chart may help here in clarifying two major and very different logics of research. In practice, of course, there are hundreds of variations on these, and the task again is to bring these varieties together. Still, it is useful at the outset to sense a divide (see Figure 6.1).

The first route starts with the big hypotheses and the search for generalizations; it makes it measurable through 'operational concepts'; searches out data to 'test' or falsify their hypotheses (the key principle of falsification); and rigorously scrutinizes the hypotheses to find false cases where it does not hold or work. Probabilities of their conclusions being true are then calculated mathematically through various procedures. Such studies usually read like technical reports – usually evidence will appear in a fair amount of statistical reporting with much technical analysis. It is a 'top-down' approach moving from the 'general' to the 'specific'. Most big survey and 'scientific sociology' uses this as its basis: we collect observations to accept or reject hypotheses.

The second route begins with observations and experiences and is based on a logic of discovery. Concepts emerge that are much less measurable but which seem to make sense of the observations and which aim to foster deeper understandings (often called sensitizing concepts). Out of such observations and concept development, small-scale theory starts to develop. Research does not establish hypotheses or even concepts in advance of various kinds of field work (observations, in libraries, looking at visual media, etc.). Usually the final study appears that contains much verbatim speech – from the people interviewed, from books, from other sources. It reads in an easier fashion and some emphasis is placed on the

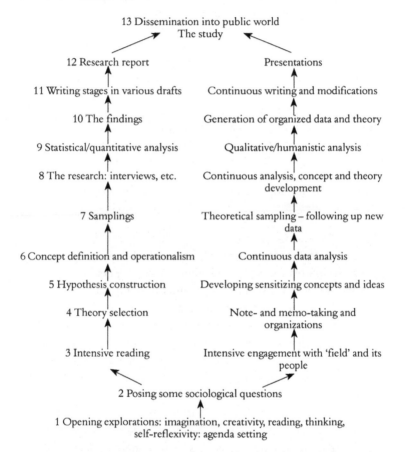

THE HYPOTHESIS–DEDUCTIVE MODEL
(the logic of demonstrations and falsification)

THE GROUNDED–INDUCTIVE MODEL
(the logic of discovery)

13 Dissemination into public world
The study

12 Research report — Presentations

11 Writing stages in various drafts — Continuous writing and modifications

10 The findings — Generation of organized data and theory

9 Statistical/quantitative analysis — Qualitative/humanistic analysis

8 The research: interviews, etc. — Continuous analysis, concept and theory development

7 Samplings — Theoretical sampling – following up new data

6 Concept definition and operationalism — Continuous data analysis

5 Hypothesis construction — Developing sensitizing concepts and ideas

4 Theory selection — Note- and memo-taking and organizations

3 Intensive reading — Intensive engagement with 'field' and its people

2 Posing some sociological questions

1 Opening explorations: imagination, creativity, reading, thinking, self-reflexivity: agenda setting

Caution: I have dangerously oversimplified these positions of the research process. Life is much more complex than our simple schemas of them: both approaches are often combined, and there are many other stances. But as an opening way of thinking about the choices available in social research, this does suggest some key different pathways.

Figure 6.1 Two 'ideal type' logics of research processes: deductive and inductive

writing craft. There is always a problem here as to whether you can truly start observing anything without prior generalizations or assumptions. It moves from observations towards case studies and only ultimately – if at all – to generalizations, abstractions and theories: it is a 'bottom-up' or grounded approach. The former is often called '**deductive**' and the latter '**inductive**'.

Sociological data are the various bits of information that sociologists analyze. When sociology was developing, it often had to 'invent methods' like 'the survey' and indeed 'the interview' to get this data – there are now studies that look at their history (e.g. Platt, 1996). But these days, the tools they use are in widespread use in society. We see interviews in the press and on the media all the time; we complete survey forms from any and every organization we are likely to encounter; life stories are a common method of documentary film and newspaper reports. Most major organizations now have 'research and development' units. There is then no longer anything

Archival documents (historical, personal, all kinds); art (painting, sculptures); artefacts and things ('stuff': personal possessions, archaeological 'finds', consumer objects); attitude scales; autobiographies; auto ethnographies; case studies; census; content analysis; conversation analysis; diaries; digital material (websites, emails, blogs, YouTube, Second Life, social networking sites); discourse analysis; documentary films; documents of all kinds (e.g. school records, club magazines); ethnotheatre; experiments (laboratory studies); fiction (novels, television drama); field research (participant observation, ethnography); films and video; focus groups; historical research; interviews of all kinds (short, long, focused, survey, in-depth, analytic); letters; life stories; maps; personal experiences; photographs; post codes; questionnaires; social surveys (national, local, longitudinal, panel); texts of all kinds; vignettes; visuals (photographs, film, videos, paintings and art).

Figure 6.2 The research tool kit

really specifically sociologically significant about research methods for sociology – they are everywhere to be found. In the past, the sociologist may have been characterized as a person who uses interviews, surveys and statistics, but not now. Research tools are used across a wide range of fields, and sociologists' work is much broader than this.

Still, to give you a quick idea of the range of tools available for gathering data, Figure 6.2 provides a quick listing of some of the tools that sociologists can use (in alphabetical order). When sociologists use a range of these tools (as they should), the process is sometimes called **triangulation**. Each one of these sources requires its own skills in analysis. (There are numerous books providing advice on each one of them.)

HOW HAS DIGITAL RESEARCH CHANGED SOCIOLOGY?

These, then, are the 'old methods' commonplace across the social and human sciences. But a change has been taking place with the digital revolution, providing new challenges for sociology. We have moved on dramatically from the methods and worlds studied by the earlier sociologists. Sociology may have been born of the Industrial Revolution and early capitalism, but it has fast had to move into the twenty-first century. In contrast with past worlds, we now live in social worlds saturated with information about society and a startling array of new everyday ways of obtaining it. The twenty-first-century world ensures that much of human social life can now be traced through a digital click. Studying society has never been easier or more widely and fully accessible. What used to take sociologists years to dig out, and often cost millions of pounds, can now be found in a few minutes or hours and cost virtually nothing. And you do not even need experts to do it! These newer resources were just never available to sociologists in the previous two centuries. There is now a new digital generation that is shifting the everyday practice of sociology. Consider just twelve of these changes sociology now incorporates into its research practice.

First, most of the *basic traditional methods have gone digital*: nowadays, interviews, questionnaires, surveys and archives can all go online. New programmes like CASIC have developed to facilitate this. (CASIC stands for Computer-Assisted Survey Information Collection.) Secondly, a wide array of *new digital tools have been developed* to assist in research: sociologists usually start with Wikipedia, Google search, Amazon books and open access journals before moving on to more advanced programmes. These have made basic research more accessible for all. Thirdly, sociologists do *live, digital-based research*, accessing people from all over the world at any time or place through their iPads, smart phones, Skype and network pages. They can use Google Maps and satnav the spaces people dwell within; deploy closed-circuit television (CCTV) to capture life as it is lived in everyday life *in situ*; and find out the lifestyles of people through consumer studies using ZIP codes and postal addresses. All this can be done globally and in an instance. More specifically, fourthly, they use *social media networks* (Facebook, etc.), with *photo sharing* (Flickr, Instagram, Picasa), *video sharing* (YouTube, Metacafe), *blogging* (Wordpress, Tumblr), *microblogging* (Twitter) and *news aggregation* (Google Reader, StumbleUpon, FeedBurner) to provide new data using user profiles, friends list, message, chats, photos and so on. A whole new world of data can be generated via social networking. And much of this aggregate data can be turned, fifthly, into '**Big Data**' research which forms massive, messy data sets that can then be extracted (mined/scraped/ harvested) and analyzed through logarithms to get meaningful patterns. It is clear that it helps to be agile in algebra, maths and logarithms to do this kind of work – it is a version of computer programming and quite far away from mainstream sociology. Sixth, much research now develops *hyperlinks* entailing hyper-reading, hyper-analysis and hyper-writing. This non-linear methodology provides a different way of thinking through, reading and presenting data. Seventh, many sociologists are developing and *using digital programmes for research*: for years now the old Statistical Package for the Social Sciences (SPSS) dominated research, but now there are hosts of new packages for all kinds of research, including CAQDAS (Computer Assisted Qualitative Data AnalysiS). ATLAS.ti, Hyper-RESEARCH, MaxQDA and NVivo are further examples. Eighth, *visual research becomes more prominent*: sociologists, like everyone else, now find they have easy and ubiquitous access to digital imaging (photo and video), making millions of images of social life available for study. At long last, the importance of the visual has started to be recognized in sociology. And these technologies have also started to change the ways modern sociology looks, incorporating video and image. Further still, optical media have also become important for 'graphic mapping' and 'data display'. Ninth, there are *new storytelling blogs, new narratives networks for journal making* and digital storytelling (with software like LiveJournal and Writers Café). Tenth, *'the digital' has itself become a major topic of investigation.* From large-scale surveys of digital use to ethnographies of digital cultures around the world; from 'the sociology of Wikipedia' to the study of all kinds of digital activities, including virtual reality, internet love, 'digital activism' and digital health. More, the digital world has created new digital modes of academic presentations: open access articles, encouraging blogs and tweets, making PowerPoint presentations and generally enhancing the range of digital modes of presentations of research. Finally, ultimately, all of this is starting to shift the very nature of sociological thinking and theory – moving it away from less ana-logue and linear thinking and becoming more concerned with *binary, hyper and digital thinking in an internet of things!*

This is not an exhaustive listing; but it is clear from this that old methods and old theories are having to change. For the contem-porary sociologist, there is now such a staggering amount of stuff about society available in digital form that it can overwhelm. And it is available to everyone, not just the sociologist! This is a very differ-ent world from that of earlier generations of sociologists, bringing often startling and very different resources available for research and study.

But all this makes the sociological questions even more pressing. Given that there is now so much social stuff out there, what is to be made of it all? It is precisely this *thought*, this serious *thinking*, which is now required when oh-so-much stuff sits at our fingertips. No data or information is just the automatic truth about society. The new technologies may change patterns of communication, create new virtual worlds and generate access to much data. *But data over-load and indiscriminate media saturation now become more and more of a problem.* Tweeting is not in-depth knowledge, and no one has ever claimed it is! So often the digital is not enough: while these new technologies certainly can inform our understanding of the social, sociologists are charged with showing how sociological thinking can help us make critical sense of this explosion of data. As sociologists, we now need to ask just *how* these newer technologies and 'digital-knowledges' may be profoundly reshaping our relationship to information and knowledge. And we need to remember the kinds of problems that a critical digitalism raises (see pp. 71–73).

THINK ON: BIG DATA V. LIVE RESEARCH

At one extreme, we have 'Big Data'. Every Google search, every tweet we send, every picture we post, every online record made, every purchase we make leaves a trace that is logged 'out there' somewhere in the big 'infosphere', becoming an amazing record of human social life. And it leads to a huge amount of potential data for sociologists and researchers to use, not just in terabytes but in petabytes (where peta- denotes a quadrillion, or a thousand trillion!). This vast scale of data is hard to imagine. Increasingly such data is 'harvested, scraped and mined' through computer logarithms and turned into useable 'Big Data'. Everything under the sun becomes 'datafied' – turned into a byte and information byte. And this means we are now swimming in a deluge of messy data that simply did not exist a few years ago.

At the other extreme we have 'live data'. Research now enables us to get very intimate with our subjects, asking them to 'wear' digital devices encouraging 'selfies' and 'self logging' (e.g. for exercises and health) and following them across places and times close up with digital audio and visual recordings, using note pads and other programmes to enable intense observation of the minutiae of everyday life *in situ*, *in flagrante delicto*, in real life, as it happens. Stories can be collected, images curated, events documented as they happen in rich contextual detail, giving us data that is richer, thicker and more 'alive' than was ever possible before.

In a curious way, the digital world reproduces the classic debates of arts and science in sociology from an earlier generation (see Table 6.1). But both kinds of data raise problems. They are both likely to produce data that is often unmanageable, unreliable, limited in what it can say, messy and even 'dirty'. It is both hard to use and hard to make sense of. More than this, all of it continues to be wide open to political and ethical issues of surveillance, confidentiality, privacy, narrative and misuse. (See: Back and Puwar, 2013; Boellstorff, 2013; Burrows and Savage, 2014; Lupton, 2015: Chapter 5; and Mayer-Schönberger and Cukier, 2013.)

ANALYTIC WORK: DATA IN SEARCH OF SENSE

We have seen that there are multiple ways of securing data for sociology: nowadays we can find such data in many places. It is there in the newspapers, on the internet, on television and in the myriad documents found in daily life. We are quite familiar now with observing the lives of others – we do it all the time when we watch 'reality programmes' like *Gogglebox* or *Big Brother* or in the many available documentary films. Indeed, some of these are quite extraordinary in giving us 'fly on the wall' accounts of life. Many of these media programmes and everyday interviews – and the reflections that go on around them – can often take you closer to what is going on in contemporary social life than a great deal of sociology published in the sociological journals! So the skills of sociology do not basically lie in their research tools. The world is now stuffed full of data for everyone to examine, and the case could now be made that we no longer need sociologists – they served a purpose in the transition from the industrial to the late modern world, but now we are all data collectors and analysts and sociologists have become dinosaurs.

This is obviously not my view. For there is a method in sociology's madness. *Sociology provides ways of making sense of this mess of data*. We know that much data is garbage, dross, that 'reality' programmes put on a show for us and are not the one 'reality' and that many surveys are biased by the commercial interests behind them (they are, after all, *market* research). The challenge for sociology is to provide *analytic tools* (as opposed to data tools) for thinking about such 'data'. In the everyday world, we might just take the 'reality' of the interview, the 'truth' of a questionnaire, the 'facts' of a survey for granted – as given. But good sociology cannot do this. It always needs to inspect the data to make critical sense of it. Sociology's cardinal methodological rule is that *truth is never easy*. In understanding social life, truth rarely simply announces itself. Social truth is a struggle arising from many perspectives and disagreements in social life. Never expect to find the truth of any social situation to simply await you from research.

THINK ON: NUMBERS AND THE SOCIOLOGIST

Sociologists are sometimes mistaken for statisticians. This is not so. True, many will have to learn the use of statistics for various research projects and run programmes that do this – like the Statistical Package for the Social Sciences (SPSS) (www.spss. com) – but this is not sociology. Yet sociologists do need to be sophisticated about numbers and acquire a critical numeracy which enable them to ask serious questions about how we use numbers in society. This is a big topic, but here are just three starting questions to ponder.

1 *Is everything measurable?* Indeed, should we try and measure everything? Can we really make sense of many things – like love, happiness, anger or God – through counting? Sociologists ask: what are the limits of numbers?

2 *What do numbers really mean?* Is a billion big and one small? Not necessarily so. Numbers are often banded around for political points, are actually incomprehensible, and can be used for very misleading ends. Sociologists ask: how can we develop benchmarks for making sense of numbers?

3 *How are statistics – of crime, of suicide, of health, of finance – produced?* What are the agencies behind them? Some sociologists study the work of statistic-producing agencies and show the everyday assumptions (even biases) they

work from in making statistics. Statistics only 'display' the work of statistic agencies, and we need to study how these displays are made. Sociologists ask: who created these statistics, when, where and why? (For more on all this, see Joel Best's *Damned Lies and Statistics*, 2012.)

AN EXAMPLE: THE DATA OF CRIME

Here is a quick example: statistics on crime and sexual violence. We are all used to hearing the saga of rising (and nowadays falling) crime rates. Here we have accounts presented by official government agents of crime statistics; huge agencies and much money is devoted to keeping these records. Indeed, how can a modern society think about crime without some large-scale statistics like these? We need them. But sociologists can *never* simply take them for granted. Instead, they have to ask just how did some people come to assemble these statistics (and not others) in these ways (and not others)? Who reports, defines and logs a crime? How do people come to make sense of what is – and is not – a crime? Once you start posing these questions, it becomes clear that statistic construction depends on a long interpretive chain of many people (victims, police, clerks, doctors, courts, judges, jurors) at different stages of vulnerability and officialdom making crucial decisions over time, often shaped by organizational needs over time. More than this, once a report is made, and crime statistics are reported to the public, we then find a whole bunch of other interpretations are made of it – the media interprets it selectively, the public has to make sense of it and the official government responds and reinterprets it. In other words, there is *a moving process of interpretation and reinterpretation of these crime statistics, and there is absolutely nothing simple about them. Criminal statistics are the work of human agencies and bureaucracies that lead to sedimented human meanings*.

There are other lessons to learn from this simple example. First, whatever crime is going on in a society, crime statistics are only one perspective or angle for getting at it: crime statistics bear a moving and difficult relationship to real or actual crime. Some crimes like rape are notoriously under-reported and suffer from severe problems of interpretation; others – a street homicide – seems much clearer to define. Processes of interpretation are done from a point of view. We can never tell or grasp the full picture. Every bit of data is told from a point of view, a perspective, a **standpoint** – and sociology has to locate this. This is the Rashomon effect, named after the famous Japanese film where one story of murder and rape is told from many perspectives and the very nature of what is true is held under a microscope. *There are always multiple perspectives on social life.* To stay with the example of rape, we can immediately see a wide range of perspectives that are available to us here. Figure 6.3 shows just a few of the angles, perspectives or standpoints that rape could be described from.

This is very simple, but surely, the more perspectives and angles we can get on this, then maybe the better our sociological account will be. Few sociologists can ever do all of this, and instead we often get descriptions of the fragments that fail to connect up. The task of sociologists is to unpack as many of these different perspectives as possible.

NARRATIVE QUESTIONS

Two linked questions follow from this. How do these perspectives get organized and shaped, and what is the wider context of the perspective? Here we enter another important feature for sociological analysis – that of **narrative** and story. Human beings are always creating meaning, and they do this primarily through stories and narratives. We are the narrating animal, and much sociology is concerned with studying the nature of social narratives, how they get

• The rape victim	• The rapist	• The rapist's family	• The victim's family
• Police responses	• Neighbours	• Rape counsellors	• Community responses
• Media reactions	• Support groups	• Politicians	• Court officials
• Men's responses (but which men?)		• Women's responses (but which women?) . . . and so on.	

In looking at any social thing, always consider the range of different perspectives that could be brought into its study.

Figure 6.3 Whose perspective? The Rashomon effect

constructed and what their consequences are. In one sense, sociology is the study of the narratives that people write and make around their lives, which then in turn reproduce new narratives of these narratives. There is a constant flow of narratives within society and sociology.

But this raises the next issue. Are all **perspectives** and narratives equally valid or dependable? If we line up all these different perspectives (as in the rape example), or analyze an array of different narratives as above, will sociology fall into relativism? Each story shows different views, and we have no baseline for adjudicating truths. Well this is not so. *Sociology looks at the relations between things, recognizes the different standpoints and perspectives, senses the narrative organization of life and then tries to balance, match and keep an eye on truth.*

We know this kind of issue from blogging or watching a reality TV programme. We see the narratives, we hear the different perspectives, but ultimately we want to find a way of bringing them together. People are different. How can we make sense of the ways in which such things interconnect and relate? How can we provide a wider, higher, broader, deeper narrative that brings these things together? This is just what sociology wants to do and it does its job when it reveals and tells these contrasting perspectives and standpoints. It is working well when it jostles contrasting standpoints together to piece together a bigger picture. And sociology does its job best of all when it brings together all perspectives and works to transcend them. (A happy day that will never ultimately come along!) We must do the best we can, and sociology's ideas of perspective and narrative help a lot.

MAKING SENSE OF DATA: GAINING ADEQUATE OBJECTIVITY IN A SUBJECTIVE WORLD

The classic way of handling method problems is derived from the adoption of the *scientific method* itself. For example, a very basic feature of science is that it tests or *falsifies data*. It does *not* accumulate more and more data that just supports a view; rather, it tries to knock down any statement, to falsify and show where conjectures are not true. It looks for negative evidence. A key tip for being scientific is usually to ask three simple questions: does this data 'measure' or truly capture what it purports (*validity*); do researchers use the same kind of tools so that like is being studied with like (*reliability*); and finally, are the subjects typical of their wider group – or not? (*representativeness*). Many research manuals flag the importance of these three key evaluative tools, and it is worth knowing about them. If, for example, you are studying, say, rape – what are you 'measuring' as rape, and are you actually tapping into what rape is? This raises serious questions about the meaning of rape. Further, is the rape a typical one, and how can we know this? Would another sociologist be able to repeat this study and come to the same kinds of conclusions?

SOCIOLOGY AS A CRITICAL IMAGINATION

But science, vital as it is, it is not without problems. Thus, sociologists cannot take for granted that the 'scientific questionnaire' will get at the facts, the interview will dig out the true story, the documentary will 'tell it as it is', or that the survey will provide accurate statistics of our world. These methods often imply that there is indeed an objective, well-ordered universe out there – one we can trap and tell the truth about. But things may not be so straightforward. Even physicists do not see the world in this simple way. Good science and good art always know this. Human social worlds do not lend themselves to 'easy' truths or findings.

What we need, therefore, is always *critique*. Think about the social life as we have been discussing it in this book (or the case of rape as we have just raised above). It is dense with contradictory and ambiguous meaning; it is always embedded in historical worlds and emerging in different spaces; there are structures and actions; there are multiple social worlds, never unitary ones; power is everywhere and hence lives, meanings and sense have to be negotiated in conflictual situations. It is lodged in worlds of intense human suffering and social inequalities. All this we have seen in this book; so how then can we study it all at such an objective and neutral distance? What we are measuring is on the move all the time, and we cannot trap the ambiguity and contradiction of social life simply through research tools. What people say at one second is often contradicted seconds later, what people say may not be what they mean – or do – and as people change, so may their 'truths'. Again, I am *not* suggesting that sociology goes down some relativist impasse where we cannot get at the truth and anything goes. Not at all. Read on. Here are more challenges.

First, all data needs to be placed in wider *contexts* – locate the wider contexts of both history and what is going on now. Knowledge never stands on its own: it needs to be related. For example, the trouble with much internet data is that it comes to us as mere 'bits'. In order to make sense of it, *we need frameworks to provide a wider sense of it.* Thus, it helps to know where this bit of data can be located within debates about it (controversies usually exist and need to be used as a frame). More, it needs also to be given some sense of historical sense – no data arrives out of the blue. There are precedents and histories – what are they? Ultimately, a range of different perspectives and narratives around it will become transparent, and these then need connecting to the wider patterns and social actions found in the wider culture as it shifts in time and space. Here I am harking back to some of the themes we saw earlier in creating a sociological imagination. Without *puzzling* these things you are lost in the moment, floating with nowhere to go. This 'puzzling' is just what good education can now help to provide.

Important here too is what is known as the **comparative method**. If we have an interview finding, we can compare it with what others have said in the past and in other cultures as well as comparing it with a more abstract ideal type. A very general idea to help in all this draws upon a nineteenth-century idea (prominent in the work of Max Weber) of the **ideal type**. Ideal types are *not* meant to be seen as ideals (or perfect types), nor are they meant to be seen as simple statistical averages. Rather, they signal the key characteristics of any phenomena – which may not actually exist in reality. It is an abstract type against which real phenomena can be matched. As Weber (1978) says: 'An ideal type is formed by the one-sided accentuation of one or more points of view and by the synthesis of a great many diffuse, discrete, more or less present and occasionally absent concrete individual phenomena, which are arranged according to those one-sidedly emphasized viewpoints into a unified analytical construct'. Sociology benefits greatly from making comparisons.

Another part of this wider critical approach is to investigate *the spirals of meanings*: how can we make sense of the meanings here, and how do they connect up with the wider culture and even the research process? *Data is always about human meanings – and as such it needs interpretations.* As we have seen, over and over, one of the key features of the social world is that it is dependent on communication, is dialogical and inter-subjective. We depend on others and their meanings. Sociological data is always congealed human meaning, and somehow we need to see how these meanings were made and then how we make sense of them; social life is encircled in meanings. Everything you touch in social life comes loaded with meaning – and hence this is always a key starting part of making sense. For Weber, the challenge was *Verstehen* (understanding); for Bourdieu, it was habitus; and for others, it was empathy. Never mind the terms; I hope you will see the importance of grasping the layers and complexities of meanings that flood social life and social research. Sociologists often refer to this as a **hermeneutic** analysis, and by this they refer to the complex ways in which humans come to make sense of their world.

THINK ON: EVALUATING DATA

Whenever you are confronted with social data – in sociology books, in the press, on websites, in reports – here are some key questions to ask:

1 *Science*: What is the evidence against this – try and falsify it. (Do not simply accumulate more and more evidence in its favour, but try to falsify it.) How typical is this? (Ask about the representativeness of the sample.) How are the validity and reliability?

2 *Context and comparison*: Locate the evidence in wider frameworks: historically (put it on a time line of similar 'facts'), geographically (how might this appear to other nations and cultures?) and theoretically (how might this appear with different thinkers and theorists approaching this same fact?).

3 *Standpoint and perspective*: What is the 'angle' here – what other perspectives might there be? All accounts are written from 'angles'. Think in particular of the background and

assumptions of the researcher and authors as far as you can. Even the most neutral of writers (a rare and not very interesting breed) work with assumptions.

4 *Language, rhetoric and narrative*: Think about how the data is being presented – usually it is trying to persuade you of its truth by using various devices. Since Aristotle's *Rhetoric* (and his debate with Plato on this), we have known about the significance of languages and the power of the poetic and storytelling to persuade audiences. Social data is a special form of rhetoric and narrative that needs understanding and examining.

5 *Hermeneutics*: Enter the circle of meaning. Data never speaks for itself – it has been given meaning by its researcher and its presenter and is now open to further interpretation. More, the data text itself can only make sense by connecting its parts; the philosopher Paul Ricoeur (1913–2005) talks about a hermeneutic circle of knowledge. As we have seen, truth and knowledge are not the straightforward things we might like to think!

6 *Reflexivity*: Consider the social impact and role of this data. Social findings feed back into social life and change it. There is no neutral presentation of findings – social facts are part of the social. This feedback needs to be considered. Crime statistics, for instance, are never simple reflections of crime but become social ideas that then change the way we think about crime (for example, they might generate 'fear of crime').

BEING PRACTICAL: A MANIFESTO FOR DOING SOCIOLOGY

I might have scared you a little in this chapter by raising some rather difficult questions about truth, meaning, knowledge and how social research is never a straightforward matter of interviewing or gathering statistics. My main aim indeed has been to make you aware of what you might do and to be critical whenever you find data. But it can be carried too far, and I have known students to give up when they found that this process was so complicated and difficult. So a balance is needed, and as usual people muddle through. Seeing sociology as an imagination, a science and a craft, you need to work on developing the tools of its trade. Learning requires patience: the voyage is from information to knowledge to wisdom. It takes time. Let me end with a series of rather more down-to-earth tips to help you on your way:

1. Get close to whatever you want to study. Stick to the concrete and ask: what is going on – by who? where? when? and why? Wherever possible stay engaged with people in their worlds and avoid becoming cut off or aloof from them. Keep yourself grounded.

2. Keep asking questions about the quality of the kind of material you are working with – your data. Think about what it is you are 'measuring', 'observing', 'describing' – are you getting at this the best way you can?

3. Think about the kind of knowledge you are aiming for and where you might stand in relationship to this. What is your own perspective, your standpoint? Maybe you are completely neutral, but this is unlikely. Learn to describe social realities from as many angles as you can. Draw some social maps of different perspectives around your topic and sense what your perspectives are leaving out.

4. Be imaginative with your research tools, making them the most appropriate tools for your study. There are a wide range of possibilities out there. You do not have to stay with the survey or the interview.

5. Cultivate good language, good concepts and good writing. Avoid jargon, shun pretentiousness and pomposity and stay intelligible as far as you can in your thinking and your writing. New words can be helpful, but go for the simpler word wherever you can. Do not be too easily impressed by complicated expressions – many academics are very poor at expressing themselves! Think of your reader, be kind and learn to write stylishly so you are a pleasure to read. Read Helen Sword's *Stylish Academic Writing* (2012), or better still, read George Orwell's classic little book *Why I Write* (1940) and his line, 'Break any rule rather than saying anything outright barbarous'.

6 Develop basic skills of numeracy, writing, thinking and 'seeing' the world. The best way to do this is to practice the skills a little every day. Develop good work habits.

7 Become sensitive to the political and ethical relations inside your research and outside of it. Recall the old adage of Francis Bacon (1561–1626) that 'knowledge is power' but also the significance of ethics, and remain empathetic to the ways you engage with people. Respect people and their worlds.

8 Stay open. Things will change and your proposals will change. This is normal. Keep a flexible eye on what you are finding and change with it. Never stick to fixed protocols if your study takes you elsewhere.

9 Know yourself and be comfortable with who you are in relation to your study. Unlike many areas of study, sociology is social. And it means you need to know a bit about what you want to study, how it links to your own life, what your reasons are for studying this, how it might be shaped and indeed impact your own life.

10 Be organized. Make plans, write lists, get files – and get a useful manual to help you (like Umberto Eco's *How to Write a Thesis*, but there are lots of them around these days).

11 Nobody can tell you how to do research, and reading guides on how to interview, design questionnaires and do content analyses, etc. are pointless until you have a project in mind. Research tips devoid of a project mean little. But once you know your project, read and study voraciously on how others have used these methods and practice them in dummy runs. Never unleash yourself on others or make data without detailed preparations.

12 Finally, the cardinal rule: let methods be your servant. Be engaged, think a lot, read widely, keep critical, stay grounded, get organized, practice daily and be passionate about what you do. Aim for adequate objectivity. And to thy own methodology be true – but make sure you have one!

SUMMARY

We look at methods and see that sociology straddles art, science and history. Methodology requires you to think hard (about what kind of knowledge you want to produce), do empirical investigation (the need for a logic of gathering data – inductive and deductive – and a wide range of research tools to draw from) and skillfully, critically analyze and make sense of data (a checklist for evaluating research is provided). The importance of digitalism in reshaping research is highlighted.

EXPLORING FURTHER

MORE THINKING

1 Clarify the distinctions between epistemological, empirical and analytic work in research. How do these distinctions appear in the emerging world of digital research?

2 Using some of the criteria suggested in this chapter, evaluate some of the research findings you find reported every day in the media and on social networks.

3 More ambitiously, write a proposal to conduct your own *sociological* study on any area of your choice, using ideas from this chapter and the previous one.

FURTHER READING

A good down-to-earth starting point is Yoland Wadsworth's *Do It Yourself Social Research* (2011, third edition). The standard textbooks (often formidably large!) can guide you through many of the issues I have only lightly touched upon in this chapter. See, for examples, Alan Bryman, *Social Research Methods* (2015, fifth edition) and Earl Babbie, *The Practice of Social Research* (2015). To get a firmer grasping of some of the philosophical issues, two classics on the philosophical problems of the social sciences are great starting places. They are Karl Popper, *The Poverty of Historicism* (1957) and Peter Winch, *The Idea of a Social Science and Its Relation to Philosophy* (1958). A good general text guide on all these issues is Gerard Delanty, *Social Science: Philosophical and Methodological Foundations* (2005) and the accompanying collection of readings in *Philosophies of Social Science: The Classic and Contemporary Readings*, edited by Gerard Delanty and Piet Strydom (2003). I have long found the work of Howard S. Becker very illuminating on all these issues; see especially *Tricks of the Trade* (1998), *Telling About Society* (2007) and most recently *What About Mozart? What About*

Murder? (2014). On digital methods, see Kate Orton-Johnson *et al.* (eds.) *Digital Sociology: Critical Perspectives* (2013); Deborah Lupton, *Digital Sociology* (2015); and Christina Silver, *Using Software in Qualitative Research* (2014, second edition).

Some challenges to orthodox methodologies include Chela Sandoval, *Methodology of the Oppressed* (2000); Les Back, *The Art of Listening* (2007); and Norman Denzin, *The Qualitative Manifesto: A Call to Arms* (2010). A critical example is Priya Dixit and Jacob L. Stump (eds.), *Critical Methods in Terrorism Studies* (2015).

TROUBLE: SUFFERING INEQUALITIES

It's the same the whole world over, it's the poor wot gets the blame;
it's the rich wot gets the pleasure, ain't it all a blooming shame.
Traditional; English music hall ballad
attributed to Billy Bennett

Very often students come to sociology with a hope of making the world a better place: they are passionate or aggrieved about some cause. They see injustice or social problems that they want to help remedy. Maybe they have read a media report on the plights of refugees or of children dying in poverty; an unemployed father has told them of the appalling conditions of work for many people; a feminist mother has taken them on a march to protest the violence, the abuse and powerlessness of many women across the world; they have seen a film about the brutalization, dehumanization and injustice of much social life; they despair at perpetual war; are angry with world homophobia and racism; they are passionate about environmental catastrophe. They are troubled about the world and ask *what is to be done?* They want to understand what is going on, why is our world turning out so badly? And they turn to sociology for help. And at its best, it is indeed sociology's mission to bring knowledge, wisdom and an acute, engaged critical imagination about the plights of humanity.

There is a lot of suffering in the world. In this chapter, I choose one which underpins many and which is the most central of all areas studied by sociologists. We look at the sufferings of inequalities.

IMAGINING THE INEQUALITIES OF THE WORLD

The leading Swedish sociologist Göran Therborn in his book *Inequalities of the World* (2006) has expressed his own personal concern about inequality so well that I will quote him; he reflects my view and that of many others too:

> Why shouldn't a new born child in Congo have the same chance to survive into a healthy adulthood as a child in Sweden? Why shouldn't a young Bihari woman have the same autonomy to choose her life pursuits as a young white American male, or an Egyptian college graduate the same as a Canadian? Why shouldn't all Pakistani and Brazilian families have the same access as British or French to good sanitation, air conditioning and/or heating, washing machines, and holiday tickets? Why should many children have to work? Why shouldn't a black HIV-positive person in Southern Africa have the same chance to survive as a white European? Why should a handful of individual 'oligarchs' be able to expropriate most of the natural resources of Russia, while a large part of the population has been pushed into pauperism? Why should big business executives be able to pay themselves hundreds of times more than the workers they are constantly pushing to 'work harder', more flexibly and at lower cost? In brief, there is inequality in this world because many are denied the chance to live their lives at all; to live a life of dignity, to try out their interests in life, and to make use of their existing potential. The inequalities of the world prevent hundreds of millions of people from developing their differences.

THE ARCHAEOLOGY OF SUFFERINGS: FROM DIFFERENCES TO INEQUALITIES

One starting point for sociology has to always be an awareness of a vast human plurality, of our **differences**. We dwell in an incorrigibly plural universe. As the Irish poet Louis MacNeice beautifully put it: the world is 'crazier and more of it than we think, the drunkenness of things various'. Human worlds are lush with multiplicities and possibilities. We have seen throughout this book how differences abound and proliferate in nations, cultures, peoples, ethnicities, religions, ages, histories, languages, meanings. Everybody's world is most certainly never just like yours, your friend's or your neighbour's, even though most days we might try to act as if it is. It is this persistent recognition of these differences and the pursuit of their understanding that is one driving hallmark of a sociological awareness.

But everywhere we look we can see these human differences growing into disagreements and conflicts, and soon differences congeal into hierarchical structures of division. All societies – human and otherwise – are distinguished by these patterns of hierarchical inequality. Ants have their workers, apes have their grooming rituals and chickens have their pecking orders. In most known human societies, there have usually been a few high in the pecking order whilst the masses are cast asunder to the lowest regions. Some have privileged and flourishing lives; some are rebellious, resisting or resilient, but many lead wasted or damaged lives. Indeed, *the history of human societies can well be read as the history of unknown billions of people going quietly to their graves with lives of almost unspeakable suffering delivered upon them from the raging inequalities and differences found in the society to which they were born but had never made.* Inequality, and unfairness, has been ubiquitous in the past and is still so today.

Societies, then, are homes to social divisions, hierarchies and structured social inequalities. There are always, it seems, the few rich and the mass poor, the elite slave owner and the wretched slave, the scapegoated migrant and the dominant host, the educated and the ignorant, the diseased and the healthy, the man and the woman, the gay and the straight, the able and the disabled, the terrorist and the terrorized, the pathological and the normal, us and them – indeed the good, the bad and the ugly! And sociology cannot fail to see this everywhere it looks. In human societies, differences are used as moral markers to establish how some are better than others. Moral worth is often attached to this labelling as boundaries are established of the normal and the pathological. The elite are superior; the mass are downcast. Borders become hierarchically arranged and a ranking or pecking order is established: outsiders, underclasses, dangerous people, marginals, outcasts – the scapegoats – are invented. Sociologists ask: just how are these 'outsiders' and ranking orders created, maintained and changed? This is the problem of social exclusion, the social 'other' and social stratification. In this chapter, I inspect a few key themes raised in the sociology of inequality.

WHAT ARE THE 'OBJECTIVE' FACTS OF WORLD INEQUALITIES?

EVIDENCE: The trends are unmistakable and quite extreme. Broadly, we live in a world where there is a 'tiny group at the top and nearly everyone else'. Although global inequalities were starting to decline in the mid-twentieth century, the past thirty years or so have seen striking growth.

According to the 2015 Credit Suisse Global Wealth Databook, about 3.4 billion people – some 70 per cent of the global population – have wealth of less than $10,000. Half of the world's riches now lie in the hands of just 1 per cent of the population. Just 62 individuals had the same wealth as 3.6 billion people! In 2015, according to Forbes magazine's annual list of The World's Billionaires, there was a record 1,826 billionaires with an aggregate of $7.05 trillion. Overall, the wealth of the richest 1 per cent in the world amounts to $110 trillion. By contrast, some 80 per cent of people in the world have just 5.5 per cent of the wealth. Indeed, most people have no wealth at all and are simply dependent on (very low) wages (usually with very poor working conditions); 80 per cent of humanity live on less than $10 a day. Countries with the least inequalities are the Nordic countries; by contrast, the UK and US have marked inequalities.

But the highest of all can be found in South Africa, China and India (see A. B. Atkinson, pp. 22–23). (To sense what a trillion pounds might mean: if you were given £1 every second until you had a trillion (1,000 billions), it would take some 32,000 years! (Sayers, p. 11)) The major inequalities of the world are now widely documented, along with their potential to cause problems for life expectancy and health, education and literacy, work and housing. The inequalities can be traced through income and wealth, both *within* countries and *between* countries around the world.

Such statistics are always problematic. There are large margins of error: it is hard to measure many of these issues in rich countries, let alone poor ones. The precision of these figures is thus often contested. Still, the figures are extreme; we can be pretty sure that overall vast billions of people live in absolute or abject poverty, whilst a few million live in almost unimaginable wealth. This is indeed very unequal.

WEBSITES: The facts of inequalities are always changing. I suggest you create your own website or blog on 'inequalities around the world'. Here are some key words to look for: *caste, class, slavery* and the *global poor*. And these connect with *poverty research, income research, 'the rich list', gender inequality, ethnic inequality, age inequality, human development, human rights* and *sexual rights*. More specifically, make sure you look out for:

World poverty
World Wealth and Income Database: http://topincomes. parisschoolofeconomics.eu/
Rich List (*Forbes*, Sunday *Times*)
Global Slavery Index: http://globalslaveryindex.org
Human Development Index (HDI): http://hdr.undp.org/en
Inequality Adjusted Human Development Index
Gender Inequality Index (GII): http://hdr.undp.org/en/content/ table-4-gender-inequality-index
See also: http://www.unwomen.org/en
Displaced migrants: http://www.internal-displacement.org/

Human Security Index: http://www.humansecurityindex.org/
See also: http://www.globalissues.org/article/26/poverty-facts-and-stats

The United Nations monitors the responses of states across the world, while Amnesty International and Human Rights Watch produce regular nation-based comparisons and reports:

Map of United Nations Indicators on Rights: http://indicators.ohchr.org/
Human Rights Watch: http://www.hrw.org/
Amnesty International: http://www.amnesty.org.uk/
Violence against Women Prevalence data (UN): http://www.endvawnow.org/uploads/browser/files/vaw_prevalence_matrix_15april_2011.pdf
Trafficking of People United Nations Global Reports: http://www.unodc.org/documents/data-and analysis/glotip/GLOTIP_2014_full_report.pdf
UNHCR Global Trends 2014: World at War: http://www.unhcr.org/556725e69.html
Carroll and Itaborahy, *State-Sponsored Homophobia: A World Survey of Laws* (2015): www.ilga.org

Visit the Vision of Humanity website and follow up on the leads it provides:

http://www.visionofhumanity.org
Global Peace Index: http://www.visionofhumanity.org/#/page/indexes/global-peace-index
Terrorism Index: http://www.visionofhumanity.org/#/page/indexes/terrorism-index
Global Cost of Violence Report: http://www.copenhagenconsensus.com/sites/default/files/conflict_assessment_-_hoeffler_and_fearon_0.pdf

FURTHER READING: The research and writing on poverty and inequality is substantial. The key works are by economists, not sociologists. The major reference points are: Oxfam, *Wealth: Having It All and Wanting More* (2015); Thomas Piketty, *Capital in the Twenty-First Century* (2014); Credit Suisse, *Global Wealth Databook* (2015). Other modern classics much discussed are: Anthony Atkinson, *Inequality* (2015); Angus Deaton, *The Great Escape* (2013/2015); Kate Pickett and Richard Wilkinson, *The Spirit Level* (2009/2015); Paul Collier, *The Bottom Billion* (2007); Joseph Stiglitz, *The Price of Inequality* (2012).

THE STRATIFICATIONS OF THE WORLD

A very good question for any sociologist to ask early on is: what is the basic map, organization or structure of the pecking order of this society or group, and how does it work? Who are its privileged and who are its devalued? Here we look at the most basic layers of hierarchy that a society has. And all societies will have such a map. The most common ones you will see across the world are the strata or layers of the slavery system, the caste system, the class system and the globally excluded. Here the idea of stratification draws on the imagery of layers: just as there are layers of the earth, so we can depict societies as falling into layers. Crudely, there are always a few at the top and many at the bottom – with quite a lot in between. Sociologists study these 'systems' in great detail, but four can be initially identified: caste, slavery, social class and the globally excluded.

CASTE

Perhaps nowhere is this more clearly seen than in the formal caste system. There is a long history of the **caste** system, notably through the Hindu religion in India. Here, people are ranked in a rigid hierarchy at birth, structured around the notions of purity and pollution. At its simplest, the Varna system denotes four major categories: Brahmins (priests and writers) who claim the highest status, Kshatriyas (warriors and rulers), Vaishyas (the merchants and landowners) and Shudras (artisans and servants). People outside the system become achhoots, 'untouchables' (nowadays called the Dahlit), and they have the most unpleasant work – handling sewage, burning corpses, scavenging. Although the system has been officially abolished in India, there is significant evidence that it is still alive in many traditional Hindu villages (and in the big cities too). It has been estimated that there are at least some 150 million untouchables in India (about 20 per cent of the population) who are abused and victimized. (Brahmins at the top make up 3–5 per cent.) This makes them one of the most subordinated and neglected groups in the world.

SLAVERY

Under systems of slavery, people are owned as property. It has been a major pattern of social organization throughout history, not just a blip of Western life. Its origins can be found deep in prehistoric hunting societies; it is dominant in ancient society – the Greeks, the Romans, the Persians, the Etruscans all had major systems of slavery. In modern times, slave trading reached a peak in the United States with a pre-Civil War slave population of 4,000,000 and then was found again through the forced labour of the Nazi regime and in the Soviet gulags. And it has not vanished today. In 2015, a modern Global Slavery Index estimates there are still some 167 countries involved in (often generational) forced labour, forced marriages, debt bondage and sex trafficking amounting to some 35.8 million (with 61 per cent in five countries: India with over fourteen million, China with over three million, Pakistan with two million, and Uzbekistan and Russia with well over one million each). (There are interesting dramatizations of slavery in films like Steve McQueen's *12 Years a Slave* (2013), Michael Apted's *Amazing Grace* (2006) and Steven Spielberg's *Amistad* (1997).)

SOCIAL CLASS

This is the major system of stratification identified with capitalism. Traditionally, sociologists have drawn upon the contrasting ideas of two key early thinkers: Marx and Weber. Marx highlighted **class** as an economic issue and identified two major social classes (there were others) who corresponded to the two basic relationships to the means of production: individuals either owned productive property or worked for others. Capitalists (or the *bourgeoisie*) owned and operated factories and used (exploited) the labour of others (the proletariat). This led to huge inequalities in the system, and in Marx's view this would lead ultimately to class conflict. Oppression and misery would drive the working majority to organize and, ultimately, to overthrow capitalism. A process would take place in which the poorer classes would become more pauperized, polarized and aware of their class position. This would lead to a class consciousness of their true economic exploitation. Max Weber made wider claims: he identified class as lying at the intersection of three distinct dimensions: class (economic), status (prestige) and power. Most recent sociologists acknowledge the centrality of the economic, measuring class through measures of income and wealth (including 'poverty studies', 'income studies', 'wealth studies' and 'rich studies') alongside occupational measures. But they also add wider dimensions of status, culture and network. Pierre Bourdieu (1930–2002) has been the most influential contemporary thinker on this, introducing the three dimensions of economic capital, **social capital** (networks and recognition) and cultural capital (cultural knowledge and skills) and arguing that class systems depend on accumulated privilege and 'reproduction' of these 'capitals'. Symbolic capital highlights the role of power and prestige: the honour and recognition one holds.

THE GLOBALLY EXCLUDED

As the world becomes increasingly transnational and globalized, a new category of stratification is becoming more visible: that of the globally excluded. The paradigmatic case in history would be concentration camps victims, stripped of everything, worth nothing and exterminated. But we can find approximate versions of this perhaps in the Rwanda genocide or even Guantanamo Bay. They are illustrated best in the vivid documentary photographs of the Brazilian Sebastião Salgado and especially in his works on *Workers* (1993), *Migrations* (2000) and *The Children* (2000). The Caribbean French philosopher-revolutionary Frantz Fanon (1925–1961) spoke of 'the wretched of the earth'. These are '*homo sacer*', the dispossessed: those suffering from 'expulsion', 'bare life'.

These 'dispossessed' arise from four key sources. First, they are the global poor; in 2011, just over one billion people live on less than \$1.25 a day. Often they have nothing at all. Here are those who experience the poverty of landless labourers and traditional peasants or those who have become the 'urban poor', who seek out an existence in the slums and *favelas* of the earth: migrants, garbage pickers, beggars, handcart pullers, sex workers, the disabled of all kinds. Second, they have no home – neither dwelling, home or country. They are the homeless, the refugees and the displaced. (At the end of 2014, there were 19.5 million refugees and over 38 million uprooted from their country (internally displaced people).) Thirdly, they often connect with unstable countries or 'states of exception' – it is estimated that out of the world's seven billion people, 26 per cent live in 'fragile states' without rights. (See Fragile States Index: Fund for Peace. In 2015, this included Sudan, South Sudan, Somalia, Central African Republic, Congo Democratic Republic, Chad, Yemen, Syria, Afghanistan, Iraq, Haiti and others.) And fourth, they are to be found in the vast and brutalizing prisons of the world. (In 2014, they 'warehoused' some ten million people.)

Such lives are precarious: people live from moment to moment, day to day, often under threat – excluded from any mainstreams of the world. Children, women and the elderly are especially likely to be impacted in this way. Zygmunt Bauman writes of *Wasted Lives* and argues that modernity (or capitalism) produces wasted populations – not just the poor and refugees but huge prison populations and other outsiders. Philosophers like Judith Butler and Giorgio Agamben write of the 'dispossessed' and 'bare life'. Curiously, we can find their counterpart in the worlds of the super rich, also ironically cut off from the rest of the world. (For a telling account of this, see Chrystia Freeland's *Plutocrats* (2012/2013).)

INTERSECTIONALITY: THE SOCIAL STRUCTURES OF LIFE'S OPPORTUNITIES

These are then four basic 'systems' of inequalities. But intersecting with them are wider *structures of opportunities* that shape their life. For some, these make life wide and expanding; for others, narrow and restricting. Seven major variables help organize these opportunities, and they interconnect and intersect. Table 7.1 outlines them.

Table 7.1 The intersecting social variables of inequalities

Whatever social thing you are looking at – schools, social work or senility – always try and ask questions about how it interconnects with at least some of the following:

		Social orders (channels of opportunities)	Supporting ideas and identities (discourses/ positionalities)
INTERSECTING ORDERS OF SOCIAL INEQUALITIES: A STRUCTURE OF LIFE OPPORTUNITIES	1	Class order	Classism and class consciousness
	2	Gender order (and patriarchy)	Sexism and gender identity
	3	Racial formation (ethnicity and race)	Racialization, racism and ethnic identity
	4	Age stratification and generational orders	Ageism and generational self
	5	Nations	Nationalism and national identity
	6	The sexual order	Heterosexism, homophobia and heteronormativity: sexual identity
	7	The disability and health order	Sickness and 'disablement' ideologies: health/ability identity

Whatever social thing you are looking at – schools, social work or senility – always try and ask questions about how it interconnects with these 'social orders' which shape our lives. Sociologists are interested in the ways they work individually (or autonomously) and the ways in which they dynamically feed into each other. Sometimes one will dominate over the others (for example, in slavery, the **racial formation** has often played a significant role, and in the exclusion of homosexuals, the sexual order works as a priority; in both cases, they are also shaped by the other six forces to some extent). In many societies, a gender order (some call it a **patriarchy**) works in which women are usually denied the same access as men to public social life – most religions are organized around ideas that women should *not* play significant roles except as mothers in the home. Ancient Greek and Roman societies were organized so that women were not only usually slaves but were also excluded fully from recognition in public life. Neither the Catholic Church nor the Muslim faith will allow women to function in any key role. Likewise, most societies organize themselves around an age hierarchy: children and youth, young people, middle and old aged. In some societies, the old are highly valued; in others, they are subordinated. Any specific order will be historically specific and unique and need careful study for all the elements outlined.

THE CLASS STRUCTURE, AGAIN

> The history of all hitherto existing society is the history of class struggles.
>
> Karl Marx, 2000

Class is critical: it is one of our main systems, but it also features as a key intersecting variable. The economists who discuss inequality (see above) rarely make much of an issue of class. It is thus a key topic for sociologists to study. Oddly though, a key preoccupation for them has been with its measurement: to study sociology and class frequently leads to debates on the range of 'class measurement ranking' scales. The most recent of these has been produced from the recently developed Great British Class Survey (GBCS). It is a little different – it draws from the ideas of Bourdieu, links to his ideas of capital and comes up with a classification that gives more emphasis to culture and networks. Here it is:

Elite – the most privileged group in the UK, distinct from the other six classes through its wealth. This group has the highest levels of all three capitals.

Established middle class – the second wealthiest, scoring highly on all three capitals. The largest and most gregarious group, scoring second highest for cultural capital.

Technical middle class – a small, distinctive new class group which is prosperous but scores low for social and cultural capital. Distinguished by its social isolation and cultural apathy.

New affluent workers – a young class group which is socially and culturally active, with middling levels of economic capital.

Traditional working class – scores low on all forms of capital but is not completely deprived. Its members have reasonably high house values, explained by this group having the oldest average age at 66.

Emergent service workers – a new, young, urban group which is relatively poor but has high social and cultural capital.

Precariat, or precarious proletariat – the poorest, most deprived class, scoring low for social and cultural capital (Savage, 2015).

THINK ON: MOBILITY AND THE PERPETUAL REPRODUCTION OF PRIVILEGE – AND UNDERPRIVILEGE

How much movement is possible between classes? This is the topic of sociological mobility studies, which usually conclude that there is much less mobility than people might think. The core problem thus becomes understanding the mechanism by which the differences keep getting reproduced – over, and over, and over again.

In general, inequalities seem to be reproduced by (a) inheritance and (b) the routines of everyday life – in families, schools, universities, workplaces, media. Pierre Bourdieu has been a key theorist to show that it is in the daily practices of choice, in liking the things that we like rather than others (heavy metal rather than opera, *Coronation Street* over the National Theatre), our fate is partially sealed. The habits – or **habitus** – of class, for instance, become settled. We may not see them as class, but they tacitly work their way through to reproduce this order.

You can find the classic discussion by Bourdieu in his book *Distinction*, and he features prominently on YouTube. A recent application to the UK can be found in the work of Tony Bennett, Mike Savage and colleagues in their book *Culture, Class, Distinction* (2009), as well as in *Social Class in the 21st Century* (2015).

PATRIARCHY AND THE GENDER STRUCTURE

> He is the Subject, he is the Absolute – she is the Other.
> Simone de Beauvoir, *The Second Sex*, 1949

All societies divide their populations into men, women and others (who do not quite fit – the **trans** world of hermaphrodites, intersex, transgenders, crossdressers and others along a wide spectrum of differences). Sex itself may have a biological foundation (chromosomes, brain structures, hormones, etc.), but the social expectations and the roles associated with being a man or being a woman are deeply social (and it is this which sociologists refer to as **gender**). They have an ambivalent relation. The precise content of what is expected of a man and a woman varies across history and across societies (and the expectations rarely match the reality), but common to most is the ways in which women are placed in subordinate roles in relation to dominant, even 'hegemonic', men. For instance, and across the world, women generally get much lower pay, have less opportunities to achieve and earn (the so-called 'glass ceiling'), do lower-status work (domestic work and care), are much less likely to become chief executive officers, and are much less likely to get on 'the rich list'. There are many fewer women in official positions of power – though in some countries this has increased. The rights to vote for women came much later than men's in most countries (and in many they remain disenfranchised). And often they have less opportunities for education. There are changes, but often the differences are quite extreme.

Men and women do indeed have different opportunities. Women simply do not fare as well as men. To try to capture this, there are several major annual reports you could look at. The World Economic Forum (WEF) has developed the Global Gender Gap Index (GGI) to measure four issues: education, economic empowerment, health and political empowerment; and the United Nations Development Programme has developed the Gender Inequality Index (GII) to measure inequalities on three dimensions: reproductive health, empowerment (political participation and women's attainment to secondary education) and the labour market. There are many controversies about such measures: they are unwieldy, complex, depend on unreliable measurements (see Chapter 6) and cannot be readily understood by the public. But worse, there are key dimensions of gender life missing such as violence and security. Still taken with other sources, such as the UN Women website, we do get a portrait of this dimension of stratification at any time. Whatever the dimension, usually the Scandinavian countries (such as Norway, Finland, Iceland and Sweden) perform best, whilst Muslim countries (notably the Yemen, Saudi Arabia, Pakistan and Turkey) come out worst.

And these days, men are often seen as under crisis . . .

THE ETHNIC AND RACE STRUCTURE

> The problem of the twentieth century is the problem of the color-line.
> W. E. B. Du Bois, *The Souls of Black Folk,* 1903

Throughout history, a process of **racialization** (in which people come to be placed in ethnic/racial categories) has been at work organizing social relations at both a macro level (the historical 'racialized' structures and ideologies found throughout societies which create unequal opportunities) and the micro level ('minority groupings' and interactions which forge identities of difference). Members of ethnic categories share cultural histories (with common ancestors, a language or a religion that, together, confer a distinctive social identity) and they are often forged out of various oppressions, discriminations, bigotries, prejudices and phobias. Here we find Islamophobia nestling with antisemitism.

Most societies round the world are composed of a range of different ethnic cultures: histories of conquest, migration and war have seen to that. In this sense, all societies are *hybridic* (combining different things) and often diasporas. In England, for example, the forebears of Pakistani, Indonesian, Irish, Caribbean, Hong Kong or Chinese Europeans – to name just a few! – may well retain cultural patterns rooted in particular areas of the world. But in each of these ethnic orders, a hierarchy of 'others' seems to emerge. There always seems to be a fear of outsiders – of the others – which runs deep. Each country and time seems to have its ethnic group which is cast out and around which all kinds of stereotypes, symbolic systems and mythical stories are invented.

The bad news is that this hostility has led to some major conflicts and issues. It becomes the basis of both slavery and caste, it is a key to the global dispossessed and we see it as playing a role in much of the world's violence, wars and terrorism.

THE DISABILITY STRUCTURE

Disabilities – from deafness, blindness and wheelchair mobility through chronic, long-term illnesses like AIDS to mental health breakdowns of all kinds – often have some kind of biological foundation and can be seen as impairments and individual differences. But how these differences are treated socially is the sociologist's core concern. The disabled have been treated differently throughout history and given an array of names: cripples, subnormality, weirdos, mad and sad people, monsters and freaks. Deformed children have been killed at birth. Freaks have been used for entertainment in circuses and films. Many have been 'put away' in asylums and made to vanish from society. And even at their best, they have been patronized by charity and welfare systems.

Sociological studies such as Erving Goffman's *Stigma* (1961/1968) suggest how the disabled get categorized, stereotyped, socially excluded and discriminated against in myriad ways. Worse, social exclusion means disabled people often experience profound levels of poverty and deprivation. It is not just the disability that causes problems but the presence of a negative, hostile or patronizing attitude from the wider society that makes life hard for them.

THE SEXUALITY STRUCTURE: HETERONORMATIVITY AND HOMOPHOBIA

Sexuality is much more than simply a biological drive. Sociologists looking at sexuality suggest that it is far from being a simple animal-like drive but is something that only functions for humans when it is weaved into social relationships and meanings. We can never just do sex – it is always enmeshed in wider rules and understandings of just *who* we can have sex with (the opposite sex?), *where* and *when* it should be done (at night in the bedroom?), just *what* can be done (vaginal–penis intercourse?) and indeed even *why* we can have sex (to have children?). The long history of religions is partially about the regulation of sex – of making acceptable contexts in which sex can be done; and histories of sexuality show enormous variations both in the kinds of sex that people have and the kinds of rules they make around it.

So sociologists are interested in such questions as how rules are made and developed about sexuality, about the range of sexual differences and how some come to be acceptable whilst others are not. They ask about the way human sexuality is given meaning – and how it often leads to the making of particular kinds of sexual identities (gay, straight, bisexual, sadomasochist, paedophile, queer). They ask about the ways in which sexuality connects to other institutions like the economy, religion, family and above all in the ways in which it intersects with other inequalities such as class, race and gender.

With this in mind, it soon becomes clear that some sexualities can be incorporated easily into a society whilst others are excluded. Homosexuality has been a key focus in recent decades, and it can be shown that there have been massively contrasting social attitudes towards it across different cultures and times. In much of the Western world, gay life has become more and more acceptable over the past twenty-five years or so – recall that in many countries it was against the law in the 1960s. Yet by the start of the twenty-first century, these same countries were legislating for gay marriages and civil partnerships, signalling 'new families of choices' and major changes in the public representations of same-sex lives. At the same time, in many other countries, hostilities to homosexuality were great: in 2016, homosexuality is still against the law in many countries, and in a good few, is liable to the death penalty.

THE AGE AND GENERATIONAL STRUCTURES

Age stratification is another key organizing difference. At the simplest level, the biological differences between infancy, youth, maturity and old age are obvious. But age is never simply biological, as every culture will generate roles and expectations geared to specific age categories. Child-rearing and infancy patterns vary enormously; not all cultures lead to the 'global youth cultures' of today (which some sociologists suggest have been shaped by class-based consumer capitalism since the Second World War). In some cultures, the elderly are highly valued for their wisdom; in others, they are more or less discarded. These age cultures, in turn, can become the basis of stereotyping, discrimination and even social exclusion ('reckless youth', 'demented elderly'). Further, we have seen the significance of generational cohorts (see Chapter 5), and these create both different 'age' structures of opportunities and the potential for conflicts between generations (Bristow, 2015).

THE STRUCTURES OF NATIONS AND THEIR OTHERS

Any selected society is *never* a unified whole. True, there is often a sense of unity that is presumed to be a national identity – but this is what social scientists call an 'imagined community'. In reality, societies are usually made of historically different groupings who over time have settled and developed – there are movements and migrations of settled peoples and the newly arrived everywhere, and they criss-cross over traditions, ethnicities, religions and politics. This is the **diaspora**. People outside their nation often develop **subaltern** identities.

You will be hard pressed to find any society in the world where there are not such schisms between minority–outsider groups, usually with long histories and troubled identities. From Sarajevo to Sri Lanka, Jerusalem to Djakarta, it seems that much of the world is engaged in a war pitting one ethnic group against its rivals. In Australia, sociologists study the tensions between Aborigines and the new Asian immigrants; in America, the focus is often on American

Indians, the blacks 'up from slavery' and a host of new immigrant groups (Mexicans, etc.). Most societies and communities are disparate and bring their own conflicts and practices from discrimination to outright genocide.

THE SUBJECTIVE REALITY OF INEQUALITIES

Sociology's task is not only to confront *objective* situations of inequality but also to ask just what are the consequences of these differences *subjectively* for those who experience them? What does it mean to people to be poor, to be excluded, to be slaves, to be outcasts? Just how is stratification actually experienced by people who live devalued, even dehumanized, lives? How is their sense of self and self-esteem shaped, and how indeed might they fight back, resist and negotiate the insults, abuses and neglects they experience in their everyday lives? Studies show a string of feelings and responses not just to poverty and hardships but also the mundane trials of everyday life – of being kept waiting, rendered invisible and made to live through symbolic assaults to their own sense of self-worth.

Table 7.2   The subjective side of inequality

There is a long history of studying the subjective experiences of those at the bottom of the pecking order. Here are some studies:

Oscar Lewis, *Five Families: Mexican Case Studies in the Culture of Poverty* (1959; 1975, new edition)

Richard Sennett and Jonathan Cobbs, *The Hidden Injuries of Class* (1977)

Lillian Rubin, *Worlds of Pain* (1977)

Nancy Scheper-Hughes, *Death Without Weeping* (1992)

Pierre Bourdieu, *The Weight of the World* (1993/1999)

Mitch Dunier, *Sidewalk* (1999)

Elijah Anderson, *Code of the Street* (1999)

Simon J. Charlesworth, *A Phenomenology of Working Class Experience* (1999)

Abdelmalek Sayad, *The Suffering of the Immigrant* (2004)

Alice Goffman, *On the Run: Fugitive Life in an American City* (2014)

Lisa McKenzie, *Getting By: Estate, Class and Culture in Austerity Britain* (2015)

As illustrated in Table 7.2, research study after study have shown the ways in which people at the lower end of the pecking order – shaped by **class, gender, ethnicity, nation**, etc. – live their lives enduring various deprivations, degradations and defilements while deploying strategies to survive them. Several striking features stand out:

1 The worlds they experience and the lives they lead are likely to be insecure and unstable. Work and wealth is never guaranteed; little can be planned; life is lived day by day. At the heart of their lives is a basic lack of any necessities for a life: little money, little work, a scarcity of food, housing is minimal – and every day requires living with this. The main task becomes a struggle for survival in a world of great instability. They live *insecure lives*.

2 These worlds are often closely linked to danger: there is the presence of violence and violent threats. Brutalization is built into the fabric of the daily life. War or conflict is often a backdrop; domestic violence is prevalent; women may experience special forms of violence such as genital mutilation; children may become soldiers. Homosexuals will be mocked or murdered. Here we have *brutalized lives*.

3 Their lives of quiet desperation can soon become trapped in a sense of devaluation and dishonour – they experience 'class contempt', racism, sexism, homophobia and the rest. All of which potentially tell them how awful they are. 'They' are accorded little respect from outside worlds and made to feel uncomfortable in the presence of the privileged. All this can bring a low sense of worth, poor self-esteem, a sense of shame, a dishonouring. These are the *shamed, dishonoured lives*.

4 Closely linked, they experience a basic lack of recognition of who they are. Their lives are surrounded by people who simply refuse to see them, who ignore them. There are the millions of people who clean offices at night, who we walk by as they beg in the street, who live in the no-go areas of slums unvisited by most, and the sick and poor whose sufferings are almost nightly displayed as 'victims' in other lands on television. These curiously live *'invisible lives'*: the great unseen.

5 But even if they are seen, it will often be through the lenses of charity and patronage, and often locked in a language

of degradation. They become the 'disreputable poor', the 'deserving poor', the 'dirty immigrants', the 'underclass', the 'pathological'. Visible, or invisible, lives are put down: they are *demeaned and dehumanized lives*.

6 People have little control over what will happen to them, and choices are restricted. But do not get me wrong. People are never passive automatons: they respond and deal with their situations. While some acquiesce and retreat in their plights, many fight back and rebel. They search for ways of dealing with their plight actively. They live *lives of resistance and fighting back*.

THINK ON: THE VOICES OF THE POOR

Here are some *Voices of the Poor* (Narayan, 2000):

Poverty is pain; it feels like a disease. It attacks a person not only materially but also morally. It eats away one's dignity and drives one into total despair.

(a poor woman in Moldova)

Children are hungry, so they start to cry. They ask for food from their mother, and their mother doesn't have it. Then the father is irritated, because the children are crying, and he takes it out on his wife. So hitting and disagreement break up the marriage.

(poor people in Bosnia)

Poor people cannot improve their status because they live day by day, and if they get sick then they are in trouble because they have to borrow money and pay interest.

(a poor woman in Vietnam)

There is no control over anything, at any hour a gun could go off, especially at night.

(a poor woman in Brazil)

It is neither leprosy nor poverty which kills the leper, but loneliness.

(a woman in Ghana)

INEQUALITIES IN IDENTITY FRAGMENTS

Objective, measurable inequalities (low income, poor literacy and the like), then, are always accompanied by subjective experiences (insecurity, invisibility, etc.). They are connected through ideas of relationships, positions and identities with others. The ideas of consciousness, subjectivities and identities can help here. In an early series of observations about all this, Marx identified the importance of class consciousness in understanding the working of the class system. For Marx, people had to become aware of their class situation as they moved from a class 'in themselves' to a class 'for themselves'. An awareness of where we are positioned in the class system becomes crucial. Class consciousness and awareness of class are key components of class analysis. But each one of our social orders provides opportunities and potentials for new identities. Thus, for example, although women and ethnic minorities are often treated unequally, history suggests that often these differences are ignored: there is little awareness of this inequality. Once a group becomes aware of itself, change becomes more possible.

Sociologists now apply these insights to a wider range of inequalities, provide a sense of (a) our location in class, race, gender, etc., (b) where we come from ('origins stories' as they are sometimes called) and (c) who we might become in the future. Our identities help give coherence to the past, present and future. Yet whilst they help us locate our positions in the world, they are open to change as we encounter different situations and relations (recently this has often been called 'positionality').

SUFFERING DIVISIONS AND HUMANITY'S INHUMANITIES

> Man's inhumanity to man makes countless thousands mourn!
> Robert Burns, 'Dirge: Man Was
> Made to Mourn', 1784

Inequalities might be understood through locating underlying common processes of division at work. Sociologists ask: *how do social processes shape our position in social life?* Ask yourself about what opportunities you have been given (or not given), of how your own life choices have been narrowed or widened. How have you been honoured and respected or shamed and treated with indifference? How have you been celebrated or stigmatized? How have you been in the mainstream of things – or banished to the margins? Some lives face perpetual danger, violence and risk and others do not. Which is yours? Think, in short, how some lives are treated humanely whilst others are dehumanized and ask where you lie in all this. When we start to think about this, several key processes raise their head.

DISEMPOWERMENT: RESOURCES AND FUNCTIONING IN THE WORLD

Max Weber (1978) defined power as 'the chance of men to realize their own will . . . even against the resistance of others' and saw it as shaped centrally by social class and status. Marx, by contrast, equated political rule with economic control. Whichever emphasis is given (they have never seemed to be incompatible positions to me), it is important to see that power is a process which flows through society – and that some people simply gain little access to it and others gain much more. The powerless come to lack the resources, the authority, the status and the sense of self that the powerful have. They lack respect. The privileged move around in different worlds: their bodies are confident, they can wear different clothes, they speak in different ways and they can cultivate a sense of respectability that marks them as valued – to themselves and in the eyes of others. They usually have autonomy and choices over their life which the powerless simply do not have. A key feature of this power is its legitimacy and the respect that others give it.

Ultimately, *the study of inequalities is about different access to resources to live with. Some people have an abundance of access to these resources, while others have almost no access.* The most obvious 'resource' is capital or wealth or economic resources. And power is an issue too – people with power usually have greater access to resources. But it goes beyond this, and these days (following often under the influence of the French sociologist Pierre Bourdieu), sociologists locate a wide array of resources. Table 7.3 is a list of key resources and, again, you might like to think about your own opportunities in relation to them.

Table 7.3   The resources of a stratified life

* *Economic resources (or economic capital)*: How much income, wealth, financial assets and inheritance do you have access to? How much does your work provide for your needs?

* *Social resources (or social capital)*: How much support do you have from family, friends, community and networks? What are your networks: who do you know?

* *Cultural resources (or cultural capital)*: How much access do you have to the knowledge, information, skills and education of your society? (Over time, such 'skills' can become part of a person's very sense of being, 'in their body', through their qualifications and sense of self.) These days, this would also include *digital resources* – access to the skills of digital communications.

* *Symbolic resources (or symbolic capital)*: How much access do you have to people giving you legitimacy and recognition and privileging your life over others?

* *Political resources*: How much autonomy do you have in your life? Are you able to control much of your day or do others control it for you?

* *Bodily and emotional resources*: In what way does your body or feelings seem to limit or control your life? How far do others regulate your body?

* *Personal resources*: How much has your own unique life and life history helped you generate personal skills for you to move easily in the world?

Understanding your own resources can perhaps help you start to see the different positions of others. Sociologists show the critical role of each of these in shaping our position in social life. Each one of the above constitutes a major area of research and thinking in sociology. Increasingly sociologists try to put these separate dimensions together and see their linkages and interconnections.

MARGINALIZATION, EXCLUSION AND THE MAKING OF THE 'OTHER'

We have seen that much social life seems to be that groups divide themselves into insiders and outsiders, creating the system of binaries – of good and bad. Many social scientists recently have called this the problem of *'alterity'* – of otherness. How do societies cope with the others? First, there is *stereotyping and stigmatization*: people categorize, simplify and devalue others, responding negatively to them – to race groups, to the disabled, to sexual minorities. Second, they *discriminate*: creating policies which exclude and dishonour. Apartheid in South Africa or racial segregation in the US are noted examples. Third, there are processes which physically separate people and eject them from the mainstream – a classic example is the creation of *ghettoization*. But sometimes people may become completely lost and absorbed through a process of *colonization*. Ultimately, they are *excluded*. A process of *expulsion* is at work. Finally, they may be *exterminated*: the striking case of genocide. Here then are key processes for a sociologist to study: stereotyping and stigmatization, discrimination, ghettoization, colonization, exclusion, expulsion and extermination. All work to reproduce inequalities in many societies.

THE PROCESS OF EXPLOITATION

Exploitation suggests people are used as means, not ends – that one group uses and benefits from another. Its most common form is economic, whereby a person's labour is used without adequate pay or compensation. A key account here suggests that a person's labour is the ultimate source of wealth (the labour theory of value). For Adam Smith (in his famous *The Wealth of Nations*, Book 1, Chapter V):

> The real price of every thing, what every thing really costs to the man who wants to acquire it, is the toil and trouble of acquiring it. What every thing is really worth to the man who has acquired it, and who wants to dispose of it or exchange it for something else, is the toil and trouble which it can save to himself, and which it can impose upon other people.

Within sociology, it was Marx, however, who developed this idea arguing that a small minority came to monopolize the labour of others (who cannot survive without working), who subsequently earn much less than is due to them whilst the owners – the capitalists – gain at their expense.

Slavery is a blatant example. But exploitation is to be found everywhere in the world. It is found in the sweatshops of unskilled, menial, low-paying labour working long hours around the world. It is found in families where women work in the home, raising children and caring for the family, without any kind of remuneration – except their husband's benevolence. It is found amongst migrating groups willing to work in dangerous jobs for low pay. And it is found in child labour. In all this, race and gender are often markers of exploitation.

VIOLENCE AS THE DIVISION OF LAST RESORT

Finally, violence may be seen as the mechanism of last resort: when all else fails, violence maintains the order. It is the ultimate mechanism to sustain inequality and difference – from state violence and war right through to the everyday bullying in families, gangs and small groups. Examples here are legion: the mass slaughtering of indigenous groups as they were invaded and colonized throughout the world's history; the chains and deaths of slaves as they were transported to their destinations; the long history of warfare between rival tribes and nations; the deaths of ten or more millions in the concentration camps and elsewhere between 1939 and 1945 – Jews, gypsies, homosexuals, vagrants, women, children; modern genocides. The list of such brutalities is long.

But there are also much less apparent mechanisms. Many feminists, for example, have claimed that 'rape is the mechanism by which men keep all women in a constant state of fear' and that it is the ultimate way in which the gender system is maintained. Others suggest there is a continuum of violence against women – from rape through pornographic representations of women as abused and on to the daily thousand little abuses and verbal harassments which keep women in their place. The system against homosexuals and trans people in some countries is ultimately upheld through the death penalty, and in others there is the perpetual fear of queer bashing and bullying. Abuse is also levied against children and old people. Nationhood, gender, class, ethnicity and sexuality are ultimately policed by violence.

SUFFERING, INEQUALITY AND THE
SEARCH FOR SOCIAL JUSTICE

So here, in a nutshell, we have a world in which for most of its human history and across most of its lands we find human beings who have managed to organize their differences into systems of stratification, hierarchy or social exclusion. *Human social worlds tend to be unequal worlds.* There is nothing hugely surprising about this – most animal societies are organized this way. It seems perfectly natural to many for there to be this hierarchy, appalling as this may be in terms of human suffering! So think a little more.

The human animal manages to transcend many other things that animals do: animals do not compose symphonies, create democracies or use mobile phones. Surely, we might have thought that human beings over millennia would have transcended these crude and restricting systems of suffering and inequality in some way. We might have thought that human beings would have tried to move beyond the brutalizing pecking order. But no: over and over again, we find cultures with a few people who have 'a lot' at the top and the many – the mass – who live 'without' at the bottom.

It is here that sociology touches many issues of social philosophy and the problems of justice, freedoms, rights and the search for human equality. Should we put up with this kind of inequality? The modern world is persistently haunted by these debates, and sociology is very much part of this. At least since the French Revolution, equality has served as one of the leading ideals of Western societies – placed often, if falsely, in conflict with ideals of freedom. Jean-Jacques Rousseau famously suggested a social contract and wrote his *Discourse on the Origin of Inequality* (1754). Karl Marx went on to write his massively influential work on class exploitation that became a major influence on the Communist revolutions of the twentieth century. And more recently, philosophers like John Rawls (1921–2002) and others have searched for principles of social justice. Rawls, for example, wanted to ensure that people with comparable talents could face roughly similar life chances and that where inequalities did occur, they nevertheless worked to the benefit of the least advantaged. He drew upon the idea of a 'veil of ignorance' whereby people – unaware of their talents and abilities, class, race, gender or religion – would be assigned a position at birth and, on the basis of not knowing any of this, be asked to choose the moral position for all to live with. Having no choice in the world we are to live in at birth, we would all probably want some kind of equality for all.

Now this is not the place to develop what has become one of the most central, complex and controversial debates in philosophy in the twentieth century. The debates between conservativism, liberalism and Marxism on equality have been long and furious, and the issue of equality has never been far away from being a central debate of our times in which sociologists have participated.

HUMAN CAPABILITIES AND FLOURISHING: THE BEST SOCIAL CONDITIONS FOR THE BEST HUMAN LIVES

At the start of the twenty-first century, one of the many lively debates has focused on human rights and human capabilities (though it is far from new – its roots go back to at least Aristotle). It has asked questions about just what human potentials and capabilities are and then linked these to ideas of a human-rights-based society. Here, we go right back to basics and consider an **ontology** of the human being: what is a human being and what is a human life for? It might help to begin this deep search with a simple answer. Human beings are bundles of needs, potentials, capabilities and differences which need appropriate social conditions in order to develop and flourish. Without the right social conditions, human life becomes flawed, damaged and prone to too much suffering: lives become 'damaged' or even 'wasted'. If the goal of a human life is to flourish and develop its potentials, we need to think about the right conditions to foster this. This seems to me to be as good as any starting point, even though there are many who disagree.

In the influential work of the Nobel-Prize-winning Indian economist Amartya Sen and the world-leading philosopher Martha Nussbaum on famine and poverty across the world, we find a major provisional listing of what these human **capabilities** could be for all human beings. They include the capability to live a *life* (being able to live to the end of a human life of normal length); for *health*; for *bodily integrity* (which means being able to move freely from place to place, being able to feel one's body secure against assault and violence and

HUMAN NEEDS/ CAPABILITIES
(What are human needs to be met – and flourish?)

1. food and water
2. breathing and sleeping
3. sense of security, physical comforts and shelter
4. employment and property
5. sense of belongingness and loving, intimacy
6. a feeling of competence
7. recognition and respect from others
8. a knowingness (understanding of world)
9. aesthetic and emotional
10. possibility of happiness

DIVISIVE PROCESSES
(How are we hindered in our capabilities and potentials?)

1. dominance and subordination
2. marginalization, stereotyping
3. exploitation
4. violence

And linked to the above: discrimination and stigmatization; ghettoization and segregation; colonization; pauperization; disempowerment; the silencing of voices; 'othering'; dehumanization; violence – and ultimately genocide

UNEQUAL ORDERS
(What are the forces which push and locate unequal positions?)

The social structures of:
1. class and economy
2. gender and patriarchy
3. ethnicity and race
4. age and generation
5. sexuality and heterosexism
6. disability and health
7. nations and nationalism

SOCIAL SUFFERINGS
(What are the subjective and objective consequences to people of inequalities?)

The thwarting of human capabilities
(A) objectively: poverty, mortality, health, malnutrition, violence *and*
(B) subjectively: flourishing lives and well-being: OR:
Damaged lives
Insecure lives
Invisible lives
Shamed lives
Demeaned lives
Brutalized lives
Resisting lives

Much has been written on these areas since the beginning of sociology. It constitutes a major area of enquiry within sociology. This figure is a worksheet: it enables the reader to connect key terms, think about how they interconnect and flow, and then link to their own life and the life of different others. The ideas are amplified in the text.

Figure 7.1 The matrix of inequalities

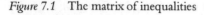

having opportunities for sexual satisfaction and for choice in matters of reproduction); for *senses, imagination and thought* (an adequate education and with guarantees of freedom of expression: political, artistic and religious); for *emotions* (to be able to have attachments to things and persons outside ourselves and to love those who love and care for us); for **practical reason** (critical reflection on the planning of one's own life – and what indeed is a good life); for *affiliation and recognition* (being able to live for and in relation to others, to recognize and show concern for other human beings); the ability to *play*; some *control over one's environment*; and finally, an ability to *live with other species* – a concern for and in relation to animals, plants and the world of nature.

Although such a list is open to change, refinement and development, it seems to me to be a very good starting point for thinking about what a human life needs to develop if it is to flourish on this earth. You might like to think about your own life and how each of these 'capabilities' appear or do not appear. Some of them – good health, etc. – seem more basic than others, but all human beings are surely in need of and capable of developing in each sphere. A life where this cannot be done is a diminished life. Still, this account does not say we are all the same. It stresses that although we do all have common human capabilities, for a good life, these all need to be developed in our own unique ways. And for many people in the world, there is currently no chance that they could develop most of them at all. It is indeed an unfair and unjust world.

One way of doing sociology is to ponder this idea of 'flourishing lives for all' and to ask what social conditions might help create this. The crucial idea here is a flourishing *for all* – not, as is so often the case, for just the few or just the elite. What must the world look like so that *all* people can live 'flourishing lives'? A world with greatly decreased inequalities in all their aspects would most surely be a part of this.

SUMMARY

Social life displays enormous differences, much of which is organized into inequalities. Four key themes can be summarized: (1) human capabilities are (2) structured through divisive processes into (3) structured inequalities which (4) have damaging effects on our lives. Sociologists study the intersections and institutions of class and economy, gender and patriarchy, ethnicity and race, age and generation, nation and culture, sexuality and heterosexism, disability and health, nations and nationalism. They investigate the beliefs (ideologies) which support them and how they might change. Key processes such as disempowerment and resources, marginalization and exclusion, exploitation and violence shape the process of divisions. Figure 7.1 attempts to bring this all together. Finally, philosophical ideas about human capabilities and a 'flourishing life for all' are raised.

EXPLORING FURTHER

MORE THINKING

1   Look at the box on 'the facts of world inequalities' (pp. 183–186). Use this as an opportunity to construct your own blog that shows the levels of inequalities in the world today.

2   How might you measure social class? Look at Mike Savage's bestselling book *Social Class in the 21st Century* (2015) and examine the new social class structure that he outlines there.

3   Look closely at Figure 7.1 and try to make sense of it. Examine the list of capabilities: how do they work in your own life? Connect these to the 'seven forces of unequal orders': how do they shape human opportunities? Finally, make a small leap into philosophy and debate with friends the idea of 'a flourishing life for all'. What do you think about the list of human capabilities listed in Figure 7.1? Are you flourishing? Who is not?

FURTHER READING

On the study of human suffering as a prime goal of sociology, see Iain Wilkinson, *Suffering: A Sociological Introduction* (2005) and Iain Wilkinson and Arthur Kleinmann, *A Passion for Society: How We Think About Human Suffering* (2016). The writing on inequalities is vast. Danny Dorling's *Injustice: Why Social Inequality Still Persists* (2015),

Göran Therborn's *The Killing Fields of Inequality* (2013) and Evelyn Kallen's *Social Inequality and Social Injustice* (2004) provide key overviews; Louise Warwick-Booth's *Social Inequality* is a clear tour of the issues (2013), while Geoff Payne's classic *Social Divisions* (2013, third edition) reviews all the major forms of inequalities. The modern classic is Kate Pickett and Richard Wilkinson's *The Spirit Level: Why More Equal Societies Almost Always Do Better* (2009; 2015, second edition). I learnt a great deal from reading Andrew Sayer's *Why We Can't Afford the Rich* (2015). Central major studies on contemporary inequality by Pinker, Atkinson, Stiglitz, *et al.* are cited in text.

More specifically: on caste, see Surinder S. Jodhka, *Caste* (2012); on slavery, see Brenda E. Stevenson, *What Is Slavery?* (2015) and Kevin Bales, *Disposable People* (2012, third edition). The writing on social class is enormous. For recent examples, see Guy Standing, *The Precariat: The New Dangerous Class* (2011); Will Atkinson, *Class* (2015); and Mike Savage, *Social Class in the 21st Century* (2015). On the globally excluded and dispossessed, see Zygmunt Bauman, *Wasted Lives* (2004); Saskia Sassen, *Expulsions* (2014); and Loic Wacquant, *Punishing the Poor* (2009). More philosophically, see Giorgio Agamben, *Homo Sacer* (1995/1998) and Judith Butler and Athena Athansaiou, *Dispossession* (2013).

Good guides to intersections are: generally, Nira Yuval-Davis, *The Politics of Belonging* (2011); on race, Nassad Meer, *Key Concepts in Race and Ethnicity* (2014, third edition); on sexualities, Jeffrey Weeks, *Sexuality* (2009, third edition) remains the classic. On disabilities, see Colin Barnes & Geoff Mercer, *Exploring Disability* (2010). On age, see Jenny Bristow, *Baby Boomers and Generational Conflict* (2015). On human capabilities, see Martha Nussbaum, *Creating Capabilities: The Human Development Approach* (2011), Angus Deaton, an economist examines the well-being of the world in *The Great Escape* (2013/2015).

VISIONS: CREATING
SOCIOLOGICAL HOPE

> The philosophers have only *interpreted* the world, in various ways.
> The point, however, is to *change* it.
>
> Karl Marx, *Theses on Feuerbach*, 1845, Thesis 11
> and engraved upon his tomb

Sociology may have been born of eighteenth-century revolutions, but it now dwells in a world of perpetual twenty-first-century conflicts. As recent centuries have unfolded, our understanding of society has not become any easier. The mass slaughtering of the twentieth century in two major world wars and holocaust genocides – justified by the ideologies of communism and fascism, and sometimes by 'pseudo-science' – generated a very dark view of twentieth-century life and its appalling possibilities. And now a multitude of public global social problems – from environmental crisis, global poverty and violence to the inequalities 'crisis', migrations and surveillance – seem unremitting. Modern media have created a greater awareness of these problems even as they have helped structure them. At its best, sociology is charged with helping us make some sense of it all. Across the world, more and more of its people see the need for this thinking sociology. And yet, this critical sociology can hardly function well in more authoritarian societies: if a society's authority is unchallengeable, then people who readily critique it can hardly be acceptable. In such cultures, sociology becomes standardized to the state's requirements and may become very narrow or go underground. Yet the modern world surely needs the sustained and serious analysis of the workings of the complex worlds we live in. That is sociology's mission. In this chapter, I look at the value of sociology, its uses or 'impacts', its 'calling' in the twenty-first century.

At its best, sociology seeks to secure an understanding of the world for the future which will help each generation. It is not utopian: it does not believe an ideal state of human life could ever be achieved or that we should be absolutist about its pursuit. But it does have utopian strivings – a learning from 'what works well' and a hope for improvement in humanity's lot. The 'Think On: On Sociology and Utopia' box shows how the notion of utopia is still around in contemporary sociology. It can bring hope. And hope is important too. Ernest Bloch's three volumes on *The Principle of Hope* (written at the end of the Holocaust) show how throughout history, all societies have needed a sense of hope. Sociologists surely want to understand the social world as it is, but they also need to bring hope to their critical imaginations to sense how we can nudge the world along into becoming a better place for all.

THINK ON: ON SOCIOLOGY AND UTOPIA

The socialist writer H.G. Wells (1886–1946) once remarked that 'the creation of Utopias, and their exhaustive criticism, is the proper and distinctive method of sociology'. Some recent sociology has picked up this idea and urged a critical return to the idea of utopia, the long-held dreams for a better world so beloved of writers down the ages. Erik Olin Wright (1947–) was President of the American Sociological Association in 2012 and suggested as his presidential themes the critical analysis of *real utopias*. For him, the sociologist should look for projects actually happening in the world today which demonstrate a better world of emancipation at work right now – lives lived that are desirable, viable and achievable. (He uses Wikipedia and participatory city budgeting as but two examples, and he has a website with many more.) The British sociologist Ruth Levitas (1949–) suggests 'utopia' might be an important sociological method in which the sociologist assembles conceptions of what a good society might look like, envisions building an architecture for a good society, then uses all this as a basis for critique and analysis of actually existing society and movements towards a better one.

In both of these useful accounts, there is an undisguised advocacy that sociology should be a normative discipline: it must take sides, be of visionary value, give hope. In both these arguments, utopia is not seen as a place; rather, it is a process in which we can learn from the best of today and help carry this forward into future generations. I think these are potentially useful ideas worth exploring in the future. We need to learn from the best of our contemporary complex human communications and to 'dream forward' to a world where more and more people can cultivate these skills. In another book, I have suggested these are 'utopian strategies of hope' (Plummer, 2015).

A caution is needed. In this chapter, I do not talk simply about the long (and sometimes pretentious and self-serving) meditations by the academically and university trained in recent times. I am also concerned with the oh-so-much more mundane activity that most people just routinely do at some points in their life. For surely, most people think at least a little about the nature of the world around them: of the gods in the air, the land they live on, the animals and nature around them, what other people are like. It is good to recognize that part of sociological thinking has this personal character. In an important sense, all people can be practical critical sociologists. We are *reflective* – people try to make sense of the world they live in.

And this in turn is *reflexive* – what we think about the world becomes social and actually plays a role reflecting back on our societies. And indeed, in these very acts of thinking, we sometimes change our societies a little. Societies – groups, tribes, civilizations, 'other people' – are always on the move through what people (you and me) think and do, and thinking about society actually helps move it on. In this final chapter, I also want to consider this linkage between everyday life practice and sociology.

A QUICK REVIEW OF THIS BOOK: MULTIPLE
SOCIOLOGIES ALWAYS ON THE MOVE

There is most surely no one way of doing any of this. Sociology is a wide open, humanistic, hybridic and ever-changing intellectual practice which aims to understand the human social worlds we live in. If there is one message that should have jumped at you in every chapter of this book, it must be *the multiplicities of sociologies*. Chapter 1 suggested that sociology can study anything under the sun. Chapter 2 suggested that the ways of thinking about the social are multiple; even studying a seemingly simple thing like 'the body' reveals a multiplicity of objects and intrepretations. The world and its theories are plural. Chapter 3 looked at a world of approaching eight billion people and the enormous varieties of religions, economies, governance – and change – we find within global multiple modernities. Chapter 4 provided a very short history of (mainly Western) sociology, only to indicate how it is itself stuffed full of different positions (a **multi-paradigm** discipline) and many potentials for the future. Sociology itself is a contested discipline. Chapters 5 and 6 took us into the heart of the sociological discipline – its imaginations, methods and theories – and once again demonstrated how it brings into play almost all other disciplines in study from the arts and the sciences – and all the 'isms' too: feminism, postmodernism, postcolonialism and the rest. Finally, Chapter 7 hurled us into the vast array of differences which congeal into dreadful patterns of social sufferings and inequalities, themselves being organized at the intersections of class, race, gender, disability, nation, sexuality and age. Complexity and multiplicity are the name of the game of sociology.

Some sociologists will not agree with me. They may claim that their way of doing sociology – as a scientific methodologist, as an analytic theorist, as a feminist, as a 'professional sociologist' – is the one 'true way'. So be it. My own view again is that in a world of such human multiplicities and complexities, many of them passionately and politically experienced, sociology can *never* be *one* fully unified discipline. It needs its many practitioners doing its many different things, bringing different angles and perspectives on a moving whole that can never in principle ever be fully or wholly grasped. And often sociological stances will be radically at odds with each other. There is no fixed object awaiting study in sociology, and there can be no fixed discipline. Indeed, what we find, and need, are many divisions of sociological labours, each of which will bring its own findings, insights and imaginations to a grasping of human social life in all its horrors and delights – each adapting and responding to its times and place. At the same time, it is not without many unifying themes and concerns, which indeed it has been one key task of this book to outline.

WHAT DO SOCIOLOGISTS DO?

The sociologist can play a number of roles in the modern world. We teach; we work in think-tanks and large (and small) research centres; we are activists; we work in both government and non-governmental agencies; we are social workers, police officers, lawyers, court workers; we work in human resources and social welfare; we work in media – and as website managers, journalists, film makers, artists. We work in international agencies and local ones. And above all, we live in everyday worlds, leading everyday lives and doing everyday things – enhanced by sociological imaginations. There are many tasks to be done, something for everyone to do and many standpoints to work from: no one person can adopt them all, but there is much to be done.

THE SOCIAL ROLES OF THE SOCIOLOGIST

A most basic function of the sociologist is that of the researcher, the gatherer (and hence creator) of social information. *We research and document the nature of the social times we live in.* Sociological information is always needed to take stock of the human world – otherwise we would be living in the dark. In the 1920s, the Chicago sociologist

Robert Park advised his students to become super-journalists; his own background was that of a journalist before he became a sociologist. Thus, at the simplest levels, and as Chapter 3 has shown, sociology maps information on such things as population size, economic functioning, the shifts in religious belief, the move to the cities, the functioning state of whole countries and regions – along with concerns over crime, migration patterns, family life, the nature of social class. World societies cannot function these days without information on a myriad of things, and this is what social science has to help provide. Just imagine living in a social world where we knew nothing about it – it is a nightmare scenario. These days a lot of such data is but a click away.

But sociologists also know that data on its own is worthless – data does not present itself automatically, and it certainly does not speak for itself. It is gathered by humans making decisions about what is significant, and it is then interpreted by multiple readers – each using it for their own ends. Ultimately, much of this will be political in nature. We need to watch the move here from *mere information* to *knowledge* to *wisdom* and the imported politics and ethics that come with it.

Thus, the second task of the sociologist is that of the thinker, the theorist – the philosopher, even – of human social life and living. As this book has tried to show throughout, *more than information and data are needed in social life: we need wider understanding and the capacity to make connections, sense links with the rich heritage of thinkers from the past, shun seeing facts in isolation and out of context.* Sociologists – however falteringly – facilitate theoretical and general thinking about society. Theory work can be difficult and can sometimes be obscure, but its aim is to foster deeper understanding of what is going on and hopefully help to provide a way for sociological knowledge to become cumulative. Wisdoms can be passed on and developed from generation to generation and may help more of us to understand social life a little better in each generation. Random facts and information are of little value.

This thinking is usually critical, and so it is but a short step for the sociologist to also become and act as critic, radical and the agent for change. *Sociology fosters a critical attitude to social life,* seeing that things are never quite what they seem and common sense never quite that common. Sociologists question and interrogate the taken for granted society, and connect it to alternative other possible worlds. They subvert the thinking as usual. In this sense, sociologists can often become idealists – seeking advance and a 'better' world. Critical theory emerged in the early twentieth century as a tool for critiquing the Enlightenment's claims of a developing rationality, science and new technological world. For them, science was never neutral, and positive thinking was never so positive. They argued for an emancipatory knowledge, one based on negative thinking and critique. This position has worked its way into sociological practice, and there is an undeniable radical leaning to much of its work.

Next comes the sociologist as educator, teacher and, these days, the media disseminator and the web coordinator of social knowledge. *We can facilitate both basic information and ways of thinking about social life* through which members of a society can try to take stock of where society has come from and where it is heading. Amongst the many things that we can do in this applied role is writing and teaching. But we can provide governments (and world organizations and NGOs) with information that helps in planning future pathways for society, and we can work in media of all kinds (from journalism to social media) so that society can find its way around social knowledge. Nowadays we are in need of a sociological Wikipedia.

There are many other roles for sociologists. We can be subterranean storytellers. *Here we reveal voices, ideas and social worlds that are subterranean in a society – subjugated knowledge, subaltern visions* that live underground and may not easily be heard. We can puncture the snoring and the sleeping in the wake of suffering. Sociologists can also be artists. *Here we generate ideas that can inform and enhance human creativity.* Sociological ideas feed into worlds of art, literature, music, poetry, film. The sociologists can be the policy shapers. Here we *advise governments and groups* on the nature of the social world. The sociologist can be the commentator and public intellectual. Here we *provide a social diagnosis of the ills of our time* and make a contribution to the human world by clarifying options, sensing alternatives and signposting directions for the future.

We might also be the dialogists. Here we *create organized dialogues across the multiple different voices to be heard in a society* (see 'Think

On: The Sociologist as Dialogist'). Sociologists must always sooner or later discover in both their research and theories that human life is always bound up with different social worlds that pose potentials for massive human conflict. As we have seen, contradiction and ubiquitous conflict have to be lived with everywhere. It is lived at every level of social life: global (e.g. wars between nation states, conflicts between men and women), national (e.g. ethnic, religious), local (e.g. community politics, splits between social movements), personal (e.g. domestic violence, breakdown of trust between friends) and social media (bullying and harassment).

THINK ON: THE SOCIOLOGIST AS DIALOGIST

Part of what sociologists invariably study is the contested relations between peoples across all spheres of social life. We examine the conflicts between countries, across groups, between and within social movements. The sociologist is regularly challenged to clarify debates, to sort out the relations across different voices – ordering them, classifying them, searching for agreements and disagreements, finding 'common grounds' (or not). This is a crucial task for sociology: its dialogic mission. So sociologists need the capacity to discuss reasonably, to talk with opposing others and to dialogue. Here are some guidelines for doing this.

THE TWELVE PILLARS FOR DIALOGIC CIVILITY (PLUMMER, 2015)

1 Recognize all of the different voices engaged around this issue (and certainly not just the dominant groups or the polarized spokespeople).
2 Avoid dehumanizing, degrading, mocking or silencing 'the other'.
3 Develop an awareness of the inequalities and the differences of power between speakers.
4 Appreciate the different social backgrounds and group belongings of participants – what religions, family, etc. mean to them.

5 Understand the differences across groups in arguing: Western 'argument culture' does not travel well. Authoritarian cultures do not readily live with debate. Develop plural voices rather than 'oppositional views'.

6 Comprehend language differences, being aware that some terms may be untranslatable and even incommensurable.

7 Reflect on your own personal prejudice and location in all this.

8 Grasp personal enmities: often there are personal likes and dislikes involved.

9 Understand the emotional and embodied basis (and history) of much life and talk.

10 Engage in reciprocity and learn the skills of negotiating conflict transformation, trust and reconciliation.

11 Maintain a sense of lightness: keep a sense of balance, humour, modesty, humanity.

12 Search for common grounds that can be agreed upon. Often the humanist values of empathy, dignity, care, justice and human flourishing can serve as a starting point: start with what might be agreed upon before entering the conflicts and differences.

Source: Plummer, 2015.

There is nothing new about such conflicts (and nor do I think they will ever end). Throughout history, wars may have always been simply the stuff of everybody's everyday life. Maybe what has happened, in effect, is a world where disagreements have now become more visible and more open to 'management'. It may be that democratizing societies generate more public spaces for a wider range of people to engage in deliberative talk about these issues than has often been known before. It may be that sociologists can *facilitate organizing principles of this deliberative talk and dialogue*. They can enable the capacity to discuss reasonably, to talk with opposing others and to dialogue. They can *foster what might be called dialogic citizenship*. It is very hard in this culture not to engage with polarized debates since this is more or less our routine way of doing things. Yet too often arguments get needlessly polarized. Because arguments become firmly attached to individual people, they actually become part of them, are identified with them, belong to them. The very people then become what is at stake in the argument as they engage in their own private monologue.

Finally, then, sociology has a wide and generic role in society: the sociologist becomes the critical citizen in society. Anyone can do this. *We can all help create a widespread social awareness and what might be called social thinking,* which is often in contrast to common sense, which usually sees the world in more individualizing and 'natural' terms. We have sociological citizenship. Sociology has to start with trying to understand the complicated nature of 'common sense', but it can also help people to challenge what is taken for granted, to look at their social world creatively and to help them to make the link between the private problems of individuals with the public problems of cultures. Sociologists can help people make social connections and help foster aware citizens who know what is going on around them. Sociology *can help create good, critical, socially aware citizens,* who can make informed and knowledgeable decisions.

AND THE WORLD GOES ROUND: THE CIRCLE OF SOCIOLOGICAL LIFE

Studying and thinking about society is itself a part of a society (in the jargon, it is 'recursive'). There is a loop which connects everyday personal, practical thinking to sociological knowledge through all the public and popular discussions we have about social issues. All this in turn feeds into wider issues of change and government and social movement change – which in turn feeds back into everyday practical life. And the world goes round . . .

Sociology is a never-ending revolving wheel with (imprecise) phases. (I call them the five 'p's.) The first phase of the circle suggests that sociological life starts with *people* – with the everyday experience, common sense and practical knowledge used by everyone in daily life. We ground sociology in these concerns and questions that people have about living in society, and we always need to return to this, however far we move in the circle. As the Canadian feminist sociologist Dorothy E. Smith once remarked: we need a sociology 'of the people, by the people and for the people'.

Put simply and diagrammatically sociology can be depicted as a never-ending wheel

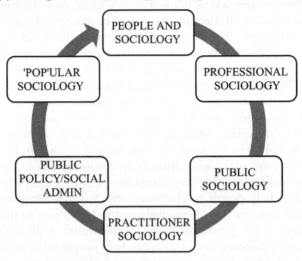

Figure 8.1 The circle of sociological life

Sociology always needs grounding in real everyday life and the people who live it.

A second phase is the *professional sociology* we outlined in Chapter 4–6. This is the sociology that is taught in universities and is organized through professional bodies like the International Sociological Association. Much of this book has been outlining the key features of this. It is a systematic, organized, sceptical and critical view of the world which does not take social things for granted but questions them. Sadly, much of it is esoteric, elite, cultlike and published in specialized journals in unreadable language.

Moving beyond this, we find what is now coming to be known as a **public sociology** – one which takes elite professional sociology and, building on the idea of public intellectuals, people well known for their ideas in public life, tries to make it publicly accessible and credible. They move onto blogs, television, radio, etc., speaking in plain language to a wider audience. The idea of a public sociology was called for in a quite famous debate in 2004 with the then-president of the American Sociological Association, Michael Burawoy. (You can find his work online and on YouTube.) Since then the idea has been advanced with much debate.

Next, there is a *practitioner sociology* – an applied sociology, those who work, for example, in teaching, sports, social work, criminology and the health professions. There are many groups who need to study sociology and apply it in their work. Typically, they will need to understand how face-to-face interactions work (microsociology), how organizations structure their work (meso-sociology) and ultimately how their work links to the wider, even global world (macro-sociology), studying the institutions and inequalities of health or education or crime or sport. Studying sociology in professional courses will bring its own textbooks like Elaine Denny and Sarah Earle's *Sociology for Nurses* (2016, third edition) or Anne Llewellyn, Lorraine Agu and David Mereer's *Sociology for Social Workers* (2014, second edition).

Sociology also has a close affinity with *public policy* and social policy. Public policy studies is mainly concerned with the ways in which politics shapes the organization of our laws and policy programmes, but social policy draws explicitly from sociological research and theories to help foster adequate responses to problems in such areas as health, crime, deprivation, poverty, city planning or the environment. At the same time, the sociological study of social policies makes it clear that the bridge from theory to practice is paved with good intentions yet littered with disasters. Much policy becomes its own form of fatal remedy, its own pyrrhic victory. In short, it often does not work at all well and can even make situations worse. Sociology has to advise caution. That said, there are many sociologists who speak out and become prominent in the political debates of their countries: Jürgen Habermas in Germany, Amitai Etzioni in the US, Pierre Bourdieu in France, Anthony Giddens in the UK, Margaret Archer at The Vatican and Roberto Mangabeira Unger in Brazil – amongst many others.

Putting all this into a loop, we return to the people, from where we started, with a *'pop'ular sociology*. Although professional sociology discusses major issues in society, it is frequently not very accessible to wider audiences. Below are some instances where you can find sociological ideas at work in more popular and lively ways. Here we have journalists with bestsellers: Owen Jones (the *Guardian* newspaper commentator) writes *The Establishment* and *Chavs*, and Naomi Klein (the environmental activist) writes *This Changes Everything*, *The Shock Doctrine* and *No Logo*. (You may not agree with their politics, but they have done a lot of research and make it accessible.) We have (a very few) sociology books that have become bestsellers: Barry Glassner's *The Culture of Fear*, Mike Savage's *Social Class in the 21st Century*. We have artists who talk about sociological issues with flair (like the work of contemporary artists Grayson Perry on identity and Anthony Gormley on the body). There are sociologists with radio programmes like Laurie Taylor's *Thinking Allowed* (weekly; see the BBC website). And there are sociological documentaries, like Andrew Jarecki's *Capturing the Friedmans* (2004), Nick Broomfield's *Ghosts* (2007), Kevin MacDonald's *Life in a Day* (2010), Sebastio Salagundi's *The Salt of the Earth* (2014) and Michael Moore's *Where to Invade Next* (2015). A lot of reality TV like *Gogglebox* and *24 Hours in A&E* might also serve as a stimulus for sociological thinking.

CRITICAL SOCIOLOGY AS A POLITICAL AND MORAL IMAGINATION

Some years ago, Norman Denzin and Yvonne Lincoln delivered a strong exhortation to sociology when they said:

> The social sciences are normative disciplines, always already embedded in issues of value, ideology, power, desire, sexism, racism, domination, repression and control. We want a social science that is committed up front to issues of social justice, equity, non-violence and peace, and universal human rights. We do not want a social science that says it can address these issues if it wants to. For us, that is no longer an option. (Denzin and Lincoln, 2005)

There is indeed a well-known cliché of sociology that it is a scientific, 'truth seeking', objective study of society, but as the quote from Denzin and Lincoln above suggests, this is a contested view. Throughout this book I have tried to show there is a continuing tension for the sociologist between being a neutral, dispassionate, objective scientific analyst of social life and being a partisan, committed, passionate person who cares about making a better world.

At the very least, we must distinguish an empirical sociology that shows how people actually *are* and a normative sociology which shows what people think we *should* do. In any event, this is a problem that has haunted sociology since its inception. The tension is built into sociology, but the positions are not necessarily wholly incompatible.

It is very clear that many of the great sociologists of the past were often passionate about changing the world. But it is also clear that they also wanted to obtain a certain objectivity and truth – none were simple relativists holding the view that 'anything goes'. They did not adopt partisan and political views from their academic pulpits, and they struggled for truth. Likewise, today, if we are to advance in the world, we need the best – or at least 'adequately objective' – knowledge we can get. But this is hard because the very subject matter of sociology is bound up with meanings, subjectivities and values and organized through power relations. Some groups (and people) have authority and status over others (and indeed congeal into massive systems of stratification, which we saw in Chapter 7). It would be naïve to think that sociologists are outside of this political process. The subject of sociology is riddled with values and power, finds itself in a rapidly changing political and moral world and is itself part of that very change. So the task of sociology is to reflexively grasp this and struggle to get at the truth of society, maybe against the odds. We have looked at some of these strategies in Chapter 6.

There is a long history of discussing the role of values and ideologies in sociology – and they usually start with our old friend Max Weber, who made key distinctions between value-free and value-relevant sociology. (You can note how often Weber has appeared in this book and sense, therefore, how important he is.) Without detailing his work here, I find his arguments lead me to think of three key ideas linked to three phases of research. You may find it helpful to get these clear:

1 *Value relevance*: be aware of your own value and political baseline. In the earliest stages of research, values become crucial in making selections and phrasing problems. Don't waste your time on worthless projects; think about what the value of your

research should be and choose your area carefully. Often you will choose a topic because it does indeed have political and moral significance.

2 *Value neutrality but ethical responsibility: be aware of the ethics of doing sociology.* Whilst doing your research, you will need to strive for adequate objectivity. Keep your eye on different perspectives, multiple representations, intimate familiarity, the balance of subjectivity and objectivity, good representativeness and sufficient contextualization, and be aware of issues of reflexivity (see Chapter 6 on all this). At the same time, sociology always deals with human life and people, and you will need to think about your responsibilities towards the people you are studying. Doing sociology in the field is riddled with ethical dilemmas. This is not just a matter of research ethics committees or institutional review boards (IRB)! It is a matter of real personal struggles to 'do the right thing'.

3 *Value implications: be aware of the politics of how your research is used.* Once research conclusions are arrived at, think carefully about the implications of who this will impact and how. Do you have responsibilities to follow the idea and findings through to a wider audience and wider political actions? Will there be political fallout because of your findings?

Values, then, are everywhere. Sociologists often feel really *subjectively passionate* about social issues – world poverty, the fate of the environment, the clash of religions, violence against women, the rising crime rate – but then find that to study them seriously, they have to do this in *an objectively detached way*. There is no point in a sociology which just adds yet another personal (even hysterical) viewpoint; some calm reflection and close observation of what is going on is needed. How can sociologists adopt *scientific attitudes* on things that harbour so much *personal involvement*? The sociologist's problem is simply put: how to be *objective* about the *subjective*, *passionate* while being *detached*, *scientific* yet *personal*, and *value free* while being *value relevant*. Sociologists walk scientific, moral and political high wires all the time.

There are some who will suggest that values should be kept strictly out of sociology. But if we look at the great sociologists of the past – and indeed many prominent sociologists today – you will soon find those who have been committed to major social change. Remember, it was Marx who was personally outraged at the exploitation and damaged lives he saw created by capitalistic industrialization; he inspired major world revolution for equality (which seriously and damagingly failed). It was Weber who said we are living in an iron cage and bemoaned – through his various depressions – the 'disenchantment of the world'. Every past sociologist has their personal and political, if often hidden, face. Many were much less radical.

Contemporary sociology is often quite explicit about its moral and political imagination. Thus, feminist sociology declares the need to remove women's inequalities; anti-racism sociology critiques **racism**; queer sociology destabilizes gender and sexual categories; post-colonial sociologies critique the supremacy of the European/American model that dominates thinking; and environmental sociologists work towards a low-carbon, sustainable society. Today, the briefest excursions into contemporary social thinkers such as Zygmunt Bauman, Ulrich Beck, Seyla Benhabib, Judith Butler, Stanley Cohen, Patricia Hill Collins, Raewyn Connell, Norman Denzin, Amitai Etzioni, Anthony Giddens, Paul Gilroy, Jürgen Habermas, Stuart Hall, Donna Haraway, Chandra Mohanty, Martha Nussbaum, Stephen Seidman, Gayatri Spivak, Alain Tourraine, John Urry, Sylvia Walby, Jeffrey Weeks and the rest will soon lead you into social science worlds that are deeply partisan and explicitly political. Amongst these, there is no pretence at all of value neutrality. We live in a land of *Contested Knowledge* which forces you to ask: whose side are you on?

All sociologists have to live with this balancing act. How to juggle their science with their politics, their ethics, their passions? Some solve it by siding with science – they may well retreat to the academy to do their studies as neutrally and dispassionately as they can. Some solve it by leaving sociology behind and joining activism of one kind or other. And some – many – become marginal, living on the borders of objectivity and subjectivity, neutrality and passion, science and art, disenchantment with the world and a hope for a better one. My view is that it is *not* a sociologist's function to tell other people what to do in social life – that would be moralistic and moralizing. But it is a challenge for sociologists to study the historical significance of different values and through such debates to work out their own system of values and politics which informs and shapes their sociological work. There are now many studies which trace the evolution of ideas around justice, caring, empathy, human rights and dignity, including Hans Joas's *The Genesis of Values* and *The Sacredness of the Person*. It is ultimately important for sociologists to understand the sociology of values and to spend time considering their own moral and political baselines in order to ask: *how should we live our lives and what is to be done?*

COMMON GROUNDS: VALUES AND VIRTUES IN SOCIOLOGY

Values (judgements of what is important), norms (accepted ways of conduct) and ethics (distinctions between right and wrong, virtuous and non-virtuous conduct) are central in human social life. Sociologists also have to take them very seriously. They study their genealogies (how values evolve across societies over history), their application in everyday life, and recognize how they shape their own work (as baseline assumptions, as ethical guidelines in research, as outcomes of their work). Values range widely and are numerous, but here are some key examples (there are others):

1 *Care and kindness*: sociologists want to understand the ways in which people look after each other – even love each other – in the world. They know that a recurring key feature of social life concerns the ways in which people look after each other in families, friendships and communities. There is even the caring for the environment. Here sociologists can investigate caring relations, make sure their research relationships are grounded in care for the other and trace the history of caring relations across societies. There is a sociology of care.

2 *Freedom, equality and justice*: sociologists grasp the tension that exists between freedom and equality: total freedom or total equality are both total nonsense. The social always constrains the free, and inequality is always shaped by the social. Sociologists investigate how freedom and justice are lived, make sure their research is grounded in such principles and investigate the genealogy of 'justice' and 'freedom'. There

are many whose lives are damaged by a lack of freedom and huge inequality, and much sociological work is hence concerned with understanding freedom and opportunities of equality.

3 *Recognition, empathy and cosmopolitanism*: sociologists find an awareness of the multiplicities of ways in which human social lives are different – across people, groups, cultures and nations – at the heart of their study. Ethnocentrism is a cardinal sin for sociologists, and a wide-awake openness to the values of others is central. Likewise, fundamentalisms of all kinds go against the grain of human diversity – and sociology! Sociologists need to recognize human differences, cultivate empathy to make sense of these other worlds, dialogue across groups, and sponsor cosmopolitanism to help understand the jostling diversities of living together.

4 *Flourishing lives for all*: sociologists are concerned with what it means to function well in a society and examine what 'human capabilities' are and the social conditions under which they can be actualized and flourish. They ask what is meant by human well-being and 'happiness'; what is meant by the good life and the wasted life; what are human capabilities and potentials; and what might be a 'virtuous' life. What are the good traits of humanity, and which need to be cherished and valued? What social conditions will bring this about? (Likewise, they can study why so many people lead lives that are 'wretched', 'damaged' and lacking in any kind of 'quality'.) Ultimately, sociologists investigate the social conditions of human flourishing and the development of *flourishing societies*.

5 *Rights and human dignity*: sociologists question what is meant by human dignity across societies and examine the rise and role of human rights debates: what it means; of modernity and universality of rights; the variety (individual and collective, i.e. group) and differentiations of human rights (civil, religious, intimate); and the international agencies and social movements for rights. Sociology analyses how human rights and dignity have become part of a world global culture helping to shape a truly '*human' society – with human rights and dignity for all people.*

Table 8.1 Future social imaginaries: grounded utopias in everyday life

The sociology, ethics and politics of 'Grounded Human Values'	Cultivating grounded institutions for 'Better Worlds For All People'
Sociology, politics and ethics of care *"looking after ourselves, each other and the world we live in"*	A Caring Democracy (Tronto, 2013) A Peace Making Society (Brewer, 2010) A Low Carbon Society (Urry, 2011)
Sociology, politics and ethics of justice, freedom and equality *"being fair and making a more equal world"*	A Fair, Just and Democratic Society (Alexander, 2006; Sandel, 2012; Sayer, 2015; Standing, 2015; Urry, 2014; Unger, 2007)
Sociology, politics and ethics of recognition, dialogues and empathy *"recognizing, appreciating and living with human differences"*	A Compassionate Society (Sznaider, 2001) An Empathic Civilization (Rifkin, 2009) A Dialogic Society (Bakhtin, 1982) A Multicultural Society (Taylor, 1994) A Cosmopolitan Society (Beck, 2006; Plummer, 2015) A Society of Belonging (Yuval-Davis. 2011)
Sociology, politics and ethics of human capabilities and flourishing *"encouraging human potentials for all"*	A Development, Flourishing, Actualizing Society (Sen 1999; Nussbaum, 2011)
Sociology, politics and ethics of human rights, **citizenship** and dignity *"living with dignity and respecting the rights of all to an equal dignity"*	A Human Society with citizenships, human rights and dignity (Marshall, 1950; Isin and Turner, 2002; Plummer, 2003; Turner, 2006b)
Sociology, politics and ethics of hope *"appreciating the inevitability of disappointment but the importance of hope"*	Real Utopias (Wright, 2010) Utopian Methods (Levitas, 2013)

CHALLENGING HORIZONS AND
SOCIOLOGICAL HOPE

What we can do is . . . make life a little less terrible and a little less
unjust in every generation. A good deal can be achieved in this way.

Karl Popper, 1948

Ultimately, sociology hurls us towards many of the really big questions of life – and many of the smaller ones. Are societies making
progress and getting better – or are we heading for Armageddon?
(And what does 'better' mean?) Why is inequality growing, and is
it inevitable? How does our social life corrupt the environment we
live in? Are war, terrorism and crime necessary – do we always need
to wage wars on the others who are not like us? Why do religions
generate hatred and war – as well as benevolence and kindness? Is
the digital world dehumanizing us? How can and do people make
sense of it all? And in all cases, what is to be done? What could
we – should we – do about it? How *should* we work to prevent
big world problems and the suffering of little human lives – how
indeed might we make the world a better place? Is justice possible
in society? Once we have entered these kinds of issues, we are a
very long way indeed from the simple facts. But then, *there are no
simple facts in sociology*. And this suggests that sociology – like it or
not – will sooner or later become embroiled in values and political
and moral life.

Studying sociology inevitably deepens the understanding of how
human social worlds work, and in doing this it helps provide a basis
for thinking of how social life can function better, of what it means
to be a good citizen in the current world, of what needs challenging.
Sociology is at its best when it starts with researching and trying
to understand, as objectively as it can, the everyday sufferings and
troubles of everyday people in their multiplicities of worlds and asks
how our social doings have helped generate 'problems' – how our
social structures and actions, our cultures and material worlds, our
biographies, histories and spaces have worked to bring these sufferings about. Sociology's ultimate mission, like all of science and art
in the end, is surely a mission for a better world. It does not do all
this serious thinking and pioneering of ideas for mere fun (though

THINK ON: CHALLENGING DIRECTIONS FOR SOCIOLOGICAL STUDY

To close, here are some emerging fields of sociological research that are developing in the twenty-first century:

The sociology of suffering. Here we need to understand the global sufferings of humanity by documenting and generating empathy for the multiple forms of personal and cultural suffering (in life, of course, but also in films, writing, art, poems), probing their depths and becoming sensitive to their pains and thinking critically about how best to theorize them, conceptualize them and explain why and how people across the world often ignore, deny, facilitate or even celebrate human suffering. We ask what the social conditions and social processes are that bring lives to suffering and despair.

The sociology of good lives. Here we listen to (and document and analyze) the stories of all people who struggle to live helpful lives, to be good people in a difficult world – even as they fail (perhaps most apparently in the lives of those in the caring professions and the like). How do they try to work to make the world a better place in their various life activities, and how do they succeed or fail? A sociology of good lives might ask how people and their groups come to look after other people and in very ordinary ways 'do good'. What are the problems this brings? We ask what the social conditions and social processes are that enable people to live caring lives.

The sociology of human capacities and flourishing. Here we assemble a sense of human capabilities and examine how some lives never have opportunities to achieve fulfilled lives whilst others do. We examine the process through which some lives become wasted, some become damaged and others flourish. Part of this will also mean sociologists develop a sociology of joy: the passion of music and dance, the skill in sport, the love of food, the pleasures of sex – and more. We ask what the social conditions and social processes are that enable people to live flourishing lives.

The sociology of the humane society and the humane state. Here we need to understand the structures of international-al economies and governance, welfare states and social protection that may facilitate capabilities; the workings of institutions that encourage the development of human rights and equality frameworks; the facilitation of care and kindness and the roles of global activism, volunteers and philanthropy. We continue to inspect the deep inter-connected structures of inequalities and social exclusion that are known to have such damaging effects on social opportunity and the quality of lives. We look to institu-tions that facilitate global empathy, cosmopolitanism and world ethics in ensuring we recognize differences and foster peace processes across our human world. We ask questions about organizing human life better at a macro scale.

The sociology of global humanity. Here we develop a persistent awareness of humanity's global interconnectedness and how this is grounded in an awareness of everyday life. It is a move away from the simple replication of the limited, narrow concerns of a small intellectual elite (largely uni-versity-based and Western) to look at the ordinary lives of ordinary people doing ordinary things all over the globe. (The YouTube film *Life in a Day* (2011) is an early exem-plar of this – showing how thousands across the world are keen to contribute in the documentation of different lives.) Avoiding the tyranny of elite knowledge, we ask how social life is lived by ordinary people across the globe. We ask how we can learn to avoid the ethnocentrism of our worlds and look out to others.

Ultimately, we need *a sociology of better worlds for all*. A key chal-lenge for sociology is the imagination of just what better human worlds may look like. Utopias may never arrive, but visions of them are important. A sociology without visions of both imagined and real utopias becomes a directionless sociology. We ask questions about our future social imaginaries, of the worlds we wish to live in, and of how our intellectual works can help move us towards them.

hopefully this may happen along the way). It is, rather, driven by a sense of a better world for all that could be ours. It is hence ultimately charged with a moral, political and critical responsibility. It seeks to develop tactics of hope, pedagogies of engagement and practices of experimentalism which sustain sociology as an emancipatory discipline which can increase the spaces in the world for kindness, justice and joy.

In the end, sociology needs to show that human social worlds are ultimately the consequence of our human social actions, even as we lose control over them. And so we had better be careful what these actions are – of how we act in the social world – and remain vigilantly aware of our past and futures. We dwell in the social, living with others of the present, alongside the dead and the about to be born. Like it or not, we are always haunted by the social whilst we shape the social world to come. The challenge for sociology is not just to understand the world but to change it.

SUMMARY

Sociology lives in human social worlds, studies them and has to take very seriously the values and politics that help shape them into the future. It can never be easily value-free. The chapter looked at some of the social roles that sociologists can perform – researcher, thinker, critic, educator, dialogist, enhancer of art and creativity, critical citizen and facilitator of unheard voices being heard. Sociology should be grounded in the people it serves, and Figure 8.1 suggests a wheel of sociological life which flows from everyday life to professional, public, practical, policy-oriented and 'pop'ular sociology. The overall goal of sociology is to help us all act as critical citizens in a world we never made but every day help to re-create. It does its work with a firm eye on making the world a better place *for all* in a hugely unequal world where billons are compelled to live damaged and wasted lives. The challenge is on for each generation to leave behind a better understanding and a mandate to act for a more humane, caring, fair and flourishing society for the generations that are to follow.

CODA: SOCIOLOGICAL EYES

We are the thinkers who puzzle and ponder.
Social critics with our eyes on the world.
Scientific artists, passionately objective.
Patchwork quilters with an eye for the queer.
Sympathetic tellers of lives damaged and draining.
Outsiders looking on margins, drowning in hope.
Wounded reformers for a better world to come.
Utopian dreamers disappointedly cheerful.
Thwarted radicals angered in worlds of injustice.
Time travellers in cyborged lands.
Critical citizens with an eye for the future.

EXPLORING FURTHER

MORE THINKING

1   Look at the ideas of Levitas and Wright mentioned in the 'Think On: On Sociology and Utopia' box (pp. 213–4). Consider these ideas of sociological utopias. What are your own ideas of a better world, and can you find instances of them in the existing world?

2   Are the values discussed in this chapter the values you hold? If not, what values do you hold? Examine how values might impinge upon sociological analysis.

3   How might your own life connect practically to the 'social roles of the sociologist' and 'the circle of sociological life'? Think what it might mean to be a good, critical, sociological citizen and the sociological research agenda it generates.

FURTHER READING

Look at some of the personal accounts of what it means to be or become a sociologist. See: Katherine Twamley *et al.* (eds.), *Sociologists' Tales: Contemporary Narratives on Sociological Thought and Practice* (2015); Peter Berger, *Adventures of an Accidental Sociologist* (2011); John Akomfrah's DVD on Stuart Hall's life, *The Stuart Hall Project* (2014); and Alan Sica and Stephen Turner, *The Disobedient Generation: Social Theorists in the Sixties* (2005), which contains essays by established sociologists on their politics in their student days. Alan Wolfe's *Marginalized in the Middle* (1998) debates the problems from a liberal sociologist's viewpoint, and Chandra Talpade Mohanty's *Feminism Without Borders: Decolonizing Theory, Practicing Solidarity* (2003) provides a rallying cry for radical change. See also contemporary blogs and websites by sociologists; starting examples might be Raewyn Connell, Saskia Sassen, Sudhir Venkatesh, Michael Burawoy, Frank Furedi and Amitai Etzioni. On the impact of various sociologists, see Oyvind Ihlen *et al.*, *Social Theory for Public Relations: Key Figures and Concepts* (2009). The contemporary debate on public sociology was re-invigorated by Michael Burawoy's 'For Public Sociology' (2005), which has generated many discussions, including Dan Clawson *et al.*, *Public Sociology: Fifteen Eminent Sociologists Debate Politics and the Profession in the Twenty-First Century* (2007). On utopias, hope and a better world, see Ernst Bloch, *The Principle of Hope* (1938–47/1986); Erik Olin Wright, *Envisioning Real Utopias* (2010); and Ruth Levitas, *Utopia as Method* (2013). On social imaginaries, see Charles Taylor, *Modern Social Imaginaries* (2003). The writing on values is truly vast. For starters, I recommend Zygmunt Bauman, *Postmodern Ethics* (1993); Iris Marion Young, *Justice and the Politics of Difference* (1990); Andrew Sayer, *Why Things Matter to People: Social Science, Values and Ethical Life* (2011); Nira Yuval-Davis, *The Politics of Belonging* (2011); and Roberto Mangabeira Unger, *The Self Awakened: Pragmatism Unbound* (2007). On people who lead exceptionally 'good' lives, see Larissa MacFarquhar, *Strangers Drowning* (2015).

CONCLUSION

THE SOCIOLOGICAL IMAGINATION: TWENTY-ONE THESES

Caution! Danger! Beware! Sociology will change your life.
Opening slide to Ken Plummer's introductory first-year
lecture at Essex University, 1987–2004

Sociology is passionate about the social. It brings a distinctive consciousness and an imagination to think outside of that limiting frame whereby everything can be explained through 'individuals' or the 'natural'. Sociology questions the 'certain blindness' of human beings' which takes the world for granted. Everywhere, it looks at the hauntings of social life. Here, as summary and challenge, are twenty-one of its key features to argue about.

1   Sociology is the systematic, sceptical and critical study of the social, investigating the characteristics, construction and consequences of human social worlds.
2   Sociology was born of radical social change and continues to dwell in major social change. Sociologists study this perpetual emergence and change.
3   Sociology brings a way of thinking – an imagination, a form of consciousness – that can/will change your life. It defamiliarizes the familiar, questions the taken for granted, and destroys the myths we choose to live by.

4 For sociologists, the air we breathe is social. We can't stop 'experiencing the social' and seeing 'the social' everywhere.

5 'The social' captures the contrasting ideas that (a) we live with others 'doing things together' at the same time as (b) we live with a distinctive reality that exists independently to constrain and coerce us in our everyday life.

6 Sociologists search for the patterns, prisons and predictabilities in human social life, creating the social structures and institutions in which we dwell.

7 Sociologists search for the patterns of meaning as humans acting in social worlds with others, creating culture and complex symbolizations to make sense of their lives and their worlds.

8 Sociologists search to grasp the contradictions between constraining structures and creative meanings: sociology sees this action/structure tension everywhere, working to find new ways of bridging the micro world with the macro world.

9 Human beings weave webs of cultures – ways of living which are composed of complex, multilayered, negotiable and ever-emergent symbolic actions. Cultures are never tight, fixed or agreed upon but are multilayered 'mosaics of social worlds'.

10 Human beings live in the brute reality of material worlds (their environments, economies, bodies) which render them vulnerable.

11 We are both animals and cultural creatures (intrinsically dual) living simultaneously in material and symbolic worlds. We are 'the little gods who shit'.

12 All social worlds are stuffed full of differences, 'incorrigibly plural', and we dwell with the tensions that arise from this. Everything in social life, including sociological thinking, brings its conflicts and contradictions.

13 Human differences are embedded in a deep swirling matrix of inequalities. Human capabilities are structured through divisive processes into structured inequalities which have damaging effects on our lives. Our opportunities for human flourishing can be thwarted by our class, gender, ethnicity, age, health, sexuality and nationhood.

14 Social life is contingent and always shaped in diverse, often unpredictable, ways by history and time, geography and space, situations and relations.

15 Social life is structured by power relations: we ask who and what can shape our lives.

16 Sociologists describe, understand and explain the social world using the best methods they can muster. Straddling art, science and history, they think hard, conduct rigorous empirical research and skillfully and critically make sense of data.

17 Digitalism is radically reforming this sociological project as it provides new tools for research, new sources of data and even new ways of thinking about social life.

18 All of social life is dialogical, not monological. Human beings are narrators and are in a constant round of telling tales of lives and societies to each other. And all knowledge, whatever else it may be, works within this social dialogue: it is always local, contested, relational knowledge.

19 Sociologists are researchers, thinkers, critics, educators, dialogists, enhancers of art and creativity, critical citizens and facilitators of unheard voices being heard. Above all, sociology fosters critical citizens who are alive and changing their own social worlds. They dwell in a flowing circle of sociological life.

20 Sociology lives in a world of values and takes such values seriously, investigating them and becoming aware of their ubiquitous use.

21 Sociology can bring hope of a better world for all. It brings tools to help us assemble future imaginaries of better worlds, study experimental actions to empower new social worlds and act as critical citizens. The challenge is on for each generation to leave behind a better place for subsequent generations.

APPENDIX

EPIGRAMMATIC SOCIOLOGY

Here are ten little sayings that thinkers about society have bequeathed us. These are just for starters. You can find many more on the website for the book. They are worth puzzling a little.

1 Dare to think. (Immanuel Kant's Enlightenment challenge, 1784.)

2 How is society possible? (A disturbing little question posed by Georg Simmel in an essay with that title, 1910.)

3 Man was born free, but everywhere he is in chains. (Jean-Jacques Rousseau's challenge in *The Social Contract*, 1762.)

4 Society is a contract, a partnership between those who are living, those who are dead and those who are to be born. (Edmund Burke's conservative attack on the French Revolution in *Reflections on the Revolution in France* (a bestseller in 1790; Oxford edition, 1993).)

5 Things are not what they seem. (Peter Berger, *Invitation to Sociology*, 1966.)

6 Things are what they seem. (Zen saying.)

7 The sociologist is a destroyer of myths. (Norbert Elias, *What Is Sociology?*, 1978.)

8 Defamiliarize the familiar. (Zygmunt Bauman and Tim May, *Thinking Sociologically*, 2001, second edition.)
9 Treat social facts as things. (Émile Durkheim, *The Rules of Sociological Method*, 1982.)
10 Consciousness does not determine life, but life determines consciousness. (Karl Marx, *The German Ideology*, 1846.)

GLOSSARY

All disciplines – from photography to physics – develop their own languages to help us see the world more clearly. In sociology you will find many dictionaries, encyclopaedias, websites and glossaries. Good examples are John Scott's compact *Oxford Dictionary of Sociology* (2014, fourth edition) and George Ritzer and J. Michael Ryan's large *Concise Encyclopaedia of Sociology* (2010). John Scott's series of books – *Sociology: The Key Concepts* (2006) and *Fifty Key Sociologists* (2007) – are worth a good look too. A glossary website can be found at www.qualityresearchinternational.com/glossary.

Below is a short 'starter' list of some key words found in this book. They are in bold in the text. The brackets indicate pages in this book where the words are raised; an author is sometimes named where more details will be found in the references.

anomie: normlessness; lack of norms or normative breakdown (more technically, a tension between cultural goals and social structures) (pp. 35, 105; Durkheim, 1984).

Big Data: the massive volume of 'messy' data consisting of billions/trillions of records generated by digital worlds (p. 166; Mayer-Schönberger, 2013).

capabilities: potentials for functioning and flourishing in various areas of life such as health, bodily integrity and thought (pp. 207–210; Nussbaum, 2011; Deneulin and Shahani, 2009).

capitalism: diverse economic systems, all of which stress private ownership, profit and usually competition (pp. 64–69; Fulcher, 2015; Harvey, 2015).

carbon economy: an economy which uses carbon intensively and extensively, creating pollution and global warming. Contrasts with a low-carbon economy (p. 74; Urry, 2011).

caste: stratification system based on inherited status (pp. 186–7; Jodhka, 2012).

Chicago sociology: first major school of US sociology (1915–1935) with a focus on the city and its problems (not to be confused with the Chicago school of neo-liberal economics) (pp. 106–7; Plummer, 2001).

citizenship: formal status as recognized member of a particular social group, such as a nation or state, which usually brings both rights and responsibilities (pp. 90, 221, 230; Marshall 1950).

class: stratification based on a hierarchy of economic and social positions. It is usually seen as having an objective side (economic) and a subjective side (class consciousness) and brings the potential for conflict (p. 104; Chapter 7; Marx, 2000; Weber, 1978).

colonialism: a situation where one country exerts direct political control of another, usually exploiting it economically and culturally (p. 117; Said, 2003; Young, 2003).

commons: cultural and natural resources available to all members of a society (p. 74; Bollier, 2014).

comparative method: used in many ways across different disciplines but always involves a contrast between social things, such as comparing different cultures, case studies, histories or economies (p. 173).

cosmopolitanism: accepting of differences; tolerance; showing common humanity (pp. 86–7; Fine, 2007).

critical theory: knowledge masks interests behind it, and critical theory unmasks these interests (p. 108; Benjamin & Horkheimer).

culture: the ideas, customs and ways of life of a group, including language and values (pp. 42–7; 132–5; Williams, 1989).

deductive method: conclusions are made logically from testing general hypotheses (top-down logic); see also inductive method (pp. 161–2).

diachronic: analyzes phenomena in terms of their development over time; contrasts with synchronic (p. 149).

dialectical: process of oppositional forces creating new forms (p. 148).

dialogue/dialogic: a recognition of multiple voices, not a single united one (pp. 219–20; Bakhtin, 1982).

diaspora: the movement and dispersals of people around the world, as in migration or the slave trade (pp. 86, 197).

differences: qualities that make one thing or person unlike another; it suggests diversities of relationships and connectedness (Chapters 2, 5 and 7; Young, 1990).

digitalism/digitization: the social process through which much of social life becomes organized through the new information technologies. Digitization refers to the process by which electrical signals in the traditional analogue system get converted to digital (pp. 70–73; 163–7; Lupton, 2015).

discourse: written or spoken communications (and often the power relations contained) that circulate in a culture (p. 41; Foucault, 1991).

dramaturgy: society analyzed as if it was a theatre and viewed through its theatrical properties (pp. 34, 135; Goffman, 1956).

embodiment: social processes that give the body meaning (p. 29; Turner, 2012).

empirical/empiricism: based on evidence and experience, not theory or speculation (pp. 123–4, 160).

Enlightenment: major seventeenth–eighteenth century movement of thought based on belief in rationality, progress, individualism and critique of main religions, monarchy and traditions (pp. 57, 98–100).

epistemology: branch of philosophy that deals with what is knowledge and truth (pp. 154, 155; Delanty & Strydom, 2003).

ethnicity: people sharing common histories, language, beliefs and lives based on common national or cultural tradition that often give them a common identity (p. 199; Fenton, 2003).

ethnocentrism: judging cultures through the eyes and prejudices of your own culture (pp. 4, 52).

ethnography: research tool that involves describing a culture and its ways of life very closely (p. 134).

ethnomethodology: Harold Garfinkel's term for the study of the ways and logics in which people make sense of everyday life (pp. 3, 34; Garfinkel, 1967).

feminism: diverse positions which are in opposition to sexism and patriarchy and usually advocate equality of sexes (pp. 114–6; Collins, 1990; Delamont, 2003; Lengermann and Niebrugge-Brantley, 1998).

financialization: processes where money and financial services become major features of the economy (p. 68; Haiven, 2014).

function: the intended and unintended consequences of any social thing or pattern for the operation of society. Functions can be negative, positive or neutral. (pp. 29, 36; Swingewood, 2000).

functionalism: examines social life and institutions in terms of their consequences and purposes. Some are direct and manifest; many are hidden or latent. It usually highlights solidarity and integration. Some consequences may be dysfunctional. Updated, it is often called neo-functionalism (pp. 36–7, 108; Parsons, 1951; Merton, 1949).

fundamentalism: conservative doctrine opposing the modern world in favour of a traditionalism based on absolute authority; usually religious (pp. 79, 87; Bruce, 2007).

Gemeinschaft: a social organization with strong social ties (and weak self interest); see also Gesellschaft (p. 103; Tönnies, 2003; De-lanty, 2005).

gender: the learnt social aspects of differences and hierarchies between men, women and others like transgenders. Gender is learnt and social, not biological (pp. 193, 199).

Gesellschaft: contrasts with Gemeinschaft; here bonds are weaker and self-interest greater (p. 103; Tönnies, 2003).

globalization: processes through which the world's countries interconnect: economically, culturally and interpersonally. Time and space reorganized (pp. 58–60; Beck, 2000; Pieterse, 2015).

glocalization: processes through which the local connects to the global (pp. 59–60; Pieterse, 2015).

habits: social behaviour that is regularly enacted and taken for granted by individuals over a prolonged period of time. A term introduced by William James; a precursor of habitus (pp. 124–6).

habitus: the habits we acquire in social life and that we carry around with us, 'transposable and durable dispositions through which people perceive, think, appreciate, act and judge in the world' (pp. 125–30; Bourdieu, 1984).

hegemony: the ability of a dominant (class) group to win over a subordinate (mass) group to their ideas and values (p. 145; Gramsci, 1998).

hermeneutics: philosophical perspective which inspects the ways in which the world is interpreted; highlights understanding and interpretation (p. 174; Ricoeur, 1981).

heteronormativity: the privileging of heterosexual relations (pp. 117, 196; Sullivan, 2003; Weeks, 2009).

homophobia: fear of same-sex relationships (pp. 117, 196; Sullivan, 2003; Weeks, 2009).

hybrid: the mixing of phenomena once seen as separate; old elements are merged into a mélange with new ones and increase diversity (p. 86).

ideal type: extracting key, abstract features (not perfect ones) from phenomena to enable comparisons with real-life examples (pp. 52, 173; Weber, 1978).

idealism: contrasts with materialism, and ultimately locates reality in mind and ideas (p. 136).

identity: the recognition of who one is and how one is recognized by others (pp. 42, 80; Mead, 1967).

inductive method: conclusions are drawn from observation and experience (bottom-up logic); see also deductive method (p. 162).

inequalities: an unfair situation whereby some people have more wealth, status, education, or power than other people (p. 3; Chapters 1, 3 and 7).

institutions: established social patterns, habits, organizations and norms clustered around specific functions in society (e.g. economy, family) (pp. 37, 125).

interpretivism: understanding of behaviour that includes the meaning of people (p. 155).

intersectionality: highlights criss-crossing connectedness of systems of oppression, discrimination and inequality such as class, gender, ethnicity, sexuality and nation-state (pp. 189–98; Yuval-Davis, 2011).

inter-subjectivity: a condition which allows people to share meanings and understandings; links to empathy, sympathy, dialogue, role-taking and self (pp. 24, 128).

macro-sociology: looks at whole societies, often comparing features of social structures (or stable patterns) and key social institutions (or organized habits) like the economy or education (Chapter 2; pp. 26–7).

materialism: the philosophy that claims that all aspects of human life flow from matter (as opposed to ideas) (pp. 135–137).

mediatization: the ways everyday social relationships, interactions and cultures become embedded in and shaped by technologically based media, both for individual use (e.g. mobile phones, social networking websites) and mass consumption (e.g. radio, television) (pp. 69–70; Hjarvard, 2013).

meso-sociology: looks at the patterns that connect micro and macro structures – the interactions in organizations like workplaces, schools or hospitals (Chapter 2; pp. 26–7).

methodology: general approach to studying how we do research (p. 123; Chapter 6).

micro-sociology: looks at social actions, face-to-face interactions and contexts, examining how people make sense of the worlds they live in (Chapter 2; pp. 26–7).

mode of production: Marxist term for a specific form and organization of material production, which involves both the forces of production (such as tools and machinery) and the relations of production (such as serf/peasant or capitalist) (p. 104).

modernity: stage of society development in the West from the Enlightenment/eighteenth century to at least the end of the twentieth century (pp. 57–59).

multiculturalism: recognition of cultural pluralism and the mixing of different cultures in a society, often ethnic (pp. 87, 114; Taylor, 1994).

multi-paradigm: the existence of many different schools and traditions of thought (pp. 111, 118, 215).

multiple modernities: the rejection of just one route or kind of modernity and the argument that there are a multiplicity of pathways into the creation of 'modernities' along with multiple futures (pp. 58–59; Eisenstadt, 2000).

narrative: a basic way of apprehending the word, usually connected to the stories we tell of our lives (pp. 42, 170; Plummer, 2001).

nation: group of people sharing the same culture; nation-state is a political unit (pp. 84–5, 199; Smith, 2009).

neo-liberalism: term which has come to be used to designate 'new right' policies and politics based on the market philosophy of Friedrich von Hayek; not to be confused with liberalism itself, which can often be radical and critical (pp. 64–9; Harvey, 2007).

norms: shared expectations of behaviour (pp. 35, 228).

ontology: a philosophical perspective on the nature of social reality; it tells us how the world is made up, what human nature is like and what the nature of things is (pp. 154, 207; Delanty, 2005).

paradigm: an established pattern of concepts and theories; a standard way of thinking (p. 154; Kuhn, 1962/2012).

patriarchy: traditionally, the rule of the father. Nowadays, a term that highlights the organization of male power (p. 191).

perspective: a specific point of view of the social world (p. 171).

pluralism: can mean two, but usually means multiple sources rather than one (p. 58).

positivism: philosophy of science which stresses logical or empirical proof (pp. 105, 155; Delanty, 2005).

post-colonialism: positions that recognize that many cultures have been built out of oppressors who have shaped the worlds and realities of those colonized (pp. 116–7; Young, 2003).

postmodernism: death of any one grand or absolute truth and the recognition of multiplicities. It can be found in discussions of types of society, social theory and methodology (pp. 87, 114; Seidman, 2012).

power: ability to achieve one's own aims against opposition (pp. 38, 144–6; Lukes, 2004).

practical reason: the everyday ability of people to make sense of their world, make themselves understood and carry out daily projects (p. 209; Bourdieu, 1990).

practices: simply, everyday habitual routines; more complexly, the ideas that bridge actions, habitus and structuration (p. 130; Bourdieu, 1990).

precariat: a class of people who experience insecurity and precarity in their lives, usually through their poor and unstable work situations (pp. 68, 72, 192; Standing, 2011, 2015).

prosumer: indicates activity when the line between consumer and producer weakens (p. 72).

public sociology: sociology which is made more relevant and accessible to the wider population outside professional sociology (p. 222; Burawoy, 2005).

queer: a questioning of all standard (usually binary) sexual and gender categories; a transgressive view of sexualities and its study (pp. 33, 117).

racial formation: linkage between racial structures and economies and meanings and cultures (p. 191; Omi & Winant, 1994).

racialization: process of ranking people on the basis of their presumed race (p. 194; Back and Solomos, 2007).

racism: ordering human life into hierarchies that bestow one ethnic majority (usually white) superiority over another (pp. 39, 71, 190, 227).

rational choice theory: highlights the ways in which people are rational beings who make calculations about the costs and benefits of alternative actions; the social is rational and self-interested (pp. 45–46; Goldthorpe, 2000; Elster, 2015).

realism: epistemology which stresses that social phenomena have an existence beyond the lives of individuals (pp. 136, 155; Delanty and Strydom, 2003).

reflexivity: reflecting on one's own actions and knowledge (p. 154).

risk society: society where global technological changes are shown to have unforeseen consequences that we cannot easily predict (p. 75; Beck, 1986, 1992).

role theory: examines the expectations, rights, duties amd norms that a person has to face and fulfill (pp. 24–5, 34).

self: in common sense terms, this often means a person's being; in sociology, it always implies others. The self is constituted through the way we see ourselves and how others see us (pp. 24–8; Cooley, 1998; Mead, 1967).

semiotics: study of signs and symbols (pp. 26, 135).

social action: social theories which highlight how people orientate their conduct to the subjective meanings of others (pp. 128–33; Stones, 2016).

social capital: friendships, networks and connections over time which create links and bonds; they often shape the quality of a life (p. 36; Field, 2008).

social constructionism: theory which suggests that the social is made by human actors giving meaning to the world (p. 34; Berger and Luckmann, 1967).

social facts: phenomena external to the individual but which act to constrain the person (pp. 2, 23; Durkheim, 1982).

social forms: underlying patterns and principles through which social life and social relations are organized (pp. 23, 125; Simmel, 1971/1908).

social imaginaries: the ways people imagine their existence together; expectations and meanings that guide daily life. (pp. 89, 230; Lemert, 2003)

social structure: highlights recurrent, patterned and stable institutions and relationships that endure to form the framework of a society (Chapters 2 and 5).

socialization: multiple processes across the life cycle through which people acquire social competence (pp. 24–8).

society: a group of people who share a common culture and usually interact in a defined territory (pp. 21, 23; Elliott & Turner, 2012).

standpoint: an epistemological position which examines the social conditions (often of oppression) which generate a version of truth grounded in a social position (like gender or race) (pp. 155, 170–1; Collins, 1990; Harding, 1986, 1998).

state: organized political community living under a single system of government that holds the monopoly of force (pp. 84–5; Weber, 2001).

structuralism: derived from linguistics and anthropology, it highlights deep and abiding forms that organize the elements of a society beneath the surface flux (p. 33).

structuration: process by which social structures are reproduced in social actions (pp. 130–2; Giddens, 1986).

subaltern: subordinate and outside the power structure; often used in debates on post-colonialism (pp. 117, 197, 218).

subjectivities: The inner world of people (as opposed to the external world) which connects meanings, attitudes, the unconscious, emotions, bodies, self and identities (Chapters 1 and 5, pp. 128–30).

sustainable development: development that meets the needs of the present without compromising the ability of future generations to meet their own needs (pp. 74, 92).

symbolic interaction: theory which studies how meanings emerge through interaction with others. Human life is to be studied through close field work. Core idea is the self (p. 25; Mead, 1967; Plummer in Stones, 2008).

synchronic: analyzes phenomena at one point in time; contrasts with diachronic (p. 149).

theory: abstract reasoning, logic and speculation, often guided by metaphor and turned into hypotheses and principles for empirical examination (Chapter 2; pp. 123–4).

triangulation: the bringing of many methods, theories and perspectives to one theme or concern (p. 163).

Verstehen: German for 'understanding', a key feature of Max Weber's sociology and interpreting meaning (pp. 134–5; Weber, 1978).

WEBLIOGRAPHY: A SHORT GUIDE TO WEBSITES

Going on line is now an essential part of sociology, and some opening guidelines for doing this have been provided in the book (see pp. 87–89. Monitoring the World; p. 184. The Facts of Inequalities). There is also a website attached to this book and you can find much more there.

CHECK IT OUT AT: kenplummer.com/sociology/
Here is a small selection of key websites

1. SOCIOLOGICAL ORGANISATIONS
Look at the websites of some key sociological associations like:

British Sociological Association (BSA) http://www.britsoc.co.uk
American Sociological Association (ASA) http://www.asanet.org
European Sociological Association (ESA) http://www.europeansociology.org
International Sociological Association (ISA) http://www.isasociology.org

These sites have sections that can assist students.

2. READING SOCIOLOGY ON LINE

Read on line some key new material written by sociologists

Discover Society

http://discoversociety.org/

Started published in 2013 this is a very lively monthly, magazine style blog for sociologists. Along with 'articles', it covers the most up to date public issues through columns like 'Viewpoints', and 'On the Frontline' alongside 'Policy Briefings'. A good read.

Contexts: Understanding people in their social worlds

http://contexts.org/

Published quarterly with Vol 15 in 2016, this magazine and blog from the American Sociological Association aims to make sociology more publicly accessible. It has discussions of the pressing issues of the day, examines social trends, and features key sociological debates. Another 'good read'.

Sociology Research On Line

http://www.socresonline.org.uk/

This is a pioneering UK-based website (Volume 20 in 2015). There are original articles that can be read online, as well as special features and editions, which try to generate sociological responses to immediate world events. For the advanced sociology student this is really worth visiting.

Sociology Review

http://www.philipallan.co.uk/sociologyreview/index.htm

Meant for school students and the 25th volume was still being published in 2016.

Contemporary Sociology

http://www.jstor.org/journals/00943061.html

This is a journal of book reviews published by the American Sociological Association.

3. BLOGS

There are remarkably few really good sociological blogs and they often have short lives. At the time of writing, these few were pretty good. They tend to highlight special interests.

This Sociological Life
https://simplysociology.wordpress.com/2012/05/
Deborah Lupton's page with a focus on digitalism, medicine, risk, parenting and bodies.

Everyday Sociology Blog
http://www.everydaysociologyblog.com

Cranky Sociologists
http://thecrankysociologists.com/

Political and Public sociology
http://averypublicsociologist.blogspot.co.uk/

The Society Pages
http://thesocietypages.org/

See also: Sociologists Without Borders
http://www.sociologistswithoutborders.org/

You can find further select lists in Deborah Lupton *Digital Sociology* pp. 218–219.

FILMOGRAPHY: A SHORT GUIDE TO SOCIOLOGY AND FILM

We live in a mediated world saturated with film and video; and most films suggest ideas about the society we live in. Films provide a good resource for sociology. Look at Jean-Anne Sutherland & Kathryn Feltey *Cinematic Sociology: Social Life in Film* (2nd ed, 2012) Pine Forge Press, which shows how to use contemporary films to develop the sociological imagination and provides an excellent filmography by theme.

Below is a list/index of films mentioned in this book.

There is a listing of others on the book's website at
http://kenplummer.com/sociology/

Amazing Grace (2006) dir Michael Apted, p. 187
http://www.imdb.com/title/tt0454776/

Amisted (1997) dir Stephen Spielberg, p. 187
http://www.imdb.com/title/tt0118607/

Capturing the Friedmans (2003) dir Andrew Jarecki, p. 224
http://www.imdb.com/title/tt0342172/

City of God (2002) dir Fernando Meirelles, Katia Lund, p. 63
http://www.imdb.com/title/tt0317248/

The Fourth World (2011) dir Mark Volkers, p. 63
http://www.imdb.com/title/tt2211047/?ref_=fn_al_tt_1

Groundhog Day (1993) dir Harold Ramis, p. 126
http://www.imdb.com/title/tt0118607/

Life in a Day (2011) dir Ken McDonald
http://www.imdb.com/title/tt1687247/

Love Actually (2011) dir Richard Curtis, p. 11
http://www.imdb.com/title/tt0314331/

The Lives of Others (2006) dir Florian Henckel von Donnersmarck,
p. 77
http://www.imdb.com/title/tt0405094/

Metropolis (1927) Fritz Lang, p. 44
http://www.imdb.com/title/tt0017136/

Modern Times (1936) dir Charles Chaplin, p. 44
http://www.imdb.com/title/tt0027977/

Q2P (2006) dir Paromita Vohra, p. 16
https://www.youtube.com/watch?v=hsJh_BamKgo
http://www.oberlin.edu/stupub/ocreview/2007/11/09/arts/Vohras_
Q2P_Film_Explores_S.html

Rashomon (1950) dir Akira Kurosawa p. 170
http://www.imdb.com/title/tt0042876/?ref_=fn_al_tt_1

The Salt of the Earth (Sebastião Salgado) (2014) dir Wim Wenders
p. 188
http://www.imdb.com/title/tt3674140/

Sliding Doors (1998) dir Peter Howitt, p. 139
http://www.imdb.com/title/tt0120148/?ref_=fn_al_tt_1

Slumdog Millionaire (2008) dir Danny Boyle, p. 63
http://www.imdb.com/title/tt0120148/?ref_=fn_al_tt_1

Stranger than Fiction (2006) dir Marc Foster, p. 125
http://www.imdb.com/title/tt0420223/

The Truman Show (1998) dir Peter Weir p. 77
http://www.imdb.com/title/tt0120382/

Where to Invade Next (2015) dir Michael Moore, p. 224
http://www.imdb.com/title/tt4897822/

12 Years a Slave (2011) dir Steve McQueen p. 187
ttp://www.imdb.com/title/tt2024544/?ref_=nv_sr_1

BIBLIOGRAPHY: READING AND REFERENCES

Adam, B. (2004) *Time*, Cambridge: Polity.

Agamben, G. (1995/1998) *Homo Sacer: Sovereign Power and Bare Life*, Palo Alto, CA: Stanford University Press.

Agger, B. (2015, 2nd ed.) *Oversharing: Presentations of Self in the Internet Age*. Abingdon, Oxford: Routledge

Agger, B. (2004) *The Virtual Self*, Oxford: Blackwell.

Albrow, M. (1996) *The Global Age,* Cambridge: Polity.

Alexander, J. C. (2006) *The Civil Sphere*, Oxford: Oxford University Press.

Alexander, J. C. (2012) *Trauma as Social Theory,* Cambridge: Polity.

Alexander, J. C. (2013) *The Dark Side of Modernity*, Cambridge: Polity.

Althusser, L. (2008) *On Ideology*, London: Verso.

Anderson, B. (1983) *Imagined Communities,* London: Verso.

Anderson, E. (1999) *Code of the Street: Decency, Violence and the Moral Life of the Inner City*, New York: Norton.

Arendt, H. (1958) *The Human Condition*, Chicago: University of Chicago Press.

Atkinson, A. B. (2015) *Inequality: What Can Be Done?*, Cambridge, MA: Harvard University Press.

Atkinson, W. (2015) *Class*, Cambridge: Polity.

Atwan, A. B. (2015) *Islamic State: The Digital Caliphate,* London: Saqi.

Babbie, E. (2005, 14th ed.) *The Practice of Social Research*, Belmont, CA: Wadsworth.

Back, L. (2007) *The Art of Listening*, Oxford: Berg.

Back, L., & Solomos, J. (Eds.) (2007) *Theories of Race and Racism: A Reader*, London: Routledge.

Back, L., & Puwar, N. (2013) 'Live Sociology', *Sociological Review*, 60: 18–39.

Bakhtin, M. (1982) *The Dialogic Imagination*, Austin: University of Texas Press.

Bales, K. (2012, 3rd ed.) *Disposable People*, Berkeley: University of California.

Ball, K., Lyon, D., & Haggerty, K. (Eds.) (2012) *The Routledge Handbook of Surveillance Studies*, London: Routledge.

Barnes, C. & Mercer G. (2010, 2nd ed.) *Exploring Disability*, Cambridge: Polity.

Baudrillard, J. (1988) *Jean Baudrillard: Selected Writings,* Cambridge: Polity.

Bauman, Z. (1991) *Modernity and the Holocaust*, Cambridge: Polity.

Bauman, Z. (1993) *Postmodern Ethics*, Oxford: Blackwell.

Bauman, Z. (1998) *Globalization: The Human Consequences*, Cambridge: Polity.

Bauman, Z. (2000) *Liquid Modernity*, Cambridge: Polity.

Bauman, Z. (2003) *Liquid Love*, Cambridge: Polity.

Bauman, Z. (2004) *Wasted Lives: Modernity and Its Outcasts*, Cambridge: Polity.

Bauman, Z. (2005) *Liquid Life*, Cambridge: Polity.

Bauman, Z. (2006) *Liquid Fear*, Cambridge: Polity.

Bauman, Z. (2007) *Liquid Times*, Cambridge: Polity.

Bauman, Z., & May, T. (2001, 2nd ed.) *Thinking Sociologically*, Oxford: Wiley Blackwell.

Bauman, Z., & Lyon, D. (2012) *Liquid Surveillance*, Cambridge: Polity.

Baym, N. K. (2015, 2nd ed.) *Personal Connections in the Digital Age*, Cambridge: Polity.

Beck, U. (1986/1992) *Risk Society*, London: Sage.

Beck, U. (2000) *What Is Globalization?*, Cambridge: Polity.

Beck, U. (2006) *Cosmopolitan Vision*, Cambridge: Polity.

Beck, U. (2008/2010) *A God of One's Own: Religion's Capacity for Peace and Potential for Violence*, Cambridge: Polity.

Beck, U. (2009) *World at Risk*, Cambridge: Polity.

Beck, U., & Beck-Gernsheim, E. (2002) *Individualization*, London: Sage.

Beck, U., & Beck-Gernsheim, E. (2013) *Distant Love: Personal Life in the Global Age*, Cambridge: Polity.

Becker, H. S. (1998) *Tricks of the Trade: How to Think About Your Research While You're Doing It*, Chicago: University of Chicago Press.

Becker, H. S. (2007) *Telling About Society*, Chicago: University of Chicago Press.

Becker, H. S. (2014) *What About Mozart? What About Murder? Reasoning from Cases*, Chicago: University of Chicago Press.

Bell, D. (2006) *Cyberculture Theorists*, London: Routledge.

Bellah, R. N., Madsen, R., Sullivan, W., Swidler, A., & Tipton, S. M. (2007, 3rd ed. [1985]) *Habits of the Heart: Individualism and Commitment in American Life*, Berkeley: University of California Press.

Bennett, T., Savage, M., Silva, E., Warde, A., Gayo-Cal, M., & Wright, D. (2009) *Culture, Class, Distinction*, London: Routledge.

Berger, P. (1966) *Invitation to Sociology*, Harmondsworth: Penguin.

Berger, P. (2011) *Adventures of an Accidental Sociologist: How to Explain the World Without Becoming a Bore*, New York: Prometheus Books.

Berger, P., & Luckmann, T. (1967/1990, 2nd ed.) *The Social Construction of Reality*, Harmondsworth: Penguin.

Bessel, R. (2015) *Violence: A Modern Obsession*, New York: Simon and Schuster.

Best, J. (2012, updated ed.) *Damned Lies and Statistics,* Berkeley: University of California Press.

Best, S. (2002) *A Beginner's Guide to Social Theory*, London: Sage.

Bhambra, G. K. (2007) *Rethinking Modernity: Postcolonialism and the Sociological Imagination*, Basingstoke: Palgrave Macmillan.

Bloch, E. (1938–47/1986) *The Principle of Hope*, three vols., Boston: MIT Press.

Blumenthal, D. (2014) *Little Vast Rooms of Undoing: Exploring Identity and Embodiment in Public Toilet Spaces*, Lanham, MD: Rowman & Littlefield.

Boellstorff, T. (2013) 'Making Big Data, in Theory', *First Monday,* 18 (10).

Bollier, D. (2014) *Think Like a Commoner: A Short Introduction to the Life of the Commons*, Gabriola Island, BC: New Society Publishers.

Booth, C. (2009) *Life and Labour of the People in London*, London: Bibliolife.

Bottero, W. (2005) *Stratification: Social Division and Inequality*, London: Routledge.

Bourdieu, P. (1990) *In Other Words: Essays Towards a Reflexive Sociology*, Cambridge: Polity.

Bourdieu, P. (1999 [1993]) *The Weight of the World: Social Suffering in Contemporary Society*, Cambridge: Polity.

Bourdieu, P. (2010 [1984]) *Distinction*, London: Routledge Classics.

Braidotti, R. (2013) *The Posthuman*, Cambridge: Polity.

Brewer, J.D. (2010) *Peace Processes: A Sociological Approach*, Cambridge: Polity.

Bristow, J. (2015) *Baby Boomers and Generational Conflict*, Basingstoke: Palgrave.

Brown, W. (2015) *Undoing the Demos: Neoliberalism's Stealth Revolution*, New York: Zone Books.

Bruce, S. (2007, 2nd ed.) *Fundamentalism*, Cambridge: Polity.

Bryman, A. (2004) *The Disneyization of Society*, London: Sage.

Bryman, A. (2015, 5th ed.) *Social Research Methods*, Oxford: Oxford University Press.

Burawoy, M. (2005) 'For Public Sociology', *American Sociological Review*, 70: 4–28.

Burke, E. (1993 [1790]) *Reflections on the Revolution in France*, Oxford: Oxford University Press.

Burrows, R., & Savage, M. (2014) 'After the Crisis? Big Data and the Methodological Challenges of Empirical Sociology', *Big Data and Society*, 1 (1).

Butler, J. (1990) *Gender Trouble*, London: Routledge.

Butler, J., & Athansaiou, A. (2013) *Dispossession: The Performative in the Political*, Cambridge: Polity.

Calaprice, A. (2005) *The New Quotable Einstein*, Princeton, NJ: Princeton University Press.

Calhoun, C. (Ed.) (2007) *Sociology in America: A History*, Chicago: University of Chicago Press.

Carr, N. (2011) *The Shallows: How the Internet Is Changing the Way We Think, Read and Remember*, London: Atlantic Books.

Carroll, A., & Itaborahy, L. P. (2015) *State-Sponsored Homophobia: A World Survey of Laws*. Retrieved from www.ilga.org

Casson, H. (1910/2015) *The History of the Telephone*. CreateSpace independent publishing platform.

Castells, M. (2002) *The Internet Galaxy*, Oxford: Oxford University Press.

Castells, M. (2009a [1996]) *The Information Age*, Oxford: Blackwell.

Castells, M. (2009b, 2nd ed.) *The Rise of the Network Society*, Oxford: Wiley Blackwell.

Castells, M. (2015, 2nd ed.) *Networks of Outrage and Hope: Social Movements in the Internet Age,* Cambridge: Polity.

Charlesworth, S. J. (1999) *A Phenomenology of Working Class Experience,* Cambridge: Cambridge University Press.

Chodorow, N. (1979) *The Reproduction of Mothering*, Berkeley: University of California Press.

Clarke, A. E. (2005) *Situational Analysis: Grounded Theory After the Postmodern Turn*, London: Sage.

Clawson, D., Zussman, R., Misra, J., Gerstel, N., Stokes, R., Anderton, D., & Burawoy, M. (Eds.) (2007) *Public Sociology: Fifteen Eminent Sociologists Debate Politics and the Profession in the Twenty-First Century*, Berkeley: University of California Press.

Cohen, R., & Kennedy, P. (2013, 3rd ed.) *Global Sociology*, Basingstoke: Palgrave.

Cohen, S. (2001) *States of Denial: Knowing About Atrocities and Sufferings*, Cambridge: Polity.

Collier, P. (2007) *The Bottom Billion*, Oxford: Oxford University Press.

Collins, P. H. (1990) *Black Feminist Thought: Knowledge, Consciousness and the Politics of Empowerment*, New York: Routledge.

Collins, R. (1998) *The Sociology of Philosophies: A Global Theory of Intellectual Change*, Cambridge, MA: Belknap Press of Harvard University Press.

Comte, A. (1824/1988) *System of Positive Politics*, London: Hackett.

Connell, R. (2005, 2nd ed.) *Masculinities*, Cambridge: Polity.

Connell, R. (2007) *Southern Theory: The Global Dynamics of Knowledge in Social Science*, Cambridge: Polity Press.

Cooley, C. H. (1998) *On Self and Social Organization*, H. Schubert (Ed.), Chicago: University of Chicago Press.

Credit Suisse (2015/2016) *Global Wealth Databook*, Zurich: Credit Suisse Research Institute.

Dahl, R. (2005, 2nd ed. [1961]) *Who Governs? Democracy and Power in the American City*, New Haven, CT: Yale University Press.

Dandaneau, S. (2001) *Taking It Big: Developing Sociological Consciousness in Postmodern Times*, Thousand Oaks, CA: Pine Forge Press.

Dartnell, M.Y. (2015) *Insurgency Online: Web Activism and Global Conflict*, Toronto: University of Toronto Press.

Davis, M. (2007) *Planet of Slums*, New York: Verso.

Deaton, A. (2013/2015) *The Great Escape: Health, Wealth and the Origins of Inequality*, Princeton, NJ: Princeton University Press.

De Beauvoir, S. (2009, new ed.) *The Second Sex*, London: Jonathan Cape.

Deegan, M.J. (1990) *Jane Addams and the Men of the Chicago School, 1892–1918*, Piscataway, NJ: Transaction Books.

Defoe, D. (1719/1992) *Robinson Crusoe*, London: Wordsworth Classics.

Delamont, S. (2003) *Feminist Sociology*, London: Sage.

Delanty, G. (2000) *Citizenship in a Global Age,* Milton Keynes: Open University Press.

Delanty, G. (2005) *Social Science: Philosophical and Methodological Foundations*, Milton Keynes: Open University Press.

Delanty, G., & Strydom, P. (2003) *Philosophies of Social Science: The Classic and Contemporary Readings*, Milton Keynes: Open University Press.

Deneulin, S., & Shahani, L. (Eds.) (2009) *An Introduction to the Human Development and Capability Approach*, London: Earthscan.

Denny, E., & Earle, S. (2016, 3rd ed.) *Sociology for Nurses*, Cambridge: Polity.

Denzin, N. (2010) *The Qualitative Manifesto: A Call to Arms*, Walnut Creek, CA: Left Coast Press.

Denzin, N., & Lincoln, Y. (Eds.) (2005, 3rd ed.) *Handbook of Qualitative Research*, London: Sage.

Diamond, J. (2012) *The World Until Yesterday: What Can We Learn from Traditional Societies?*, New York: Penguin/Allen Lane.

Diamond, L. (2012) *Liberation Technology: Social Media and the Struggle for Democracy,* Baltimore, MD: Johns Hopkins University Press.

Dixit, P. & Stump J.L. (Eds.) (2015) *Critical Methods in Terrorism Studies*, Oxford, Routledge.

Dorling, D. (2013) *Population 10 Billion*, London: Constable/Little, Brown.

Dorling, D. (2015, 2nd ed.) *Injustice: Why Social Inequality Still Persists*, Bristol: Policy Press.

Du Bois, W.E.B. (1995, new ed. [1889]) *The Philadelphia Negro*, Philadelphia: University of Pennsylvania Press.

Du Bois, W.E.B. (2007 [1903]) *The Souls of Black Folk*, Oxford: Oxford University Press.

Dunier, M. (1992, 2nd ed.) *Slim's Table: Race, Respectability and Masculinity*, Chicago: University of Chicago Press.

Dunier, M. (1999) *Sidewalk*, New York: Farrar, Straus and Giroux.

Durkheim, E. (1982 [1895]) *The Rules of Sociological Method*, Glencoe, IL: Free Press.

Durkheim, E. (1984 [1893]) *The Division of Labour in Society*, London: Palgrave Macmillan.

Durkheim, E. (2002, 2nd ed. [1897]) *Suicide*, London: Routledge.

Durkheim, E. (2008, student ed. [1912]) *The Elementary Forms of Religious Life*, Oxford: Oxford University Press.

Eco, U. (1977/2015) *How to Write a Thesis*, London: The MIT Press.

Economist (2015, 25th ed.) *Pocket World in Figures*, London: Profile Books.

Ehrenreich, B. (2002) *Nickel and Dimed: Undercover in Low-Wage America*, London: Granta.

Eisenstadt, S. N. (2000) 'Multiple Modernities', *Daedalus*, 129(1): 1–29.

Elias, N. (1978) *What Is Sociology?*, London: Hutchinson.

Elias, N. (2000, 2nd ed. [1939]) *The Civilizing Process*, Oxford: Blackwell.

Eliot, G. (1874/2003) *Middlemarch: A Study of Provincial Life*, Middlesex: Penguin Classics.

Elliott, A. (2013, 3rd ed.) *Concepts of the Self*, Cambridge: Polity.

Elliott, A. (2014, 2nd ed.) *Contemporary Social Theory*, Oxford: Routledge.

Elliott, A. & Lemert C. (2006, 2nd ed., 2009) *The New Individualism: The Emotional Costs of Globalization*, London: Routledge.

Elliott, A., & Turner, B. S. (2012) *On Society*, Cambridge: Polity.

Elster, J. (2015, 2nd ed.) *Explaining Social Behaviour*, Cambridge: Cambridge University Press.

Etzioni, A. (2001) *The Monochrome Society*, Princeton, NJ: Princeton University Press.

Evans, D. (1993) *Sexual Citizenship*, London: Routledge.

Evans, M. (2006) *A Short History of Society*, Maidenhead: Open University Press.

Fenton, S. (2003) *Ethnicity*, Cambridge: Polity.

Fevre, R., & Bancroft, A. (2010) *Dead White Men and Other Important People: Sociology's Big Ideas*, Hampshire: Palgrave.

Field, J. (2008, 2nd ed.) *Social Capital*, London: Routledge.

Fine, R. (2007) *Cosmopolitanism*, London: Routledge.

Foster, R.J. (2008) *Coca-Globalization: Following Soft Drinks from New York to New Guinea*, Basingstoke: Palgrave.

Foucault, M. (1961/2001) *Madness and Civilization*, London: Routledge Classic.

Foucault, M. (1963) *The Birth of the Clinic*, London: Tavistock.

Foucault, M. (1969/2002) *The Archaeology of Knowledge*, London: Routledge Classic.

Foucault, M. (1976) *The History of Sexuality*, London: Allen-Lane.

Foucault, M. (1991, new ed. [1975]) *Discipline and Punish: Birth of the Prison*, Harmondsworth: Penguin.

Foucault, M. (2001 [1969]) *The Order of Things*, London: Routledge.

Fox, K. (2005) *Watching the English: The Hidden Rules of English Behaviour*, London: Hodder and Stoughton.

Frank, A.W. (1995) *The Wounded Storyteller*, Chicago: Chicago University Press.

Freeland, C. (2012/2013) *Plutocrats,* London: Penguin.

Freud, S. (2002 [1930]) *Civilization and Its Discontents*, London: Penguin.

Fuchs, C. (2013) *Social Media: A Critical Introduction*, London: Sage.

Fukuyama, F. (1993) *The End of History and the Last Man*, London: Penguin.

Fulcher, J. (2015, 2nd ed.) *Capitalism: A Very Short Introduction*, Oxford: Oxford University Press.

Fulcher, J., & Scott, J. (2011, 4th ed.) *Sociology*, Oxford: Oxford University Press.

Garfinkel, H. (1967) *Studies in Ethnomethodology*, Englewood Cliffs, NJ: Prentice Hall.

Giddens, A. (1973) *Capitalism and Modern Social Theory*, Cambridge: Cambridge University Press.

Giddens, A. (1986) *The Constitution of Society*, Cambridge: Polity Press.

Giddens, A. (1999) *Runaway World: How Globalization Is Reshaping Our Lives*, London: Profile.

Giddens, A. (2009) *Politics of Climate Change*, Cambridge: Polity.

Giddens, A., & Sutton, P. (2013, 7th ed.) *Sociology*, Cambridge: Polity.

Gladwell, M. (2001) *The Tipping Point: How Little Things Can Make a Big Difference*, London: Abacus.

Glassner, B. (2000) *The Culture of Fear: Why Americans Are Afraid of the Wrong Things*, New York: Basic Books.

Glenn, J.C., Florescu, E., & the Millennium Project Team (2015) *2015–16 State of the Future*, United Nations Millennium Project.

Goffman, A. (2014) *On the Run: Fugitive Life in an American City*, Chicago: University of Chicago Press.

Goffman, E. (1959 [1956]) *The Presentation of Self in Everyday Life*, Harmondsworth: Penguin.

Goffman, E. (1961/1968) *Stigma: Notes on the Management of Spoiled Identity*, Harmondsworth: Pelican.

Goffman, E. (1991 [1961]) *Asylums*, London: Penguin.

Goldthorpe, J. (2000) *On Sociology*, Oxford: Oxford University Press.

Gordon, A. (2008) *Ghostly Matters: Haunting and the Sociological Imagination*, Minneapolis: University of Minnesota Press.

Gouldner, A. (1970) *The Coming Crisis of Western Sociology*, London: Heinemann.

Graham, H. (2009) *Unequal Lives: Health and Socioeconomic Inequalities*, Maidenhead: Open University Press.

Gramsci, A. (1998 [1929–35]) *Prison Notebooks: Selections*, London: Lawrence and Wishart.

Habermas, J. (1989 [1962]) *The Structural Transformation of the Public Sphere*, Cambridge: Polity.

Habermas, J. (2001) *The Postnational Constellation*, Cambridge: Polity.

Habermas, J. et al. (2010) *An Awareness of What Is Missing: Faith and Reason in a Post-Secular Age*, Cambridge: Polity.

Hable Gray, C. (2002) *Cyborg Citizen,* London: Routledge.

Haiven, M. (2014) *Cultures of Financialization: Fictitious Capital in Popular Culture and Everyday Life*, Basingstoke: Palgrave.

Hall, R. (2015) *The Transparent Traveler*, Durham, NC: Duke University Press.

Halsey, A. H. (2004) *A History of Sociology in Britain*, Oxford: Oxford University Press.

Harari, Y. N. (2011/2015) *Sapiens: A Brief History of Humankind*, London: Vintage Books.

Harding, S. (1986) *The Science Question in Feminism*, Milton Keynes: Open University Press.

Harding, S. (1998) *Is Science Multicultural?: Postcolonialisms, Feminisms and Epistemologies*, Bloomington: Indiana University Press.

Harper, S. (2006) *Ageing Societies*, London: Hodder Arnold.

Harvey, D. (2007) *A Brief History of Neo-liberalism*, Oxford: Oxford University Press.

Harvey, D. (2015) *Seventeen Contradictions and the End of Capitalism*, London: Profile Books.

Harvey, M., Quilley, S., & Benyon, H. (2002) *Exploring the Tomato: Transformations of Nature, Society and Economy*, Cheltenham: Edward Elgar.

Hearn, J. (2015) *Men of the World: Genders, Globalizations, Transnational Times*, London: Sage.

Hjarvard, S. (2013) *The Mediatization of Culture and Society*, London: Routledge.

Hobbes, T. (2008 [1651]) *Leviathan*, London: Penguin.

Hochschild, A. R. (1983) *The Managed Heart: The Commercialization of Human Feeling*, Berkeley: University of California Press.

Holman, R. J. (2009) *Cosmopolitanisms: New Thinking and New Directions*, Basingstoke: Palgrave.

Holmwood, J., & Scott, J. (Eds.) (2014) *The Palgrave Handbook of Sociology in Britain*, Basingstoke: Palgrave.

Horkheimer, M., & Adorno, T. (1944/1997) *Dialectic of Enlightenment*, London: Verso.

Hughes, J., Sharrock, W., & Martin, P. J. (2003, 2nd ed.) *Understanding Classical Sociology*, London: Sage.

Hulme, D. (2015) *Global Poverty*, London: Routledge.

Humphreys, L. (1975) *Tearoom Trade: Impersonal Sex in Public Places,* Edison, NJ: Aldine Transaction.

Ihlen, O., Fredrikson, M., & van Ruler, B. (2009) *Social Theory for Public Relations: Key Figures and Concepts*, London: Routledge.

Ingham, G. (2008) *Capitalism*, Cambridge: Polity.

Inglis, D., & Thorpe, C. (2012) *An Invitation to Social Theory*, Cambridge: Polity.

Isin, E.F. & Turner, B.S. (Eds.) (2002) *Handbook of Citizenship Studies*, London: Sage.

James, W. (1977) *The Writings of William James*, Chicago: University of Chicago Press.

Jaspers, K. (1951/2003) *Way to Wisdom: An Introduction to Philosophy*, New Haven, CT: Yale University Press.

Jenkins, R. (2002) *Foundations of Sociology: Towards a Better Understanding of the Human World*, Basingstoke: Palgrave Macmillan.

Jenks, C. (Ed.) (1998) *Core Sociological Dichotomies*, London: Sage.

Joas, H. (2000) *The Genesis of Values*, Cambridge: Polity.

Joas, H. (2013) *The Sacredness of the Person: A New Genealogy of Human Rights*, Washington DC: Georgetown University Press.

Jodhka, S. S. (2012) *Caste*, Oxford: Oxford University Press.

Jones, O. (2012, revised ed.) *Chavs: The Demonization of the Working Class*, London: Verso.

Jones, O. (2014/2015) *The Establishment: And How They Got Away with It*, Middlesex: Penguin.

Jordan, T. (2015) *Information Politics: Liberation and Exploitation in the Digital Society*, London: Pluto Press.

Juergensberger, M. (2015) *God in the Tumult of the Global Square: Religion in the Global Civil Sphere*, Berkeley: University of California Press.

Kafka, F. (1925/2000) *The Trial*, Middlesex: Penguin Modern Classics.

Kallen, E. (2004) *Social Inequality and Social Injustice: A Human Rights Perspective*, London: Palgrave Macmillan.

Keen, A. (2015) *The Internet Is Not the Answer*, London: Atlantic Books.

Kelly, L. (1988) *Surviving Sexual Violence,* Cambridge: Polity Press.

Kennedy-Pipe, C. (2015) *Terrorism and Political Violence*, London: Sage.

Klein, N. (2000/2010) *No Logo*, London: Fourth Estate.

Klein, N. (2008) *The Shock Doctrine: The Rise of Disaster Capitalism*, Middlesex: Penguin.

Klein, N. (2015) *This Changes Everything*, Middlesex: Penguin.

Kluckhohn, C. (1948) *Personality in Nature, Society and Culture*, New York: Knopf.

Kuhn, T. S. (1962/2012) *The Structure of Scientific Revolutions*, Chicago: University of Chicago Press.

Kumar, K. (1978) *Prophecy and Progress: Sociology of Industrial and Post-Industrial Society*, London: Viking.

Kymlicka, W. (1996) *Multicultural Citizenship*, Wotton-under-Edge: Clarendon Press.

Lapavistas, C. (2013) *Profiting Without Producing: How Financialization Exploits Us All*, London: Verso.

Lazzarata, M. (2007) *The Making of the Indebted Man*, Los Angeles: Semiotext.

Lemert, C. (2011, 5th ed.) *Social Things: An Introduction to the Sociological Life*, New York: Rowman & Littlefield.

Lemert, C. (2013, 5th ed.) *Social Theory: The Multicultural and Classic Readings*, Boulder, CO: Westview Press.

Lengermann, P. M., & Niebrugge-Brantley, J. (1998) *The Women Founders: Sociology and Social Theory, 1830–1930*, London: McGraw-Hill.

Levine, D. (Ed.) (1971) *Simmel on Individuality and Social Forms*, Chicago: University of Chicago Press.

Levine, D. (1995) *Visions of the Sociological Tradition*, Chicago: Chicago University Press.

Levitas, R. (2013) *Utopia as Method: The Imaginary Reconstitution of Society*, Basingstoke: Palgrave.

Lewis, O. (1975, new ed. [1959]) *Five Families: Mexican Case Studies in the Culture of Poverty*, New York: Basic Books.

Ling, R. (2008) *New Tech, New Ties: How Mobile Communication Is Reshaping Social Cohesion*, Cambridge, MA: MIT Press.

Lister, R. (2003) *Citizenship: Feminist Perspectives*, London: Palgrave Macmillan.

Llewellyn, A., Agu, L., & Mercer, D. (2014, 2nd ed.) *Sociology for Social Workers*, Cambridge: Polity.

Long, K. (2015) *The Huddled Masses: Immigration and Inequality*, Marston Gate: Amazon.

Lukes, S. (2004, 2nd ed.) *Power*, Basingstoke: Palgrave.

Lupton, D. (2015) *Digital Sociology*, London: Routledge.

Lynd, R., & Lynd, H. (1929/1959) *Middletown*, New York: Harcourt Publishers.

Lyon, D. (2001) *Surveillance Society*, Milton Keynes: Open University Press.

Lyotard, J.-F. (1984) *The Postmodern Condition*, Manchester: Manchester University Press.

McCaughey, M. (2014) *Cyberactivism on the Participatory Web*, London: Routledge.

McDonald, K. (2013) *Our Violent World: Terrorism in Society*, Basingstoke: Palgrave Macmillan.

Machiavelli, N. (2004 [1513]) *The Prince*, London: Penguin.

MacFarquhar, M. (2015) *Strangers Drowning: Voyages to the Brink of Moral Extremity*, London: Allen Lane.

Macionis, J., & Plummer, K. (2012, 5th ed.) *Sociology: A Global Introduction*, Harlow: Pearson.

McKenzie, L. (2015) *Getting By: Estate, Class and Culture in Austerity Britain*, Bristol: Policy Press.

McLennan, G. (2011) *Story of Sociology: A First Companion to Social Theory*, London: Bloomsbury.

MacNeice, L. (2007) *Louis MacNeice: Collected Poems*, London: Faber and Faber.

McRobbie, A. (2000, 2nd ed.) *Feminism and Youth Culture*, Basingstoke: Palgrave Macmillan.

Malesevic, S. (2013) *Nation-States and Nationalisms*, Cambridge: Polity.

Malthus, T. (2008) *An Essay on the Principles of Population*, Oxford: Oxford Classics.

Mann, M. (2004) *The Dark Side of Democracy: Explaining Ethnic Cleansing*, Cambridge: Cambridge University Press.

Mann, M. (2012) *The Social Sources of Power: Globalizations*, 1945–2011 Volume 4, Cambridge: Cambridge University Press.

Marshall, T. H. (1950) *Citizenship and Social Class and Other Essays*, Cambridge: Cambridge University Press.

Martell, L. (2010) *The Sociology of Globalization*, Cambridge: Polity.

Marx, K. (2000) *Karl Marx: Selected Writings*, D. McLellan (Ed.), Oxford: Oxford University Press.

Marx, K., & Engels, F. (1846/1987) *The German Ideology*, London: Lawrence and Wisehart.

Mason, P. (2015) *Postcapitalism: A Guide to Our Future*, London: Allen Lane.

Mathiesen, T. (2013) *Towards a Surveillant Society: The Rise of Surveillance Systems in Europe*, Sherfield on Loddon: Waterside Press.

Mauss, M. (1915/2011) *The Gift*, London: Martino Fine Books.

Mayer-Schönberger, V., & Cukier, K. (2013) *Big Data: A Revolution That Will Transform How We Live, Work and Think*, London: John Murray.

Mead, G. H. (1967 [1934]) *Mind, Self and Society*, Chicago: University of Chicago Press.

Meer, N. (2014, 3rd ed.) *Key Concepts in Race and Ethnicity*, London: Sage.

Merton, R. K. (1949/1968) *Social Theory and Social Structure*, New York: MacMillan.

Miliband, R. (1973) *The State in Capitalist Society*, London: Quartet Books.

Mills, C. W. (1956) *The Power Elite*, Oxford: Oxford University Press.

Mills, C. W. (1959/2000) *The Sociological Imagination*, Oxford: Oxford University Press.

Mohanty, C. (2003) *Feminism Without Borders: Decolonizing Theory, Practicing Solidarity*, Durham, NC: Duke University Press.

Molotch, H. (2012) *Against Security: How Things Go Wrong at Airports, Subways and Other Sites of Ambiguous Danger*, Princeton, NJ: Princeton University Press.

Molotch, H., & Noren, L. (2010) *Toilet: Public Restrooms and the Politics of Sharing*, New York: New York University Press.

Morris, A. (2015) *The Scholar Denied: W. E. B. Du Bois and the Birth of Modern Sociology*, Berkeley: University of California Press.

Narayan, D. (2000) *Can Anyone Hear Us?: Voices of the Poor*, Oxford: Oxford University Press.

Nehring, D. (2013) *Sociology: An Introductory Textbook and Reader*, Harlow: Routledge.

Nisbet, R. (1976) *Sociology as an Art Form*, Oxford: Oxford University Press.

Nisbet, R. (1993 [1966]) *The Sociological Tradition*, Edison, NJ: Transaction Publishers.

Nolan, P., & Lenski, G. (2014, 12th ed.) *Human Societies: An Introduction to Macrosociology*, Boulder, CO: Paradigm.

Nussbaum, M. (2011) *Creating Capabilities: The Human Development Approach*, Cambridge, MA: Belknap Press of Harvard University Press.

Oakley, A. (1974) *The Sociology of Housework*, London: Martin Robertson.

Omi, M., & Winant, H. (1994, 2nd ed.) *Racial Formation in the United States*, London: Routledge.

Ong, A. (1999) *Flexible Citizenship*, Durham, NC: Duke University Press.

Orton-Johnson, K., & Prior, N. (Eds.) (2013) *Digital Sociology: Critical Perspectives*, Basingstoke: Palgrave Macmillan.

Orwell, G. (1949) *1984*, London: Secker and Warburg.

Orwell, G. (2004 [1940]) *Why I Write*, London: Penguin.

Outwaite, W. (2015) *Social Theory: Ideas in Profile*, London: Profile Books.

Oxfam (2015) *Wealth: Having It All and Wanting More*, Oxfam Issue Briefing, January 2015.

Pagden, A. (2013) *The Enlightenment and Why It Still Matters*, Oxford: Oxford University Press.

Palley, T. (2014) *Financialization*, Basingstoke: Palgrave.

Park, R. E., & Burgess, E. (1921) *Introduction to the Science of Sociology* [The Green Bible], Chicago: University of Chicago Press.

Parsons, T. (1951) *The Social System*, London: Routledge.

Payne, G. (Ed.) (2013, 3rd ed.) *Social Divisions*, Basingstoke: Palgrave.

Perrow, C. (2011) *The Next Catastrophe*, Princeton, NJ: Princeton University Press.

Pew Centre (2015) The Future of World Religions: Population Growth 2010–2050. http://www.pewforum.org/files/2015/03/PF_15.04.02_Projections FullReport.pdf

Pickerill, J. (2010) *Cyberprotest: Environmental Activism Online*, Manchester: Manchester University Press.

Pickett, K., & Wilkinson, R. (2015, 2nd ed./2009) *The Spirit Level: Why More Equal Societies Almost Always Do Better*, London: Allen Lane.

Pieterse, J. N. (2015, 3rd ed.) *Globalization and Culture: Global Melange*, Lanham, MD: Rowman & Littlefield.

Piketty, T. (2014) *Capital in the Twenty-First Century*, Cambridge, MA: Belknap Press of Harvard University Press.

Pinker, S. (2012) *The Better Angels of Our Nature: Why Violence Has Declined*, New York: Viking Books.

Pirandello, L. (1965 [1921]) *Six Characters in Search of an Author*, Harmondsworth: Penguin.

Platt, J. (1996) *A History of Sociological Research Methods in America, 1920–1960*, Cambridge: University of Cambridge Press.

Platt, J. (2003) *A Sociological History of the British Sociological Association*, London: Routledge.

Platt, L. (2011) *Understanding Inequality*, Cambridge: Polity.

Plummer, K. (2001) *Documents of Life 2: An Invitation to a Critical Humanism*, London: Sage.

Plummer, K. (2003) *Intimate Citizenship*, Seattle: University of Washington Press.

Plummer, K. (2010) 'Generational Sexualities, Subterranean Traditions, and the Hauntings of the Sexual World: Some Preliminary Remarks', *Symbolic Interaction*, 33(2): 163–91.

Plummer, K. (2011, 4th ed.) 'Critical Humanism and Queer Theory' with new afterword and comment, 'Moving On'. In N. Denzin & Y. Lincoln (Eds.), *The Sage Handbook of Qualitative Research* (pp. 195–201).

Plummer, K. (2012a) 'My Multiple Sick Bodies: Symbolic Interaction, Auto/ethnography and the Sick Body'. In B. S. Turner (Ed.), *Routledge Handbook of Body Studies* (pp. 75–93), London: Routledge.

Plummer, K. (2012b) 'Critical Sexualities Studies'. In G. Ritzer (Ed.), *Wiley-Blackwell Handbook of Sociology* (pp. 243–68), Oxford: Blackwell.

Plummer, K. (2013) 'A Manifesto for Critical Humanism in Sociology'. In D. Nehring, *Sociology: A Text and Reader* (pp. 489–517), London: Pearson/Routledge.

Plummer, K. (Ed.) (2014) *Imaginations: Fifty Years of Essex Sociology*, Wivenhoe: Wivenbooks.

Plummer, K. (2015) *Cosmopolitan Sexualities: Hope and the Humanist Imagination*, Cambridge: Polity.

Popper, K. (1948) 'Utopia and Violence', *Hibbert Journal*, 46: 109–16.

Popper, K. (2002 [1957]) *The Poverty of Historicism*, London: Routledge.

Putnam, R. D. (2000) *Bowling Alone: The Collapse and Revival of American Community*, New York: Simon and Schuster.

Ransome, P. (2010) *Social Theory for Beginners*, Bristol: Policy Press.

Rawls, J. (1999 [1971]) *A Theory of Justice*, Boston, MA: Harvard University Press.

Ricoeur, P. (1981) *Hermeneutics and the Human Sciences*, Cambridge: Cambridge University Press.

Riesman, D., Glazer, N., & Denney, R. (2001 [1950]) *The Lonely Crowd*, New Haven, CT: Yale University Press.

Rifkin, J. (2009) *The Empathic Civilization*, Cambridge: Polity.

Rigney, D. (2001) *The Metaphorical Society: An Invitation to Social Theory*, Boulder, CO: Rowman & Littlefield.

Ritzer, G. (2014, 8th ed. [1993]) *The McDonaldization of Society*, Thousand Oaks, CA: Pine Forge Press.

Ritzer, G. (2015, 2nd ed.) *Globalization: A Basic Text*, Chichester: Wiley.

Ritzer, G., & Ryan, J.M. (Eds.) (2010) *Concise Encyclopaedia of Sociology*, Oxford: Blackwell.

Rose, N. (2007) *The Politics of Life Itself*, Princeton, NJ: Princeton University Press.

Rousseau, J.-J. (2008 [1762]) *The Social Contract*, Oxford: Oxford University Press.

Rousseau, J.-J. (2009 [1754]) *Discourse on the Origin of Inequality*, Oxford: Oxford University Press.

Rubin, G. (1984) 'Thinking Sex'. In C. Vance (Ed.), *Pleasure and Danger*, London: Routledge.

Rubin, L. (1977) *Worlds of Pain*, New York: Basic Books.

Said, E. (2003 [1978]) *Orientalism*, Harmondsworth: Penguin Classics.

Salgado, S. (1993/1997) *Workers*, Woking: Aperture Books.

Salgado, S. (2000) *Migrations*, Woking: Aperture Books.

Salgado, S. (2000) *The Children*, Woking: Aperture Books.

Sandel, M.J. (2012) *What Money Can't Buy: The Moral Limits of Markets*, London: Allen Lane.

Sandoval, C. (2000) *Methodology of the Oppressed*, Minneapolis: University of Minnesota Press.

Sassen, S. (2006) *Cities in a World Economy*, Thousand Oaks, CA: Pine Forge Press.

Sassen, S. (2006) *Territory, Authority, Rights: From Medieval to Global Assemblages*, Princeton, NJ: Princeton University Press.

Sassen, S. (2014) *Expulsions: Brutality and Complexity in the Global Economy*, Cambridge, MA: Belknap Press of Harvard University Press.

Savage, M. (2015) *Social Class in the 21st Century*, London: Penguin.

Sayad, A. (2004) *The Suffering of the Immigrant*, Cambridge: Polity.

Sayer, A. (2011) *Why Things Matter to People: Social Science, Values and Ethical Life*, Cambridge: Cambridge University Press.

Sayer, A. (2015) *Why We Can't Afford the Rich*, Bristol: Policy.

Scheper-Hughes, N. (1992) *Death Without Weeping*, Berkeley: University of California Press.

Scott, J. (2006a) *Social Theory: Central Issues in Sociology*, London: Sage.

Scott, J. (2006b) *Sociology: The Key Concepts*, London: Routledge.

Scott, J. (2007) *Sociology: Fifty Key Sociologists*, London: Routledge.

Scott, J. (2014, 4th ed.) *Oxford Dictionary of Sociology*, Oxford: Oxford University Press.

Seidman, S. (2012, 5th ed.) *Contested Knowledge: Social Theory Today*, Oxford: Blackwell.

Sen, A. (1999) *Development as Freedom*, Oxford: Oxford University Press.

Sennett, R., & Cobbs, J. (1977) *The Hidden Injuries of Class,* New York: Random House.

Sevenhuijsen, S. (1998) *Citizenship and the Ethics of Care,* London: Routledge.

Shakespeare, W. (2007) *Complete Works*, J. Bate & E. Rasmussen (Eds.), Basingstoke: Macmillan.

Shaw, C. (1966 [1930]) *The Jack-Roller: A Delinquent Boy's Own Story*, Chicago: University of Chicago Press.

Shaw, M. (2003) *War and Genocide: Organized Killing on Modern Society*, Cambridge: Polity.

Sica, A., & Turner, S. (2005) *The Disobedient Generation: Social Theorists in the Sixties*, Chicago: University of Chicago Press.

Silver, C. (2014, 2nd ed.) *Using Software in Qualitative Research*, London: Sage.

Simmel, G. (1900/2011) *The Philosophy of Money*, London: Routledge.

Simmel, G. (1910) 'How Is Society Possible?' *American Journal of Sociology*, 16(3): 372–91.

Skeggs, B. (1997) *Formations of Class and Gender*, London: Sage.

Smart, C. (1976) *Women, Crime and Criminology*, London: Routledge.

Smith, A. (2008 [1776]) *The Wealth of Nations*, Oxford: Oxford University Press.

Smith, A. (2009) *The Cultural Foundations of Nations*, Oxford: Blackwell.

Smith, A. (2010 [1759]) *The Theory of Moral Sentiments*, Middlesex: Penguin Classic.

Smith, D. E. (1998) *Writing the Social: Critique, Theory and Investigations*, Toronto: University of Toronto.

Smith, G. (2007) *Erving Goffman*, London: Routledge.

Standing, G. (2011) *The Precariat: The New Dangerous Class,* London: Bloomsbury.

Standing, G. (2015) *The Precariat's Charter,* London: Bloomsbury.

Stanley, L., & Wise, S. (1983) *Breaking Out: Feminist Consciousness and Feminist Research*, London: Routledge.

Stanley, L., & Wise, S. (1993) *Breaking Out Again: Feminist Ontology and Epistemology*, London: Routledge.

Stein, A. (1997) *Sex and Sensibility: Stories of a Lesbian Generation*, Berkeley: University of California Press.

Stein, A. (2014) *Reluctant Witnesses: Survivors, Their Children and the Rise of Holocaust Consciousness*, Oxford: Oxford University Press.

Stevenson, B. E. (2015) *What Is Slavery?* Cambridge: Polity.

Stevenson, N. (2003) *Cultural Citizenship: Cosmopolitan Questions*, Milton Keynes: Open University Press.

Stiglitz, J. (2012) *The Price of Inequality*, London: Allen Lane.

Stones, R. (2008, 2nd ed.) *Key Sociological Thinkers*, Basingstoke: Palgrave.

Sullivan, N. (2003) *A Critical Introduction to Queer Theory*, Edinburgh: University of Edinburgh Press.

Swingewood, A. (2000, 3rd ed.) *A Short History of Sociological Thought*, London: Macmillan.

Sword, H. (2012) *Stylish Academic Writing*, Cambridge, MA: Harvard University Press.

Sznaider, N. (2001) *The Compassionate Temperament: Care and Cruelty in Modern Society*, Oxford: Roman & Littlefield.

Taleb, N. (2008) *The Black Swan: The Impact of the Highly Improbable*, London: Penguin.

Taylor, A. (2014) *The People's Platform: And Other Digital Delusions*, London: Fourth Estate.

Taylor, C. (1994) *Multiculturalism: Examining the Politics of Recognition*, Princeton, NJ: Princeton University Press.

Taylor, C. (2003) *Modern Social Imaginaries*, Durham, NC: Duke University Press.

Taylor, C. (2007) *A Secular Age*, Cambridge, MA: Harvard University Press.

Taylor, I. (2013) *Revolting Subjects*, London: Zed Books.

Therborn, G. (2004) *Between Sex and Power: Family in the World, 1900–2000*, London: Routledge.

Therborn, G. (2006) *Inequalities of the World: New Theoretical Frameworks, Multiple Empirical Approaches*, London: Verso.

Therborn, G. (2010) *The World: A Beginner's Guide*, London: Sage.

Therborn, G. (2013) *The Killing Fields of Inequality*, Cambridge: Polity.

Thomas, W.I. (1966) *Social Organization and Social Personality*, Chicago: University of Chicago Press.

Thomas, W.I., & Znaniecki, F. (1918–20/2012) *The Polish Peasant in Europe and America*, Chicago: University of Chicago Press/Nabu Press.

Tilley, C. (2004) *Social Movements, 1768–2004*, New York: Paradigm.

Tong, R. (2015, 4th ed.) *Feminist Thought*, Boulder, CO: Westview.

Tönnies, F. (2003 [1887]) *Community and Society*, London: Dover Publications.

Tronto, J. (2013) *Caring Democracy: Markets, Equality and Justice*, New York, New York University Press.

Turkle, S. (2013) *Alone Together*, New York: Basic.

Turkle, S. (2015) *Reclaiming Conversation*, Middlesex: Penguin.

Turnbull, C. (1984) *The Human Cycle*, New York: Simon and Schuster.

Turner, B.S. (2006) *Dictionary of Sociology*, Cambridge: Cambridge University Press.

Turner, B.S. (2006b) *Vulnerability and Human Rights*, Pennsylvania: State Pennsylvania University Press.

Turner, B.S. (2008, 3rd ed. [1984]) *The Body and Society: Explorations in Social Theory*, London: Sage.

Turner, B.S. (Ed.) (2012) *Routledge Handbook of Body Studies*, London: Routledge.

Twamley, K., Doidge, M., & Scott, A. (Eds.) (2015) *Sociologists' Tales: Contemporary Narratives on Sociological Thought and Practice*, Bristol: Policy Press.

Unger, R.M. (2007) *The Self Awakened: Pragmatism Unbound*, Cambridge, MA: Harvard University Press.

United Nations, Department of Economic and Social Affairs, Population Division (2013) *World Population Ageing 2013*. ST/ESA/SER.A/348.

United Nations, Department of Economic and Social Affairs, Population Division (2014) *World Urbanization Prospects: The 2014 Revision, Highlights*. ST/ESA/SER.A/352.

United Nations High Commissioner for Refugees (UNHCR), *UNHCR Global Trends 2014: World at War*, 18 June 2015. Retrieved from www.refworld.org/docid/558292924.html

United Nations (2014/2015) *Human Development Report 2014/15*, Basingstoke: Palgrave Macmillan.

Urry, J. (2000) *Sociology Beyond Societies: Mobilities for the Twenty-First Century*, London: Routledge.

Urry, J. (2003) *Global Complexity*, Cambridge: Polity.

Urry, J. (2007) *Mobilities*, Cambridge: Polity.

Urry, J. (2011) *Climate Change and Society*, Cambridge: Polity.

Urry, J. (2014) *Offshoring*, Cambridge: Polity.

Vaidhyanathan, S. (2012) *The Googlization of Everything*, Berkeley: University of California Press.

Voltaire, F. (1759/2006) *Candide, or Optimism*, Middlesex: Penguin Classics.

Wacquant, L. (2008) *Urban Outcasts: A Comparative Sociology of Advanced Marginality*, Cambridge: Polity.

Wacquant, L. (2009) *Punishing the Poor: The Neo-liberal Government of Social Security*, Durham, NC: Duke University.

Wadsworth, Y. (2011, 3rd ed.) *Do It Yourself Social Research*, Walnut Creek, CA: Left Coast Press.

Walby, S. (1990) *Theorizing Patriarchy*, Oxford: Blackwell.

Walby, S. (2009) *Globalization and Inequalities: Complexities and Contested Modernities*, London: Sage.

Walby, S. (2015) *Crisis*, Cambridge: Polity.

Wallerstein, I. (1999) *The End of the World as We Know It*, Minneapolis: University of Minnesota Press.

Warwick-Booth, L. (2013) *Social Inequality*, London: Sage.

Weber, M. (1978) *Economy and Society*, G. Roth & C. Wittich (Eds.), Berkeley: University of California Press.

Weber, M. (2001 [1904]) *The Protestant Ethic and the Spirit of Capitalism*, London: Routledge.

Weeks, J. (2009, 3rd ed.) *Sexuality*, London: Routledge.

Wells, H. G. (1906) 'The So-called Science of Sociology', *Sociological Papers*, 3: 367.

Westmarland, N. (2015) *Violence Against Women: Criminological perspective's on men's violences*, London: Routledge.

Wilkinson, I. (2005) *Suffering: A Sociological Introduction*, Cambridge: Polity.

Wilkinson, I., & Kleinmann, A. (2016) *A Passion for Society: How We Think About Human Suffering*, Berkeley: University of California Press.

Williams, R. (1989) *Resources of Hope: Culture, Democracy, Socialism*, London: Verso.

Willis, P. (1978) *Learning to Labour*, Farnham: Ashgate.

Winant, H. (2004) *The New Politics of Race: Globalism, Justice, Difference*, Minneapolis: University of Minnesota Press.

Winch, P., & Gaita, R. (2007 [1958]) *The Idea of a Social Science and Its Relation to Philosophy*, London: Routledge.

Wolfe, A. (1998) *Marginalized in the Middle*, Chicago: University of Chicago Press.

Wolfson, T. (2014) *Digital Rebellion: The Birth of the Cyber Left*, Champaign, IL: University of Illinois Press.

Wouters, C. (2007) *Informalization: Manners and Emotions Since 1890*, London: Sage.

Wright, E. O. (2010) *Envisioning Real Utopias*, London: Verso.

Young, I. M. (1990) *Justice and the Politics of Difference*, Princeton, NJ: Princeton University Press.

Young, R. J. C. (2003) *Postcolonialism*, Oxford: Oxford University.

Yuval-Davis, N. (2011) *The Politics of Belonging: Intersectional Contestations*, London: Sage.

Zerubavel, E. (2003) *Time Maps: Collective Memory and the Social Shapes of the Past*, Chicago: University of Chicago Press.

Zuckerman, P. (2003) *Invitation to the Sociology of Religion*, New York: Routledge.

INDEX